THE NEW BALLGAME

THE NEW BALLGAME

The Not-So-Hidden Forces
Shaping Modern Baseball

Russell A. Carleton

TRIUMPH
BOOKS

Library of Congress Cataloging-in-Publication Data available upon request.

This book is available in quantity at special discounts for your group or organization. For further information, contact:

Triumph Books LLC
814 North Franklin Street
Chicago, Illinois 60610
(312) 337-0747
www.triumphbooks.com

Printed in U.S.A.
ISBN: 978-1-63727-226-8
Design by Patricia Frey

For Natalie, Leah, Miriam,
Timothy, and Kieran, my five facts.

Contents

Chapter 1
The Jim Poole Problem

On the night of May 28, 1988, my dad took me to a baseball game. That night, Cleveland sat in second place, a game and a half out of first in the American League Eastern Division, but in the 1980s in Northeast Ohio, we knew not to get our hopes up. We'd all been burned too many times. Since the founding of the AL East, 19 years earlier, Cleveland had never finished higher than fourth place and had eked out a winning record only three times. The year before, *Sports Illustrated* magazine had put outfielders Joe Carter and Cory Snyder on the cover of its baseball preview issue and predicted a World Series win on the shores of Lake Erie. The team responded by losing 101 games. Cleveland was a rough place to grow up as a baseball fan, but in late May of 1988, there was again whispered talk of a pennant race coming to town for the first time in forever. It didn't. I remember the whispers, but mostly I remember being an eight-year-old kid who got to go to a baseball game and eat a footlong hotdog.

The game was held at Cleveland Municipal Stadium, a venue that was not only monstrous in size—it could hold 70,000 tortured souls—but also monstrous for its fan amenities. If you ever went to a game at "Muni," you know exactly what I mean. The (false) legend was that the stadium was built as part of an unsuccessful bid for Cleveland to host the 1932 Summer Olympics. Whatever its genesis, no one had bothered to stage an exodus from it. Five decades later, there were still baseball games being played (and mostly lost) there, only now the concrete was crumbling and the steel pylons

1

were rusting. Muni was a strange first ballpark to fall in love with, but it was mine. Fenway Park and Wrigley Field hold people's imaginations as quaint and quirky ballparks from a bygone era that played host to decades of losing and heartbreak. For this, their rust is labeled "charming." Muni was just a dump, and when it was eventually demolished in 1996, its ruins were unceremoniously pushed into the lake.

That night at Muni, Cleveland took on Milwaukee. The Brewers were starting 35-year-old journeyman Odell Jones on the mound, because their "ace" pitcher, Teddy Higuera, had been injured in the first inning of his previous outing five days earlier. Jones had replaced Higuera that day and thrown five innings of one-run ball, so with Higuera still unable to pitch, Brewers manager Tom Trebelhorn again turned to Jones. It was the first time that he had started a game in seven years, and the hope was that he could get through four or five innings and hand the game over to the bullpen. On the way to the game in the car, my father and his friend J.B. wondered who on earth Odell Jones was.

ON THE AFTERNOON of September 1, 2014, I took my five-year-old daughter to a baseball game. So much had changed in the 26 years since the Odell Jones game that had brought me to both fatherhood and Atlanta, but my love of baseball remained constant. I had promised my daughter that we'd see a game and on that Labor Day afternoon, I delivered. At that point in the 2014 season, Atlanta still had hopes of reaching the playoffs, standing a game out of a Wild Card spot. The late summer of 2014 wasn't kind to them and they sputtered to a sub-.500 finish. My daughter didn't care. She just wanted to see a baseball game and drink a root beer.

The game was held at Turner Field, which was an odd stadium for its time. "The Ted" (after broadcasting magnate Ted Turner) was built as the Olympic Stadium when Atlanta hosted the 1996 Summer Games. After the Olympics, the stadium was retrofitted into a baseball park which "re-opened" in 1997, at a time when everyone else was moving into small parks which sought to mimic the intimacy of Fenway Park and Wrigley Field. The Ted was serviceable as a ballpark, but lacked the Fenway backstory.

That day, Atlanta was facing the Phillies, with Cole Hamels toeing the rubber for Philadelphia. By that point, Hamels was widely known, if only as a holdover from when the Phillies won the 2008 World Series. Hamels had been named MVP of that series, not that my daughter, who at the time was a blue line on a pregnancy test, would have remembered that.

Hamels wasn't sharp for the Phillies. He walked both Jason Heyward and Emilio Bonafácio, Atlanta's first and second hitters of the day, but somehow rallied to strike out both Freddie Freeman and Justin Upton, and then induced Chris Johnson to fly out to left. In the third inning, the Phillies pushed across the game's first run against Atlanta starter Julio Teherán on a Ben Revere sacrifice fly. In the bottom of the frame, Hamels was at it again. He walked Heyward and Freeman, but again escaped with no damage. During that inning, my daughter told me that she wanted to stay all the way until the end of the game, even though it was being played in upper 80s heat with little breeze. Apparently, I was doing something right as a dad.

ODELL JONES AND Cleveland starting pitcher Rich Yett traded zeroes through the first three innings on that night in 1988, with Jones somehow setting down Cleveland's hitters in order in all three. In the fourth, Milwaukee shortstop Dale Sveum singled in Rob Deer to give the Brewers a 1–0 lead, and Jones retired Julio Franco, Willie Upshaw, and Joe Carter in order for the second straight time. In the fifth, Cory Snyder, Mel Hall, and Brook Jacoby couldn't muster anything against him. In the sixth, Pat Tabler, Andy Allanson, and Jay Bell all walked back to the dugout in disgust. It's said that an infinite number of monkeys at an infinite number of type-writers would eventually reproduce a page of Shakespeare. I don't know whether they would have ever thought to produce the line, "Odell Jones is perfect through six innings." If they did, they surely would have been laughing right after typing it.

My father told me in the top of the seventh inning that I was witnessing something special, although I was a bit too young to appreciate how special it was. In the bottom of the seventh, Franco, Upshaw, and Carter were dispatched without incident. There were more than 38,000 fans that night at Muni, and I think we were all marveling at the improbable event unfolding in front of us. In the eighth inning, Snyder flied to right to become Jones's 22nd consecutive victim, but the next batter, Mel Hall, drew a walk, and the Cleveland faithful exploded in cheers. They were short-lived as Jacoby flew to left and Tabler grounded to third. Maybe we wouldn't see a perfect game that night, but Odell Jones was three outs away from a no-hitter, and that was a rare bird unto itself.

I would love to say that I witnessed history that night in Cleveland, but with one out in the ninth inning, Cleveland pinch-hitter Ron Washington did something that had proved incredibly hard for the rest of his teammates and lined a single to right field. Jones's bid for the most unlikely no-hitter of all time was over. He left the game and Brewers closer Dan Plesac came on for the final two outs. I almost got to see something worth writing about that day.

It's an odd thing to watch the pitcher from a visiting team creep closer to a landmark achievement like a no-hitter, because you don't know whether to root, root, root for the home team or to root for history to take place. Life is full of conflicts, and that day, eight-year-old me had to confront that one. I've never quite solved that dilemma in my own head.

COLE HAMELS'S HIGH-WIRE act lasted into the sixth inning. He had settled down in the fourth and fifth and retired the side in order and only allowed a leadoff walk to Freddie Freeman in the sixth, but after 108 pitches in the hot Atlanta sun, Hamels was lifted for pinch-hitter Grady Sizemore and told to report to the showers. He finished his day having walked five batters and hit one, but he hadn't given up a run. Or a hit. Somehow through all of that, Atlanta still didn't have a hit in this game.

The Phillies, who by this point had pushed their lead to a more comfortable 5–0, brought in relievers Jake Diekman and Ken Giles, both of whom normally would have been reserved for games which were a little more in doubt, to preserve the thing that you're not allowed to talk about while it's happening. If you're not going chase a little history now and then, why bother showing up to the ballpark? Diekman and Giles did their jobs and didn't surrender any runs or base hits. In the ninth, now up 7–0, the Phillies brought in their closer, Jonathan Papelbon, officially to protect the lead, but more importantly to protect their shot at history.

Life sometimes rhymes in unexpected ways. As I sat with my daughter, I told her that she was witnessing something special and that I wished she was older so that she could appreciate it. The outcome of the game itself wasn't in doubt. The only remaining question was whether this would be another near-miss or a day where I could say "I was there." It's an odd thing to watch the fourth pitcher of the day from a visiting team creep closer to a landmark achievement like a no-hitter, because you don't know whether to root, root, root for the home team or to root for history to take place. That day, 34-year-old me had to confront that one. I still haven't quite solved that dilemma in my own head.

A band of kids in the upper deck at Turner Field started a chant of "Get a hit!" perhaps hoping to not only scuttle the no-hitter, but to produce the eight runs the home team would have needed to win. My daughter and I joined in, but it didn't work. Papelbon got the job done in nine pitches, dispatching José Costanza, Chris Johnson, and Phil Gosselin in order. I looked out and noted the neat symmetry on the scoreboard. Philadelphia had scored seven runs on seven hits that day. Atlanta had scored no runs on no hits. They say that if you stick around a baseball game long enough, you'll eventually see something that you've never seen before. That day, my daughter witnessed her first no-hitter. And I witnessed mine.

"SO, DO TWINS run in your family?" She wasn't talking about the Minnesota variety. It was a strange question to ask. It was 2016, and my wife and I had just gotten back from a Christmas trip to Cleveland where we had shared with my parents the joyful news that we were expecting Baby Number Four. That day, we had an appointment to see the newest member of our family for the first time. So, while I appreciated the small talk from the ultrasound tech, I was hoping to focus on….

Oh. That's why she was asking. Make that Baby Number Four *and* Baby Number Five. My wife, Tanya, had told me a few days earlier that she was feeling "twice as morning sick" during this pregnancy. She was wondering whether that meant anything. Apparently, it did. Seven months later, when we welcomed our sons into the world, we became co-investigators in one of the longest-running natural experiments in human history.

The idea of twins as a storytelling device reaches back to the earliest days of humanity. Literature is filled with twins being separated at birth and reunited by circumstance. There's often a scene where the twins meet and compare notes about their upbringing, followed by the two facing some sort of challenge and meeting it in different ways. It's a way for the author to isolate some piece of the human experience and to say "Here's what could have happened if things had been a little different." In literature, it's easy to draw bright, clean lines between those differences in upbringing and whatever divergent paths the twins took. The science of the matter is a little fuzzier.

Twins are just as much a staple in the scientific study of child development and for the same reason. They provide the closest thing to a natural control group that a scientist will ever find to answer questions like what would happen if things were a little different. Identical twins share nearly complete copies of their DNA. Fraternal and sororal twins share half their DNA, and twins are usually raised in the same environment. They're wonderful, little science projects. Even before I was a dad to twins, I was familiar with that science. In addition to being a son of Cleveland, a transplant to Atlanta, a dad, and a baseball fan, I hold a Ph.D. in child and adolescent clinical psychology. I'm a researcher. I feed my kids by studying other kids through data.

When I introduce myself to someone I've never met, I usually recite some version of that same paragraph. I'm from Cleveland. I live in Atlanta. I have a job as a researcher in the field of child psychology. I am married and the proud father of five amazing kids. I love baseball. The "five facts" speech is one of those things that everyone does, but no one realizes that they do it until someone points it out. As part of the culture we live in, we are expected to recite the geography of our childhood, and then our adulthood, what we do for a living, our relationship and family status, and a hobby. It's an odd set of facts. After all, what do you really know of me from those five facts? What if things had been a little different?

Before I was born, my father worked at Cleveland Hopkins Airport as the assistant manager in their parking lot. He was good at what he did and the company asked him if he was interested in a promotion to manager. The catch was that the job was in Salt Lake City. As he and my mother were expecting their firstborn in a few months (me!), he declined, but what would have happened if he had said yes? I would never have known it, but my life would have been at least a *little* different. I would have still had the same DNA and same parents, although in a different house and in a different neighborhood in a different state, and with an entirely different cast of people around me. Would I have turned out differently as a human being or would I have simply been the same person with different names for my childhood friends? More importantly, would I have even grown up as a baseball fan with no major league team around for a few hundred miles? There's no question that something about me would be different today, but what? What about my life story exists *because* I grew up in Cleveland?

Before I became a full-time researcher and tried to answer those sorts of questions, I worked as a mental health counselor, providing therapy to patients who would introduce themselves with their own "five facts" speech. Part of working as a therapist is getting past those surface facts and delving into sometimes uncomfortable places in people's lives. I was at the distinct disadvantage that I couldn't force people to reveal anything to me. Sometimes, people who are seeking therapy are eager for a place where they can talk about the things that they have held inside for a long time. Sometimes, they keep their guard up because they don't want to be there. Sometimes, what they need to say isn't easy to say out loud. In the therapy room, you have to be a good detective and try to figure out what a person isn't telling you based on the few things that they have.

To place myself on the proverbial couch for a moment, my own "five facts" reveal some more telling things about who I am now as a person, but they only become apparent if we look at them *in conjunction* with one another. I grew up in Cleveland, yet I live in Atlanta. That means I made a decision to leave my home. I've had to live as an outsider in a new city. As I raise my five kids, my extended family isn't an easy drive away. I've had to say some tough goodbyes. Those statements probably explain more about me than simply saying "I grew up in Cleveland and I now live in Atlanta" but to understand how I got to where I am, you have to work to make those connections.

I PROMISE THAT this is still a book about baseball. After all, my love of baseball is my fifth fact. It's true that I still carry a fondness for my beloved Cleveland Guardians (see fact one), despite raising five Atlanta fans (see facts two and four), but it's my third fact that drives most of this book. I'm a researcher and—I make no apology for this—I'm a numbers guy. "Analytics" is a term that's become very loaded in baseball. It's always a little tense in the room when the subject comes up. You might be better off asking Uncle Larry about his political opinions over Thanksgiving dinner. Some think of analytics as the search for obscure and useless facts, like that Ozzie Smith got a hit off of a left-handed pitcher in road games on the 15th day of the month a total of six times during his career. That's a true statement, but it's pointless trivia. It doesn't tell us anything deeper about baseball. I'm looking for something a little more meaningful.

Baseball has always been a game played in two languages. Usually, that refers to English and Spanish, but baseball has two other tongues that we rarely acknowledge: a narrative language and a numerical one. For the most part, they run alongside each other, intersecting where they need to; the phrase ".300 hitter" is both a decimal describing a player's previous at-bats and shorthand for a "good hitter."

For a century and a half, a staple of the sports section of the daily paper has been the box score, a small data set which summarized the previous day's game in matrix form. It was invariably paired with a paragraph or two which summarized the critical moments in the game and perhaps a few thoughts from the game's participants. The numbers and the narrative both had their section. There was always a small disconnect between the two, because the box score could only provide a very sterile notation, such as, "HR—Justice (1, off Poole, 6th inning, none on)," as if that were just another instance of a player hitting a home run. Where I live in Atlanta (fact two), fans of a certain age can tell you exactly where they were when David Justice hit a solo home run off Cleveland reliever Jim Poole in the sixth inning of Game 6 of the 1995 World Series. It was the only run scored that night, and Atlanta's 1–0 victory clinched the first World Series championship in the city's history. I remember where I was when that home run left the Atlanta Fulton County Stadium playing field too. I was in the doorway between the kitchen and living room in my parents' house in Cleveland (fact one). I have a somewhat less fond view of that home run than my neighbors.

The box score has always had a special place in the way we document baseball. The importance of Justice's home run can easily be spelled out in a paragraph, and in a way that the box score can't. To figure that all out from the box score, you have to be able to read its notation and work to connect the line about Justice's home run with the fact that the final score was 1–0. Even then, you need some knowledge of how the 1995 World Series progressed. It's likely that you, who have picked up a book about baseball, are well-versed in how to read one, but for a moment consider how weird the box score is to an outsider.

The box score does have one advantage: everyone who plays gets a line that shows off their accomplishments for the day, whether they hit for the cycle or went 0-for-4. It doesn't limit itself to just the moments of high emotion. That level of detail would be too cumbersome for a game story that might have a 100-word limit, but the box score documents everyone's efforts, despite the fact that most of them weren't all that relevant to the outcome. Somewhere out there, there's a box score about a forgotten game in August between two teams that didn't break .500 that year in which someone named Jones played left field and went 1-for-4, despite the fact that his team lost 10–4. It doesn't tell us much about Jones as a player for that season or his career, nor give us much other information, but it still exists to tell us how his day went. We don't question its existence. Baseball documents even the things that don't seem important. The box score sees everything.

I like box scores for the fact that if you know where to look, there are stories about each game hiding inside. In the line "HR—Justice (1, off Poole, 6th inning, none on)," most people who remember the 1995 World Series will remember Justice for hitting the blast, but to me, the most interesting piece of that notation is the seemingly inconsequential "off Poole." The story of how Jim Poole, a left-handed reliever who spent 11 gloriously average years in the majors playing for eight different teams, happened to be in the middle of the diamond to give up the most important home run in Atlanta baseball history tells us something about the game. If we know where to look, we can find the story hiding in plain sight.

We can see that Poole was the first reliever to exit the Cleveland bullpen after starter Dennis Martínez lasted only 4⅔ innings. Martínez allowed nine baserunners, and yet somehow didn't give up a run. The box score shows us that Atlanta stranded 11 runners during the game, a tribute to how much danger Martínez flirted with. The fifth inning had started out promisingly, with Martínez striking out Tom Glavine and then inducing Marquis Grissom to pop up to second baseman Carlos Baerga. But after

October 28, 1995—Cleveland at Atlanta (Game 6, 1995 World Series)

Cleveland	AB	R	H	RBI	Atlanta	AB	R	H	RBI
Lofton, cf	4	0	0	0	Grissom, cf	4	0	1	0
Vizquel, ss	3	0	0	0	Lemke, 2b	2	0	1	0
Sorrento, ph	1	0	0	0	Jones, 3b	3	0	2	0
Baerga, 2b	4	0	0	0	McGriff, 1b	4	0	0	0
Belle, lf	1	0	0	0	Justice, rf	2	1	2	1
Murray, 1b	2	0	0	0	Klesko, lf	1	0	0	0
Ramirez, rf	3	0	0	0	Devereaux, lf	1	0	0	0
Embree, p	0	0	0	0	López, c	3	0	0	0
Tavárez, p	0	0	0	0	Belliard, ss	4	0	0	0
Assenmacher, p	0	0	0	0	Glavine, p	3	0	0	0
Thome, 3b	3	0	0	0	Polonia, ph	1	0	0	0
Peña, c	3	0	1	0	Wohlers, p	0	0	0	0
Martínez, p	1	0	0	0					
Poole, p	1	0	0	0					
Hill, p	0	0	0	0					
Amaro Jr., rf	1	0	0	0					

Cleveland	000 000 000		0 1 1
Atlanta	000 001 00x		1 6 0

2B—Justice (1); HR—Justice (1, off Poole, 6th inning, none on); SH—Lemke (1); SB—Lofton (11), Grissom (5); CS—Belle (1), Lemke (1); DP—Cleveland 1, (Martínez-Vizquel-Baerga-Murray); E—Thome (2); LOB—Cleveland 3, Atlanta 11; T—3:02; A—51,875

Cleveland	IP	H	R	ER	BB	SO
Martínez	4.2	4	0	0	5	2
Poole, L (0–1)	1.1	1	1	0		1
Hill	0	1	0	0	0	0
Embree	1	0	0	0	2	0
Tavárez	0.2	0	0	0	0	0
Assenmacher	0.1	0	0	0	0	1

Atlanta	IP	H	R	ER	BB	SO
Glavine, W (2–0)	8	1	0	0	3	8
Wohlers, S (4)	1	0	0	0	0	0

Mark Lemke drew the fifth and final walk that Martínez surrendered that night, Chipper Jones reached on an infield single to the right side, pushing Lemke to second. It was a tough spot for Poole to enter. Runners at first and second, with two outs in a scoreless game.

Cleveland manager Mike Hargrove was probably quietly fuming that Baerga hadn't gotten to Jones's slow roller a little quicker. Perhaps a more defensively gifted second baseman would have converted it into the third out of the inning. The box score doesn't record an error for Baerga, because he didn't bobble the ball or throw it away. He just didn't quite get there in time, and it made Hargrove's job much more difficult. The next three scheduled hitters for Atlanta, Fred McGriff, Justice, and Ryan Klesko, were all left-handed and Hargrove wanted a lefty on the mound to face them. In anticipation of this moment, Poole had been warming up, but with the game being played in a National League park, Hargrove had to think about something other than who would face the left-handed triumvirate. In fact, Poole's line in the box score gives away the plot.

Poole, p   1   0   0   0

Jim Poole would eventually come to the plate in the top of the sixth inning, though at the time Mike Hargrove pointed to the left-field bullpen to summon Poole, that wasn't a given. Managing under ye olde National League rules where pitchers were called on to bat, Hargrove had to make a painful decision. It was clear that Martínez's day was finished, but how to get Poole into the game mid-inning? The pitcher's spot in the lineup would be due up second in the sixth inning. If Poole entered the game as a direct substitute for Martínez, Poole might be called on to hit.

Hargrove's hope was that Poole could retire Fred McGriff to end the fifth and then come out to face Justice and Klesko in the bottom of the sixth. Seventh-spot hitter and future Hall of Famer Jim Thome had made the final out of Cleveland's half of the fifth inning. Should Hargrove use a double switch, likely bringing light-hitting utility infielder Álvaro Espinoza into the game to play third and hit in the pitcher's spot? Was it more important to keep Thome's prodigious bat in the game or to keep a bat out of Poole's hands in the top of the sixth? Maybe the veteran Martínez had one more batter left in him? How does one even begin to make that decision?

If things had been a little different and Baerga had gotten the out, Hargrove could have simply pinch-hit for the clearly gassed Martínez in the top of the sixth, cleared the pitcher's spot, and then inserted Poole into the game to face McGriff, Justice, and Klesko. Perhaps even more infuriating, he should never have had to make that call. At the time, home-field advantage in the World Series alternated from year to year between the National League and the American League. For several decades, the American League team had hosted Games 1, 2, 6, and 7 in its park in odd-numbered years, while the National League team had the honor in even-numbered years. As 1995 was an odd-numbered year, Game 6 would normally have been played in Cleveland, under American League rules with a designated hitter, and Hargrove wouldn't have had to worry about the pitcher hitting at all.

However, a little more than a year earlier, Major League Baseball began its longest and most famous labor stoppage, a players' strike that canceled the last month and a half of the 1994 regular season, along with the playoffs and the Fall Classic. To make up for the cancelation, the National League was given home field for the 1995 World Series. Had labor peace prevailed in baseball, Mike Hargrove might have had an easier night. Alas, none of that happened and the box score tells us that Hargrove chose to have Poole enter the game as a direct substitute for Martínez. When Poole struck Fred McGriff out on three straight pitches to end the fifth, Hargrove had to be smiling for the moment. His plan had worked.

In the top of the sixth, Cleveland was once again facing Tom Glavine, in his Hall of Fame prime. The box score records that Glavine surrendered one hit that night in eight innings of work, but even before we knew the glory of Glavine's effort, it was clear that he was locked in. The box score tells us that the owner of that hit was catcher and eighth-place hitter Tony Peña. What it doesn't tell us is that his hit was a single to lead off the sixth inning. Now with Peña on first, Hargrove had another decision to make. Thome's bat was still in the lineup and Poole had retired McGriff to end the threat in the fifth inning, but the public address announcer at Atlanta-Fulton County Stadium had to announce *someone* as Cleveland's next batter. That someone would be given the task of facing Glavine, on a night where he was clearly in command of the game, at a point where Cleveland had finally gotten a baserunner on, in the sixth inning of a still-scoreless game which they literally *had* to win.

Hargrove had a full bench and some options. If Poole, who to that point in his career had never taken a major league at-bat, went up to the plate, he would obviously be bunting, but could he bunt? Would switch-hitting outfielder and eventual MLB general manager Rubén Amaro Jr., who had made the postseason roster because he could be called on to bunt, be a better pick?

Hargrove had two other left-handed relievers available, Alan Embree and Paul Assenmacher, both of whom would eventually get their own lines in the box score. Hargrove could still have a left-handed pitcher ready to face Justice and Klesko in the next frame, though he knew that the McGriff-Justice-Klesko alley would come up again at least once more in this game, and maybe more. Burning Poole here *might* mean that later in the night, Fred McGriff would be strolling to the plate and Hargrove would be out of southpaws. Then again, maybe Hargrove should have worried about the eighth inning when he got there and seized the possible opportunity to break through in the sixth. Was having a real MLB hitter up to potentially move Peña over more important or was possibly not having a lefty available later in the game for the heart of the Atlanta order? How does one even begin to make that decision?

The box score again tells us what Hargrove decided. Poole stepped to the plate and didn't even try to hide the fact that he was squaring up to sacrifice. After fouling off two attempts, he popped his third bunt into the air and first baseman McGriff got to retire the man who had made him look foolish a few minutes earlier. Cleveland's rally fizzled before it started, and they returned to the field, scoreless, though they still had the lefty Poole on the mound.

The fact that Mike Hargrove bent over backwards to ensure that a nondescript, but left-handed, journeyman reliever stayed in the biggest game of the year might not seem like a lesson in analytics, but it is. Even casual fans of baseball will recognize Hargrove's insistence on having a left-handed pitcher to face a string of left-handed hitters as "the platoon effect." We know that when the hitter and pitcher are of the same handedness, the pitcher has a small, though real advantage. It shows up in the numbers, and while it doesn't turn the batter into a video game character with cheat codes on, it is an edge.

Table 1. Batting outcomes, by pitcher and batter handedness, 2022

Matchup	Batting Average	On-Base Percentage	Slugging Percentage
RH batter vs. RH pitcher	.245	.307	.393
RH batter vs. LH pitcher	.252	.320	.417
LH batter vs. LH pitcher	.225	.300	.347
LH batter vs. RH pitcher	.239	.314	.394

The idea of using handedness platoons was one of the first triumphs of "analytics" in the game's history. We just didn't call it that back then. The numbers clearly showed that handedness mattered, and all else being equal, managers should strive to get that advantage when they could. Jim Poole was pitching in that moment because the numbers said he had a not-so-hidden super power in his left arm. I'm sure that as David Justice drove the ball over the right-center-field fence and a stake into my 15-year-old heart, Mike Hargrove comforted himself with the knowledge that the numbers said he was perfectly justified in having Poole out there.

Or was he? Poole had a career ERA of 4.31, which put him right around average for the high-scoring 1990s, and an ERA of 3.75 during the 1995 season. We should give him some additional credit for the fact that he was facing a left-handed batter, but was his left arm all that mattered? Hargrove also had relievers Julián Tavárez (2.44 ERA in 1995) and Eric Plunk (2.67) in his bullpen, both better than Poole overall, but they threw with their right arms. Was the platoon advantage enough to cancel out that gap? Was Hargrove better served by saving the righties for later in the game when other right-handed batters came up?

It's not polite to second-guess Mike Hargrove's decisions that night. It's also entirely unsatisfying, because we'll never know the answer to the question, "What if things had been a little different?" It's possible that Rubén Amaro Jr. would have popped up his bunt, and then Alan Embree or Eric Plunk would have given up the same home run to Justice. It's possible that in the alternate timeline or perhaps just my own teenage imagination, Cleveland could have won Game 6 and then Game 7. Maybe I would have moved to Salt Lake City as a baby and never even noticed. The thing about baseball is the same questions have a way of coming around again and again. Managers still agonize over decisions where there is no obvious answer.

The major contribution that analytics has made to baseball hasn't been discovering something new about the game. Everyone in baseball knows about the platoon advantage. Everyone knows that some pitchers are better than others. Is it more important to have the platoon advantage with a lesser pitcher or is it more important to have the better pitcher on the mound, no matter his handedness? Anyone can make a decision when all the arrows are pointing the same way. Analytics is a framework for thinking about problems that are complicated. Analytics puts different pieces of the game into perspective *relative to each other*, so that when you are forced to decide between two arrows that are pointing in different directions, you know which one is bigger.

If you want to understand *a* game of baseball, you should read the newspaper article from the next day. History is written by the victors, or at least the beat writers for the winning team. Afterward, we know whether the decisions that the manager made worked, but there's no skill involved in predicting the past. If you want to understand *the* game of baseball, you're going to need some box scores. You're going to need the numbers. You're going to need analytics.

There are hundreds of decisions that happen during a game. Some have obvious answers. Some don't. What if one of them had been decided differently? We'll never know the answer to the question for that specific game, but the beauty of baseball's near-obsessive record keeping, combined with its daily, grinding schedule, is that it generates a lot of box scores. We can go back and find other similar moments where someone else made a different call and see what happened. We can look to see which decision turned out to be the right one more often. Nothing works all the time, but if you can be right more often than you're wrong, eventually, you end up ahead.

A GAME OF baseball is a nine-act play unfolding over three hours with its heroes and villains taking the stage and then exiting. A batter gets a hit, another performs a selfless feat of martyrdom and bunts him over, and a third drives him home with the go-ahead run in the eighth inning. The bunt works wonderfully as a narrative device, especially if everything works out in the end. Multiple players worked together, one of them using a skill that is quite difficult to acquire—in 2022, about 45 percent of bunt attempts in Major League Baseball resulted in the bat striking the ball and the ball going into fair territory—not for his own sake, but in service of the team's goals. In United States culture, our bunter will be seen as a hero. He endured baseball's version of "death for a cause." Even if the team doesn't score after the bunt, our hero "did his job." It's not surprising that the emotional pull of the bunt has persisted.

A funny thing happened on the way to the ballpark though. It's hard to put into words, because teams do still use the bunt every now and then, but it feels like someone killed the bunt. Where words fail us, perhaps we can instead speak of that vague feeling in our collective tummies with a graph. Figure 1 below shows us what has happened from 1950 to 2022. Bunting situations are defined here as a runner on first with no outs, and we can see the percentage of time in which the batter (pitchers batting are excluded) laid down a bunt.

Figure 1. Percentage of "bunting situations" where the batter bunted (pitchers batting excluded), 1950–2022

The graph shows us that over time, the bunt had been slouching toward extinction. The trade in the sacrifice bunt play has always been an out (an obvious bad thing for the batting team) for the runner being able to move up a base (a good thing). Managers could point to the fact that they were moving the runner closer to home, which is the point of the game, but this assumed that the base was more valuable than the out that the play required in payment. What modern analytics showed (and here, credit should be given to writers John Thorn and Pete Palmer and their 1985 book, *The Hidden Game of Baseball*) was that the out was worth more than the base, and that teams were surrendering runs even on a "successful" sacrifice. It's not that teams didn't score sometimes after a bunt, but they scored more often when they didn't. No one had ever calculated which arrow was bigger.

In 2012, something happened. That year, 6.3 percent of all these "runner on first" situations were met with a bunt. By 2022, only 2.5 percent were. Not only did the bunt mostly die, but we can even see the moment on the graph when someone pushed it over the edge. Ed from Lakewood on your local sports talk radio station will tell you that society is surely collapsing because no one can bunt anymore. In reality, the cause of the bunt's demise was math. However noble or sublime a play the sacrifice bunt is, it's not the most effective way to score runs. As teams began to realize that the arrow for the out that you have to surrender was larger than the arrow for the 90 feet of real estate you gain, they all but stopped doing it. That's what efficient baseball looks like.

WE'RE GOING TO need a little help if we're going to study *the* game of baseball. There are 2,430 regular season games played every year, each lasting around three hours on average. If you queued up all of them and started watching as everyone sang *Auld Lang Syne* on January 1, you wouldn't quite be done by Halloween, even if you watched 24 hours a day. And even if you clipped all the box scores from the paper each day, making any sense of them isn't a project that could be done by hand. To process that much information, humans need a friend to help them.

The neat thing about computers is not only that they can process large amounts of information, including a few decades worth of baseball data, but that they can do it in a few minutes. At least, now they can. The phrase "big data" is something that has only come into our cultural lexicon since the turn of the millennium, and for good reason. Big data used to require (literally) big computers which were only available on the campuses of big universities. The ability to even ask the question "How many runs were scored in Situation A vs. Situation B?" is a development that has taken place within my lifetime. For a long time, there were questions—both in baseball and in the rest of life—that had never been answered because they had never been functionally answer-able. Now they had answers. There were ideas—both in baseball and in the rest of life—that had stood largely unquestioned. Some of them were revealed to be wrong. Stories—both in baseball and in the rest of life—that were considered to be the product of unseen and unknowable forces now had very logical and tangible explanations. Big data ruined some of the mystery in life.

This is the part where people sometimes get a little uncomfortable and close the book, though they can't quite put into words why. As a psychologist (fact three of my five facts), it's sometimes my job to help people verbalize the things that make them uncomfortable. Storytelling is one of the activities that make us human. We are all narrators of our own story. The five facts speech itself progresses from childhood (I was born in Cleveland) to adulthood (and now I live in Atlanta) and usually covers our professional journey (I am a mental health researcher), our close relationships (a husband and father of five), and where we found meaning along the way (and I love baseball). There is a narrative arc and a hero (me!) Sure, things could have been different, and along the way, there were moments that were critical in me finding this particular path, but I have a hard time imagining my life any other way.

There's a good reason for that. In life, there's not usually a way to go back and check how things would have worked out had this one thing been different. Eventually, you have to deal with the reality in front of you. We can't become consumed with the question "What if?" or we won't be able to function in daily life. But that question never fully goes away. What if the 1994 strike had never happened? What if Hargrove had pinch-hit Amaro Jr.? What if I had grown up in Salt Lake City or fallen in love with Sally or sociology or soccer instead? One of the functions that art plays is to allow us to occasionally indulge those questions and quietly reckon with them. But the book always has a back cover and the film always has credits. There's an end to it all after which we need to get back to regular life. We relegate these "what ifs" to the fiction section, and when we are ready to come back to reality, we can soothe ourselves with the thought that "We'll never really know."

Along comes someone with a computer. While we'll never have *the* answer to "What if?" we sometimes come face-to-face with the fact that we probably should have picked a different option. Maybe everything could have been different if we had only known better. We are willing to indulge "What if?" but only so far. Computers and analytics can look at questions like "What if?" in ways that humans can't, but also in ways that encroach on our sense of who we are. That's going to feel a little icky.

A lot of books on the "numbers and baseball" shelf spend their time talking about the statistical measures of baseball. The book *Moneyball* famously extolled the virtues of on-base percentage (OBP) over batting average, mostly because batting average pretends that walks never happened. Those books talk about why runs batted in (RBI) and pitching wins are bad stats to measure a player by, because they are so heavily influenced by what a player's teammates did. Eventually, someone mentions Wins Above Replacement (WAR) and it's Hades from here to Halifax. That book is out there if you'd like to read it. This one is a little different.

If you've watched *the* game of baseball for a few decades, you've probably noticed a few changes. There wasn't a point where someone said, "We're going to phase out the complete game for pitchers," but little by little, it happened. In this book, I want to ask, "How did we get here?" How did we get to games that take forever to play, where teams use six pitchers each, strikeouts run rampant, even the National League teams use the designated hitter, and every team seems to be run by a computer? How did we get from the baseball of my youth to this new ballgame?

This is also the part of the book where analytically inclined writers usually start beating people over the head with math. There will be some numbers as you turn these pages, but the numbers aren't the point. My goal is to show you that if we look closely at *the* game of baseball, the reasons for those changes make sense. You may or may not like the way the game has evolved, but those changes didn't just come from left field. Most of them came from people studying the game over time, and asking, "What if things had been different?" and then realizing that there was nothing stopping them. There's always another game tomorrow night.

This might not be a comfortable book. The psychologist in me knows that dealing with change is difficult. As obvious as my own five facts seem to me now, there was once a time when I had never been to Atlanta, nor taken a course in psychology, nor had I become a husband and father. Most shockingly, there was a time before I knew what baseball was. As surely as I have changed, the game of baseball has changed too and there's no way to un-crack those eggs for either one of us. I offer you this book as a journey that we might walk together to better understand *the* game of baseball, how we got to this new ballgame, where we're going, and yes, what we lost along the way.

Will you come along with me?

Chapter 2

Fire Up the Time Machine

There are certain days in your life that end up being more important to writing your five facts than the rest. Sometimes, you realize it while it's happening. Sometimes you don't. I thought September 26, 1999, was going to be one of those days. It was the beginning of my sophomore year at Kenyon College, and I had dreams of working in radio. I didn't have the athletic talent to play in MLB, but I was the kid who would call play-by-play for my baseball video games. I figured that one day, I might do that for a real game.

That night, I strolled into the musty basement studios of WKCO to do the first night of my station internship. Luckily for me, there was no communications major at Kenyon, and the only qualification for hosting a show was promising not to swear on the air. Much. Not that anyone was actually listening. The reason I didn't start until my sophomore year was that the year before, the Federal Communications Commission notified the school that they were operating their radio transmitter on an expired license. It had been out-of-date for two years before anyone had noticed.

I showed up half an hour ahead of time because I was so excited. My mentor, Jeremy, showed up five minutes before the show began. The mechanics of working the radio station mixing board weren't hard and he taught me in 20 minutes. Jeremy told me that the harder—and more important—part was developing a DJ persona. Most people ended up making a two-hour mix tape for themselves, occasionally mumbling the station's call letters. I was already ahead of him on this one. I planned to open my show with a song called "Pizza Cutter" by the band Letters to Cleo, and so I was The Pizza Cutter. I planned a segment called "The Foreign Intelligence Files," where I would read silly news stories and play silly sound effects. Listening back to the shows that I taped, they weren't great, but the show meant a lot to me. I put real work into it. I taught myself basic audio production, cutting promos and ID tags in my spare time. By my senior year, it sounded halfway decent.

While in the studio, I saw all the work that happened behind the scenes. While the three people listening were enjoying whatever song Jeremy played, he was searching through the station's CD collection (hello 1999!) for the next song, lining up the next PSA, and planning out what would happen 15 minutes down the line. Radio, even music-centered radio, was more complicated than just showing up and talking in a stream of consciousness. These were the guts of radio that I never appreciated when all I heard was the end product.

The next week, Jeremy was heading out of town for a wedding and told me that I should shadow whatever replacement DJ was there. I arrived half an hour early again, but this time, no real DJ showed. Since I already knew how the sound board worked, the DJ who was mumbling the call letters for the last time said, "Well, you're here. Why don't you just do the show?" You will never know terror until you see that flashing red light bulb and the microphone is pointed at you.

I faked my way through the next two hours, trying out my "Pizza Cutter" character, and it happened that the station manager had come down to the studio to check on something while I was on the air. Hearing my work, he liked that I had a plan for the show, however goofy it was, and offered me a DJ slot on the spot. That night, the Pizza Cutter was born. I spent three years on the air at WKCO. I was mostly just a college student playing around with a radio transmitter. With the hindsight of a couple of decades, I now know that my voice—both literally and figuratively—wasn't made for radio, though having done a little broadcasting gave me a perspective on how hard it all really is.

It's easy to mouth the words that go with a baseball broadcast. I'd encourage anyone who thinks that they can do it to pull out a tape recorder and try to call an inning of a real game. You'll announce the batter and say where the ball went, but if you're not actively working on it, you'll just be flatly reciting the script of a game. You have to know when to pause. You have to be able to work in the promotion for the local auto parts superstore. You need to be able to use the tone of your voice to communicate the building action, but still keep the dull moments interesting. In baseball, there are a lot of dull moments. If you really listen, you start to notice that announcers have little factoids and stories and insights to fill the time between pitches, and then you realize that someone had to prepare all of those. Sometimes, you'll be in the middle of something else and the batter hits a drive into deep left field to make it a 4–0 game. It's all a lot harder than just watching a game and talking.

As I walked out of WKCO on that September night, I didn't know that life would end up taking me in another direction. I was convinced that this was going to be one of *those* moments in my life, the start of something that would become one of my five facts. I figured I would look back on that night as my first time seeing real radio being made. Maybe someday, years later, I would write about it in my famous baseball announcer memoir. While September 26, 1999, wasn't the glorious beginning to my broadcast career, it still turned out to be pretty memorable. Ten minutes after I left the radio station, I met my wife.

THERE'S A LONG-RUNNING baseball podcast called *Effectively Wild* that I have been privileged to be a small part of over the years. It was started as an offshoot of *Baseball Prospectus,* the website where I have written for more than a decade. I've been a guest (and drawing on my extensive radio experience, occasionally a co-host) on the show many times. *Effectively Wild* isn't usually a "recap show" that plays highlights of yesterday's games or discusses the latest roster moves. There's room for that if something interesting happens, but the podcast is always at its best when discussing *the* game of baseball, rather than *a* game of baseball.

Like a lot of podcasts that have withstood the test of time, a group of fans has grown up around it and the hosts often take e-mail questions from listeners. The questions tend to be one part baseball, one part science fiction. Poor Mike Trout, the soft-spoken generational talent, has been subjected to any number of theoretical experiments on the show in the name of understanding the game. What would happen if the right-handed Trout had to bat left-handed? How long would it take people to figure it out if a fan with minimal baseball playing experience were to switch bodies with Trout? What if things were to be a little different? Or perhaps, *very* different?

The questions might seem strange at first, but science fiction exists within human culture for a reason. It allows space to explore ideas without worrying about the limits of reality. Mike Trout is clearly a gifted athlete and has honed his talent as a baseball player for his entire life, but what part of Trout's greatness was the result of his physical gifts and what part drew from his years of experience playing baseball?

One day, in the podcast's Facebook fan group, I saw a similar question posed by a listener that made me think for a bit. "How far back in time would you have to send an average team of modern-day players before they would be the greatest baseball team on the planet?" Time travel is an old stand-by among sci-fi plot devices and baseball arguments. What would happen if the Big Red Machine of the 1970s had faced off against the Murderers' Row Yankees of the 1920s? We'll never be able to answer that question, but it's fun to talk about. Sometimes it even leads to insight about *the* game of baseball.

In 2018, relief pitcher Adam Ottavino made the controversial claim that if he were to face Babe Ruth, he would "strike him out every time." Ottavino argued that Ruth's long swing would have been overpowered by modern-day velocity and Ruth's training regimen, primitive by modern standards, would have left him comparatively out of shape. As Ottavino himself pointed out, it was a different game back then.

There's a concept in the field of psychology known as the Flynn Effect. It's named after researcher James Flynn, who noted that over several decades, the average score on standardized intelligence tests has crept slowly upward. It's not entirely clear why this is. It's possible that humans are getting smarter. It's also possible that humans have gotten better about designing intelligence tests that flatter themselves more thoroughly. As comedian Emo Philips observed: "I used to think that the brain was the most wonderful organ in my body. Then I realized who was telling me this."

Humans are measurably better off in some ways than they once were. The Centers for Disease Control and Prevention (CDC) estimates a person born in 2020 in the United States will live for 77.0 years, which is up from 69.7 years in 1960 and 47.3 years in 1900. Every four years, the Olympic games provide a guidepost for the limits of a variety of human athletic endeavors, and over time, the Gold Medal marks for most events have trended toward harder, better, faster, and stronger. We enjoy the benefits (and problems) of technologies that weren't even thought of a century ago. There now exists a set of wires which gives you near-instant access to vast oceans of human knowledge and cat videos and is accessible from a device that fits in your pocket. Even better, for a yearly subscription fee, you can use those same wires to watch any MLB game as it unfolds live.

The pitchers and hitters of today might keep pace with each other, but what would happen if we introduced a time machine into the equation? If a team of hitters from the present day were sent to 1927 and faced off against the pitchers of that era, would they keep Babe Ruth company at the top of the home run leaderboard? Would they blow past him? How far back might we need to send a team of average present-day players—a team that would go 81–81 now—before they became the team that everyone feared?

THIS QUESTION HAS a hitch in it, and it has nothing to do with temporal paradoxes. Baseball's double-accounting system makes these sorts of cross-era comparisons difficult. A home run hit by the batter is a home run given up by the pitcher. If we see that home run rates are up, should we conclude that hitters have gotten better or that pitchers have gotten worse? Maybe it's both. Maybe it's neither. Maybe there's some other factor at work.

Midway through the 2015 season, close observers of MLB noticed that suddenly, the ball was looking a little livelier. Before the All-Star Game that year, teams were hitting 0.94 home runs per game. Afterward, with the same batters facing the same pitchers in the same parks, the rate surged to 1.09 round-trippers per game. It doesn't sound like much when you first read it, but that's a random 15 percent increase in the middle of the season when presumably nothing else had changed. That's going to raise a few eyebrows. It came on the back of a decline in scoring around MLB that had seen runs per game fall from 5.14 in 2000 to 4.07 in 2014. There had been worry that MLB was entering a new dead ball era. Something was going on, even if no one knew exactly what.

As a point of comparison, during the 10-year period between 1994 to 2003, MLB averaged 1.07 home runs per team per game, and there were widespread suspicions that there had been a chemical cause for that power surge. In 2003, MLB began testing for performance enhancing drugs and afterward home run rates started falling. Whether those two facts are related is hard to prove, but by 2014, run scoring had fallen to its lowest levels since the late 1980s and early 1990s. Somehow, in the middle of the 2015 season, teams went from the lowest offensive output MLB had seen in a few decades to hitting like it was the middle of the (ahem) "power era" 1990s.

Table 2. Home run rate, per team per game, 2013–2022

Year	Home run rate
2013	0.95
2014	0.86
2015	1.01
2016	1.16
2017	1.26
2018	1.15
2019	1.39
2020	1.28
2021	1.22
2022	1.07

Did MLB try to goose the game midway through 2015 so that it included more dingers? The league denied actively meddling in the matter, but when they investigated the issue for themselves, they found something interesting. Baseballs are not all the same size, although those variations aren't always visible to the naked eye. The rulebook allows a range of a few millimeters of diameter and ounces of weight for what's acceptable, and the mix in late 2015 had tilted toward the smaller side of that range. The smaller balls were more likely to travel a little farther off the bat. It was enough to turn a few fly balls to the wall into fly balls *over* the wall.

One hypothesis was that MLB exerted pressure on its ball supplier, the Rawlings Corporation (which MLB eventually co-bought in 2018), to make the balls more uniform. Research by Ph.D. astrophysicist (and avid knitter) Meredith Wills, who collected and dissected foul balls sent to her by fans, found that the yarn used to stitch the ball together (the "laces" of the ball) had changed from year to year, and that seemed to stretch the leather a little more tightly and change how the ball traveled. Sometimes, little decisions have bigger effects than you might expect. Of all the threads that run through and shape baseball, I doubt anyone would have thought to name the production line at the Rawlings factory in Costa Rica sourcing yarn from somewhere else as the force that most changed the game.

When we interpret data in baseball, especially historical data, we need to be careful. At the very least, we need to be humble. Baseball is a complicated system, and in any system, sometimes you have to admit that you don't know how all the parts work together. A game of baseball might be decided by the players on the field, but there are forces—some hidden, some not-so-hidden—beyond the field that shape the game. It's usually only over time that we can see how. On our journey through this book, we will be looking for those not-so-hidden forces as we try to figure out how we got to this new ballgame.

Let's have our average MLB team put on their seat belts, fire up the DeLorean, and figure this question out. We assume that they will set down in whatever year we program the time machine for and quietly infiltrate and replace one of the already existing teams in the league. No one will notice or think that it's weird that the 1927 Yankees seem to have signed a bunch of new players. That Ruth guy was probably going to strike out every time anyway.

When you play the time machine game, you first have to answer the question *what would they be allowed to take with them?* "How would Babe Ruth perform if magically transported from 1927 to the present?" has a different answer than "How would Babe Ruth perform if he had been born in modern times and then played in today's MLB as a 32-year-old, as he was in 1927?" The question that we're really asking there is how much Ruth would benefit from modern medicine and science. It's an ultimately unanswerable question, but it makes for a good discussion.

They Can Take Their Bodies with Them

What if our time-traveling team could only take their physical bodies with them? If we set them down in 1978, they would find nothing weird about living in the world of disco and Jimmy Carter and polyester uniforms. One of the first things that our time travelers would notice is that they were much bigger than most of the other players in the league.

Figure 2. Average body-mass index (BMI) of MLB players, 1950–2022

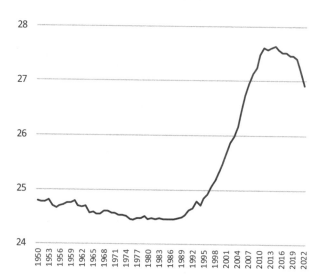

While player heights have been inching upward over the years, the modern player is significantly heavier than ever before. We see the point where the scales tipped in the mid-1990s. The median (50 percent larger, 50 percent smaller) player in present-day MLB would be larger than 90 percent of players who played in any year before the 1990s. There have always been a few "big guys" in MLB, but half of the players on our time travel team would be as big or bigger. Given the timeframe, some readers are already speculating about the cause of that rather obvious jump.

That increase in size comes with a cost. We don't have good data on how fast players from bygone eras ran, but from game data, we can see signs of slowing. In Table 3 below, we see two pieces of evidence. One is the number of triples hit in the league each year divided by the total numbers of doubles and triples. This tells us how often a batter was fast enough to stretch out an extra-base hit to three full bags. The other is the percentage of time in each season that a runner took an "extra" base on another batter's base hit. This could be going from first to third on a single, first to home on a double, or second to home on a single. We can see that over time, there's been less motion on the basepaths.

Next, I included a couple of indicators of power, starting with home runs per fly ball*. I put an asterisk next to fly ball*, because data on the types of batted balls hit (e.g., line drives, ground balls) aren't available back into the 1950s, '60s, and '70s. I improvised. That's actually HR / (HR + 2B + 3B + air outs caught by outfielders). I did the same thing for how often batters hit an extra-base hit (double or triple) as a percentage of fly balls* hit. To make sure we aren't picking up the well-known power enhancing effects of Coors Field, I excluded games played there.

Then there's the last indicator, which is league-wide BABIP, short for Batting Average on Balls in Play. Strikeouts, walks, hit batsmen, and home runs aren't included, because the ball isn't "in play" for the defense. If BABIP goes up, it means that more balls are getting past the fielders and are going for hits.

Table 3. Baserunning, power, and fielding indicators

Year	3B / (2B + 3B)	"Extra" Base Rate	HR/FB*	XBH/FB*	BABIP
1952	17.1%	47.2%	7.4%	17.5%	.270
1962	16.4%	49.9%	10.6%	18.2%	.282
1972	13.8%	47.4%	8.0%	17.0%	.272
1982	13.2%	46.3%	8.5%	18.4%	.284
1992	11.4%	45.2%	7.6%	18.5%	.285
2002	9.6%	43.2%	10.7%	20.6%	.292
2012	10.0%	42.8%	11.0%	20.5%	.295
2022	7.5%	42.9%	11.7%	19.1%	.290

Let's address the elephant in the room and say the word "steroids" because it's probably part of the story, though perhaps not in the way you might think. It's widely accepted that there were players who used anabolic steroids in the 1990s to increase muscle mass. Some have publicly confessed to doing so. Because there was no official testing during that era, it's impossible to know how much of an effect steroids had. We also don't know how many players (or which ones) were building muscles through a healthy diet and exercise and how many found their super power in a syringe. Even after MLB implemented a stringent testing program for performance enhancing drugs, the trend toward larger players has continued. By 2022, the average shortstop (193 pounds) weighed almost as much as the average first baseman from 1982 (194 pounds).

Up to the 1990s, player sizes changed very little over several decades, then seemingly all at once, MLB saw an influx of larger players, across all positions.

Some of the bulk may have been ill-gotten, but whatever else steroids did, they showed that bigger boppers batted better. A third baseman or a right fielder with a little heft might not be as good on defense or the basepaths, but the extra home runs might be worth it anyway. Even after the cheaters were weeded out, there were plenty of players who had developed muscles the natural way, but who might have been previously considered "too big" or "not mobile enough" for MLB. Maybe the real legacy of steroids was changing what teams thought of an as an acceptable body type for a major league player.

LET'S SEND OUR time travel team back to 1972 and have them play a season against the teams from that year. It's impossible to know exactly what would happen next. We're already in the land of science fiction after all, but maybe we can get some idea of the advantages (and disadvantages) that they'd have based on their size.

For one, our present-day team would be facing vintage 1972 hitters, who were more likely to test the defense, averaging 4,426 balls in play per team, compared to 3,971 per team in 2022. One reason that present-day position players can be larger and less mobile is that more outs are now gotten by strikeout and there are fewer balls in play for them to have to chase down. Hitters from 1972 would be facing defenders who were about 2 percent less likely to turn those balls into an out than they were used to. That means that our modern-day defenders would give up an extra 80 hits that 1972 defenses would have gotten an out on.

Or would they? We just made the simultaneous case that modern players are slower and less mobile, which would certainly make them worse defenders, but that they also hit the ball harder as a result. Is the reason for the downward trend in modern-day defense a problem with slower players or the fact that everyone hits rockets in the new ballgame? These questions end up being difficult to resolve, but we will let our estimate of 80 extra hits stand for the moment.

A good quick conversion rule is that changing an out to a hit is worth about three-quarters of a run. If you're someone who has never seen fractions used to describe runs, the idea is that, other than hitting a home run, a batter can't produce a run all by himself. If a batter singles, he not only gets to first base and becomes a potential run, but he also pushes the other runners who might be out there along and some of them might score. Plus, by not making an out, he gives another one of his teammates a chance to do something helpful. The math gets a little complicated, but the average number of runs a team might expect to score after a single, rather than an out, goes up by about .75. Over the course of a season, 80 outs changed into hits means our modern team will allow 60 more runs because of their relatively poor defensive skills. That's a lot.

On the flip side, the defense can't catch a ball that goes over the fence, and here's where our time travelers will have a big advantage. Modern hitters, when they manage to lift the ball into the air, are more likely to hit a home run, by a whopping 4.3 percent margin over our 1970s hitters. The average team in 2022 hit 1,476 fly balls. Over that same number of fly balls, our modern hitters would have a 63 home run advantage, obliterating the defensive disadvantage we saw a moment ago. We haven't even accounted for the extra extra-base hits that they'd also tally. Even after adjusting for the fact that our modern players wouldn't be as spry on the basepaths, the net effect favors the bigger players.

Again, we need to be humble about the limits of our data. We're talking about projected averages over the course of a season in a thought exercise that involves a time machine. But when we add it all up, our bigger batters would score *somewhere around* 30 runs more due to their size advantage. We need to stress that "somewhere around" rather heavily. It's an estimate. We can't swear to that number down to the decimal place, but we also know that the numbers are on the correct order of magnitude. We're pretty sure that our larger players are less mobile and worse defenders, which is a bad thing, but also better power hitters, which is a good thing. Because the arrows are pointing in different directions, we need to know which arrow is bigger, and we see that the extra power has the larger effect.

The effect also isn't huge. Another one of those "on average" guidelines is that if a team scores 10 extra runs or gives up 10 fewer runs (or some combination of both), then they will win one extra game. Our average, 81–81 present-day team would likely win a couple of extra games on account of their size advantage over the players from 1972. That won't turn them into the best team in baseball. It probably wouldn't even make them a playoff team. So yes, size matters, but it isn't everything.

Here we see the first of our not-so-hidden forces shaping baseball. *Baseball has evolved into a game of the arms, rather than the legs.* The very name of the game "baseball" suggests that the primary action of the game should be the running of the bases. That is, after all, how the points are scored. The new ballgame is moving away from that. While players still run the bases and have to chase down the ball, the act of hitting has become the priority. There are plenty of people who prefer the "running style" of the game, but it's a power game now. Stolen base attempts are fun to watch. A good defensive play or a throw to nab a runner is a thing of beauty, but if someone offered you 90 runs in exchange for 60 runs, you'd be a fool not to make that trade. Baseball has changed because the "power game" works. There's probably an upper limit to how many tank-shaped fielders a team can put out there before the defense completely collapses and the tradeoff for the extra home runs isn't worth it anymore, but as of yet, teams don't seem to have found it.

They Can Take Their Arms with Them

Between 2002 and 2022, the average velocity on a fastball has increased by 4.6 miles per hour. Sadly, we don't have complete data on pitch speeds before 2002, but anecdotally, we know that while there have always been a few flamethrowers in the game, what might have been an average fastball in the past is merely on the fringe now.

Figure 3. Average velocity of fastballs (mph), 2002–2022

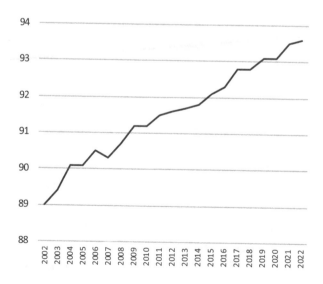

It's not just the ol' speedballs that can make you look like a fool in the new ballgame. When we look at other pitch types (sliders, curves), they have also sped up by about the same amount. Some of that comes from how pitching roles are structured now. In the past, starters were expected to go deep into games if not finish them. Relievers were also expected to stick around for a while too. Until 1987, the majority of relief appearances lasted more than one inning. Pitchers needed to ration their energy. In 2022, the average start lasted a little more than 15 outs, and the majority of relief appearances lasted for three or fewer outs. When pitchers aren't asked to do as much, they can use "max effort" on their pitches more times during a game and reach back for that "little extra." You don't have to worry about the seventh inning if you know someone else will be pitching it.

There were players who threw 95 back in the 1980s, but they were a rare find. A pitcher who could hit 100 mph was near mythical. In 2022, there were 65 different pitchers who threw a pitch at 100 mph during a game. It's possible that there were always pitchers who could have thrown that fast over a short burst, but who would have shorted out after an inning. Because they were considered ill-suited to providing enough "length" in their outings, they were passed over in favor of players who were more suited to the "energy conservation" style. Our time-traveling team would be going back to an era in which they wouldn't face quite as much velocity as they do now. Their opponents would constantly be facing what they had previously only known as "the hardest-throwing guy in the league." It's difficult to model exactly what would happen, but we do have some evidence that our team from 1972 might have a hard time keeping up.

MLB provides data on the speed and spin of every pitch thrown from 2015 onward, along with what happened as a result. I looked at fastballs at each mile per hour step (i.e., fastballs that were 89 mph, 90 mph, 91 mph, etc.). In addition to some simple metrics like swing percentage and contact rate (per swing), I also looked at what happened when batters struck the ball. We can look at both the exit velocity of the ball off the bat and at outcomes like the batting average and slugging percentage on those balls.

Table 4. Results on fastballs, by speed

Velocity	Swing %	Contact %	Exit Velocity (mph)	Batting Average	Slugging Percentage
88 mph	41%	87%	84.4	.357	.629
89 mph	42%	87%	84.4	.362	.630
90 mph	44%	86%	84.2	.360	.634
91 mph	45%	85%	84.2	.362	.626
92 mph	46%	84%	84.1	.365	.627
93 mph	47%	83%	84.0	.362	.612
94 mph	49%	82%	84.0	.360	.606
95 mph	50%	80%	84.0	.362	.600
96 mph	51%	79%	84.0	.357	.578
97 mph	52%	78%	84.1	.359	.569
98 mph	53%	77%	84.0	.354	.563
99 mph	54%	75%	83.8	.365	.565
100+ mph	56%	73%	83.2	.353	.517

If those batting average and slugging numbers look high, it's due to the fact that those columns only count balls hit into play, which means strikeouts are by definition taken out. The pattern here is pretty obvious. As fastball velocity goes up, players swing more and make less contact, which will inevitably lead to more strikeouts. When they do make fair contact with the ball, their ability to get a hit, and especially an extra-base hit, takes a dive as well. There's a pleasant myth that a pitcher who throws hard ends up "supplying the power" to the batter. This isn't correct. Against faster fastballs, batters have trouble making contact and are less likely to drive the ball. You might catch up to a 100-mph heater, but can you hit the ball *square*? If not, you might just end up popping it up.

All of those numbers come from present-day batters, who have the advantage of being used to a world where a lot of pitchers throw 95 or better. Now imagine the unsuspecting hitters of 1972 who may have faced off against Nolan Ryan at some point. They'd have never seen consistent velocity like this, and in a game situation, they'd probably have trouble making contact with it too. If the average fastball of 2002 was below 90 mph, it's likely that it was lower still in the 1960s and 1970s. Even if we assume that it was 89 mph back then, we can see from our modern-day chart that 89 and 93 mph fastballs have a 4 percent difference between them in how often hitters make contact. Our 1972 hitters would probably swing and miss more.

There's an understandable frustration that the new ballgame has become flooded with strikeouts. In 2002, 16.8 percent of batters walked back to their dugout after hearing the umpire call "steeerike three!" In 2022, that number was 22.4 percent. Ed from Lakewood probably has a theory about how hitters so much more selfish than they used to be. I'd suggest that the problem is really the human brain mixed with the laws of physics. The pitching rubber is located 60 feet and 6 inches from home plate, though the pitcher pushes forward and extends his arm toward home when throwing the ball. The actual distance that the ball travels from the hand is about 54 feet. At 89 mph, that journey would take 414 milliseconds (ms), which is less than half a second. The problem is that the human brain needs between 200 and 250 ms to respond to literally anything. MLB players tend to be on the quick side of that spectrum, which is one of the things that makes them elite athletes, but they are still human. With an 89-mph fastball, a batter has about 214 ms to respond to a pitch. Bump that fastball up to 93 mph, and batters have 196 ms of actionable response time. The increase in fastball velocity from 2002 to 2022 has resulted in the loss of about 8 percent of the response time that the batter used to have. Hitting the ball has gotten harder and that's before we consider things like how much the ball breaks and moves.

Here's another of those not-so-hidden forces that is shaping the game: *As players have gotten bigger and as the ball moves faster, neither the basic size and shape of the field nor the laws of physics have changed.* The pitching rubber has remained 60 feet and 6 inches away since the turn of the 20th century, but the pitches are covering that distance ever faster. There's a fundamental asymmetry of baseball that other sports don't have. If they made the hoop bigger in basketball, the average final score of an NBA game would go up, but since both teams shoot baskets, there wouldn't likely be an advantage to one side or the other. In baseball, if pitchers learn to throw harder, batters can't just throw the ball back harder in response. It's an entirely different skill on the batter's part that has to compensate for the increased velocity, and there are limits to how fast the human brain can process information.

They Can Take... the World Baseball Classic with Them?

The World Baseball Classic was dreamed up to be baseball's answer to soccer's World Cup. Professional soccer players have clubs that employ them, but there has always been a strong culture in the sport around national teams. Despite its annual championship being called the "World" Series, 97 percent of all MLB teams play in the same country. Baseball has never had the same level of connection to its national jerseys. There are high-profile international amateur competitions, like the Summer Olympics, but until a few decades ago, the game was so thoroughly dominated by the United States that there seemed little point in trying to stage an international competition among professionals.

It's not surprising that the majority of players in MLB hail from the United States. The game was invented somewhere in New York (where exactly and by whom depends on whom you ask). The foremost league in the world is located in the United States (and Toronto), but the United States is no longer the only country where baseball is played on a wide scale. The game has taken root and grown in countries like the Dominican Republic, Japan, Venezuela, South Korea, and Mexico, and many of the best players from those countries have made their way to MLB. The first World Baseball Classic was held in 2006, and it featured MLB players (and others) wearing their country's flag on their sleeves. While the United States team was formidable, teams from the other countries weren't just there to provide the U.S. someone to win against.

March 20, 2006—Japan vs. Cuba (WBC Gold Medal Game)

Japan	AB	R	H	RBI	Cuba	AB	R	H	RBI
Kawasaki, ss	5	1	0	0	Paret, ss	5	1	2	2
Miyamoto, ss	0	0	0	0	Enríquez, 3b	5	0	0	0
Nishioka, 2b	4	2	2	0	Gourriel, 2b	5	2	1	0
Suzuki, rf	4	3	2	1	Borrero, 1b	4	1	1	0
Matsunaka, dh	4	3	3	0	Cepeda, lf	4	1	2	3
Tamura, lf	3	1	1	2	Urrutia, rf	4	0	2	1
Fukudome, ph-lf	1	0	1	2	Garlobo, dh	4	0	1	0
Satozaki, c	2	0	0	0	Pestano, c	4	1	1	0
Ogasawara, 1b	2	0	0	3	Ramírez, cf	4	0	1	0
Imae, 3b	5	0	1	2					
Aoki, cf	2	0	0	0					

Japan —   400 020 004   10 10 3
Cuba —   100 002 021   6 11 1

2B—Suzuki (1), Ramírez (1), Cepeda (1), Pestano (1); HR—Paret (1, off Matsuzaka, 1st inning, none on), Cepeda (1, off Fujita, 8th inning, 1 on); SH—Satozaki (1); SF—Ogasawara 2 (2); SB—Nishioka (1); CS—Nishioka (1); PO—Nishioka (1); IBB—Matsunaka (1); HBP—Tamura (1, by Odelín) DP—Japan 2 (Nishioka-Kawasaki-Ogasawara, Kawasaki-Nishioka-Ogasawara); E- Kawasaki 2 (2), Watanabe (1), Enríquez (1); PB—Satozaki (1); LOB—Japan 7, Cuba 6; T—3:40; A—42,696

Japan	IP	H	R	ER	BB	SO
Matsuzaka, W (1–0)	4.0	4	1	1	0	5
Watanabe	3.0	4	3	2	0	2
Fujita, H (1)	0.1	1	1	1	0	0
Otsuka, S (1)	1.2	2	1	1	0	2

Cuba	IP	H	R	ER	BB	SO
Romero, L (0–1)	0.1	2	3	3	1	0
Odelín	0.1	1	1	1	1	1
N. González	3.1	3	2	2	2	3
Pedroso	0.1	1	0	0	0	0
Palma	4.0	2	4	2	1	3
Maya	0.0	1	0	0	1	0
Y. González	0.1	0	0	0	0	0
Martínez	0.1	0	0	0	0	0

Watanabe faced one batter in the eighth; N. González faced two batters in the fifth; Maya faced two batters in the ninth.

AS A DOCUMENT of *a* game of baseball, the box score from the championship game of the 2006 WBC is mildly interesting. Tsuyoshi Nishioka somehow managed the trifecta of stealing a base, being caught stealing, and being picked off in one game. Japan scored 10 runs with the benefit of only one extra-base hit (an Ichiro Suzuki double). Cuba used three pitchers to get out *of the first inning.* Late in the game, Cuba managed to pull within a run of Japan, but a four-run ninth put the game away for the eventual champions.

As a document about *the* game of baseball, this box score is remarkable. Several players from the game were either already playing or would eventually play in MLB, but the championship game to a major international baseball tournament was being contested by two nations, one politically alienated from the United States, the other a hemisphere away. It was a testament to how far the seeds of baseball had spread and how deep the roots had grown when those seeds landed. Baseball might still be "America's Pastime" but no longer could the United States claim supremacy over the rest of the world. Baseball has become a world game.

Figure 4 shows how the number of MLB players born outside the United States has grown over the years. (The numbers include Puerto Rico, which is a territory of the United States, but is recognized as a separate entity for international athletic competitions, including the World Baseball Classic.)

Figure 4. Percentage of MLB players born outside United States, 1950–2022

The expansion of the game, both within the United States and around the world, is positive for baseball. There are more baseball fans who love the game, and a bigger talent pool means better players on the field. It's also going to leave a mark on how the game is played. Teams can now find more humans capable of throwing a ball 95 mph. That's going to crowd out some of the pitchers who can "only" throw 92 mph.

Coming back to our team of time travelers, imagine for a moment that MLB passed a rule that said no more than 10 or 15 percent of a team's roster could be composed of players who were born outside the United States. In 2022, 28 percent of MLB players were born in countries not starting with the letter "U." The average team would have to cut roughly 15 percent of its roster, or about four players. MLB would never do this, but if they did, teams would do the only logical thing that they could. They would replace the four players they had to cast off with lesser players born in the United States. Some teams would be more affected than others, but all teams would have less talent than they started with.

By going back in time, our average team from today would be entering a world where this rule had effectively been put into place. The investments that MLB has made over time in international outreach hadn't yet paid their dividends. There were probably kids who had the talent to be MLB players, but who never got into baseball or never got in front of the eyes of an MLB scout. Because teams of today get to take advantage of those global investments of yesteryear, a team going back in time would be able to take a few extra players with them whom their opponents would have never known about.

It brings us to the third of our not-so-hidden forces in the game. *The most important ratio in baseball is the size of the talent pool relative to the number of MLB roster spots available.* If you've ever played in a fantasy baseball league with 10 teams, you know this intuitively. The worst player on your roster is a pretty good everyday player on one of the 30 actual MLB teams. It's not that we can put an exact number to this ratio, but we can certainly recognize how this ratio has changed over time.

Here's how that might play out. Below, I've created eight fake players, each with a made-up "talent" score, that play in a five-team league.

Table 5. Eight Fake Players

Player	Talent Score
Angelo, Michael	97
O'Neil, April	93
Nardo, Leo	91
Atello, Don	83
Phael, Ray	77
Wayne, Bruce	85
Prince, Diana	82
Kent, Clark	75

The first five players on that list are currently rostered and Angelo, O'Neil, and Nardo are secure in their jobs, although Bruce Wayne (85) has more talent than Don Atello (83) and Ray Phael (77) and should have already been in the majors. It's just that up until last year, no one thought to scout Gotham for baseball talent. Once Wayne is found though, he'll make a roster. Don Atello becomes the worst regular player in the league, and poor Ray Phael is out of a job. Clearly though, the overall talent level in the league has gotten better.

Ray Phael will probably go to the minors, but even there, he'll meet Diana Prince who is a super friend of Wayne's, and who is better (82) than Phael (77). If someone gets injured, she'll be the one called up, and her talent score is only one tick below that of Don Atello (83). As a result of the talent pool expansion, the gap between the end of the roster and the top of the marginal pool is smaller. Don Atello and Diana Prince look a little more interchangeable. On the flip side, if the league expands to eight teams, suddenly, Clark Kent (75) will be seeing significant playing time. Expansion waters down the talent pool.

The MLB talent pool can expand in a number of different ways. Jackie Robinson's breaking of the color barrier (or as we should properly call it, "the racism line") in 1947 provided one major influx of talented players in a short period of time, but there have been other forces pushing on this ratio. The population of the United States and other baseball-playing countries steadily increased throughout the 20th and early 21st centuries. The internet has increased the ability of teams to find players who might not have been reached before. A scout can stand on a ballfield in the middle of nowhere, record video of a player, and almost immediately upload that video to a team server. More players are able to be seen, and some of them turn out to be very good.

The other way in which the size of the talent pool changes is that roles within the game are sometimes re-defined, and players who would not have been previously considered can become potential major leaguers. We saw a little while ago that teams have been moving toward larger, more powerful, and less mobile players. The ones who can run and hit for contact are still out there and some of them still have MLB jobs, but if teams are willing to take chances on more body types, it means that the available talent pool of potential MLB players has expanded.

On the other side of that ratio, the primary way that the number of roster spots has changed is through expansion of the league. The American and National Leagues had eight franchises each in 1901 and didn't expand until 1961. Since then, the size of both leagues has nearly doubled. Despite that, the size of the major league roster has remained relatively stable over the decades. After the 2019 season, MLB teams agreed to expand the roster to 26, up from the 25-spot roster that had originally been set in 1910.

In the short-term, expansion dilutes the talent pool by creating more roster spots, and those will be filled by players who would not have been good enough to be in the league otherwise, but the talent pool can expand too. If the talent pool expands faster than the number of roster spots, it's going to affect the game on the field. In this book, we're going to talk a lot about how changes in that ratio have played out between the foul lines.

THE ARC OF baseball history has blessedly bent toward greater inclusion, though baseball has some well-known skeletons in its closet. In 1884, Moses Fleetwood Walker played 42 games for the Toledo Blue Stockings of the American Association. His brother Welday played five games alongside him. The Walkers were the only acknowledged Black players in Major League Baseball until Jackie Robinson's debut. In 1879, William Edward White, then a student at Brown University, played a single game at first base for the Providence Grays of the National League. White had been born in Georgia prior to the Civil War to an enslaved Black woman and the man who held her captive. Because of his light skin, White "passed" as Caucasian and was therefore allowed to play in an era where racist segregation was the norm. The Society for American Baseball Research now considers him to be the first Black player in Major League history.

There was never a formal declaration that Black players were not welcome in Major League Baseball, but some players, notably Hall of Famer Cap Anson, would refuse to take the field against them, and as a result, no one reached out to sign them. There was no question that there were exceptional Black players. In the 1920s, a series of parallel baseball leagues, known as the Negro Leagues, sprung up. The numbers make a very compelling case that the talent level in these leagues was on par with the American and National Leagues, then considered the two "major" leagues in existence. During the 1920s through the 1940s, teams made up of Negro League players would sometimes play against teams made up of Caucasian players in barnstorming exhibition games. While these games didn't count in any standings, records for many of them still exist and Negro League players had a winning record against teams composed of active players from the American and National Leagues.

Even after Jackie Robinson joined the Brooklyn Dodgers, there were still only a few teams willing to sign Black players. It wasn't until the end of the 1953 season, when Ernie Banks debuted for the Chicago Cubs, that half of the 16 American and National League teams existing at the time had even one Black player on their roster. When players did move from the Negro Leagues into the AL or NL, they tended to maintain their level of performance relative to the competition. If the best players in AAA were to be promoted to MLB today, they would likely be bench players. For that reason, the two AAA leagues in the United States (the Pacific Coast League and the International League) are acknowledged as "minor" leagues. However, players who had been high-level performers in the Negro Leagues were also high-level performers when they came to the American and National Leagues, even as they had to endure racist abuse from their new fans. In 2020, Major League Baseball acknowledged that the Negro Leagues were and should be considered to be part of its history, including its statistical history. During the time period between 1920 and 1950, there were three major leagues.

For those who grew up learning the history of only the American and National Leagues, it's important to remember that what happened prior to the breaking of the racism line in those leagues was done in the context of a shallower talent pool. Some of the pitchers whom batters faced would not have been in the league, but for the racism line. The same goes for some of the batters whom those pitchers struck out. When we compare numbers across eras in baseball, we have to take that into account. There were times when the talent pool had been artificially watered down.

AS FANS, WE tend to look at the modern game and wonder why it isn't played like it was in the past. Perhaps, with the aid of a time machine, we might ask the same question, but in reverse. Why didn't teams in the past do what is obvious now? One possibility is that they didn't because they couldn't at the time. Teams used to take trains from city to city because commercial airplanes literally didn't exist. As a dad of five kids (fact four), I sometimes have to remind myself that the realities that my kids face as they grow up are different than the ones that I faced. I'm old enough to remember the question "Do you have an e-mail address?" Had I hopped out of the time machine in the 1970s and encountered my own parents, they wouldn't have understood the question.

Maybe *the* game of baseball really was in some way better "back in the day." I am wildly unqualified to tell anyone how they should feel on the matter, because there isn't a Platonic ideal of baseball. Baseball has the illusion of sameness, and while many of its rules have remained stable over time, the world has changed around it. As the world turns, baseball turns with it, a little at a time. Things have always been a little different than they once were. Those changes matter.

It's common among baseball fans to talk about "The Greatest Player" of all-time. There's a list of players who usually make the cut, most of them long-retired Yankees outfielders. But what does it mean if Adam Ottavino was right? Ottavino has never been anywhere near the best player in baseball even in his own time. What if, magically transported back to 1927, he really would have struck Babe Ruth out every time, along with all of his contemporaries? Does that diminish what Ruth accomplished? Can Ruth be

The Greatest Player in Baseball History if he played against a shallower talent pool, and one that excluded Black players?

I don't think we should look down on Ruth, but we do need to understand that while the rules of the game are (mostly) the same as a century ago when Ruth walked the diamond. Ruth was a product of his time and we have to understand his accomplishments in the context of that time. Ruth was much better than the contemporaries placed in front of him and that's about as far as we can go. We have to live with not being able to answer the question "Who was the greatest?" with any certainty, mostly because time travel is impossible. A century later, it's a new—and different—ballgame. The forces that have changed the world since the days of Ruth have shaped baseball in very real and profound ways. It's many of those same forces that are going to explain why the new ballgame seems a little different than we may remember it.

Chapter 3

Separated at Birth

I sometimes wonder whether anyone has ever wound up in the emergency room over the designated hitter. Baseball fans can get passionate about the details, but nothing seems to stoke the passions like the question of whether the pitcher should step into the batter's box or whether some impostor should take his place. If you want to start an argument—and perhaps a knife fight—at a sports bar, just bring up the two most divisive letters in baseball, "DH."

I grew up cheering for an American League team in Cleveland (fact one), and so the Designated Hitter was always part of the hot dog scented air that I breathed. The American League first experimented with a proto-designated hitter in Spring Training in 1969 and 1970, but it wasn't until 1973 that a designated hitter appeared in a game that counted. It means that there are fans of the game, including myself, who are officially "middle aged" and have never known a world without the DH. For nearly five decades, until the National League also adopted the rule in 2022, the pitcher would bat in certain major league parks. In others, someone else was designated to take his turn.

If there's a not-so-hidden force that shaped baseball during those years, it's the fact that prior to 2000, the American and National Leagues were two separate and rival business entities. While both now effectively function as two conferences of the global conglomerate that is Major League Baseball Inc., each league used to maintain independent offices, have a separate president and administration, and of course, separate rules. The reason that the American League could adopt the designated hitter while the National League did not was that the AL didn't have to ask permission.

I went to my first game at Cleveland Muni in 1986. In that game, eventual Hall of Famer Reggie Jackson walked to the plate in the top of the first inning for the visiting California Angels and then walked back to the dugout after striking out for the third out of the inning. He didn't join his teammates on the field. No one blinked. In the bottom of the fourth inning, Cleveland's designated hitter Andre Thornton hit the first major league home run that I witnessed in person. I didn't watch a pitcher bat live and in person until I was in college and my family took a trip to Pittsburgh to see a game.

Even as the National League has fallen, with no sign of going back, the DH still has a reputation as being *the* most divisive issue in baseball. Scientific random-digit dialing polls among the public on the designated hitter issue are hard to come by. (I'm told that there are other, more pressing concerns out there.) There are plenty of internet polls, but internet polls are dominated by internet trolls. In 2018, a polling group at Seton Hall University found a roughly even split among the public about the DH. Even then, polling proved to be fickle. By March of 2021, the same Seton Hall group found that respondents favored the DH being added to the National League by a ratio of about 2-to-1. A year later, the fans got their wish.

Because of my work as a researcher and writer at *Baseball Prospectus*, I consider myself something of an expert on polling. In the Summer of 2021, before the implementation of the universal DH, I decided to try my hand at it. I created a list of 39 controversial statements about the game of baseball (e.g., I prefer a style of play with more bunting; I think a computer/machine should call balls and strikes during MLB games). I asked respondents to rate their agreement with each on a six-point scale. The first statement was, "I think pitchers should have to bat for themselves." It didn't say "designated hitter," although the next question, "I think both leagues should adopt the same rule with respect to the designated hitter" did. Based on my own limited resources, I had no illusion that this would be the sort of market research study that MLB might conduct privately about its product. I've been writing about the joys of analytics in baseball for more than a decade. The people who were likely to read my work and respond to my poll are the sort of biased sample who would produce this sort of distribution:

"I believe that analytics plays too large a role in baseball today."

	1	2	3	4	5	6	
Disagree	40.6%	27.3%	11.9%	9.9%	5.5%	4.8%	**Agree**

Even if the bias in the sample means we can't estimate what percentage of all MLB fans prefer their hitters to be designated, we can at least look at some interesting findings *within* the survey. I also asked respondents to identify the team that they grew up cheering for and the team for whom they cheered as an adult. In a cross-tab that should surprise no one, here are ratings for the statement "I think pitchers should have to bat for themselves." (Higher scores mean more agreement.)

Table 6. Support for pitchers batting, by league allegiance

Team Cheering For Was In	Growing Up	Currently
American League	2.21	2.15
National League	3.42	3.48

There's an obvious split in there, with AL fans more supportive of the DH and NL fans more supportive of the pitcher batting. The numbers didn't change much whether I looked at childhood allegiances or adult ones, but that's because most folks still cheered for the same team that they grew up with. I did have a subsample of respondents, big enough to look into, who had switched their allegiances over their lifetime.

Table 7. Support for pitchers batting, including league switchers

Teams Cheered For	Rating
Cheered for different teams, both in AL	1.88
Always cheered for the same AL team	2.08
NL team growing up, AL team currently	2.83
Always cheered for the same NL team	3.46
AL team growing up, NL team currently	3.48
Cheered for different teams, both in NL	3.80

Surprisingly, the factor most influencing a person's views on the DH was the league of the person's currently favored team. People weren't prisoners of their childhoods. We all grow and change. In the poll, people who believed that pitchers should bat for themselves were much less likely to believe in standardizing the rule across both leagues. Those who favored the DH were more likely to endorse a single rule. I think that the "let the pitchers hit" segment of the audience had already given up any hope that the American League would return to its pre-1973 form, but wanted to keep the pitcher-hitting rule for the National League.

If DH opponents have one thing that they can hang their baseball caps on, it's that when someone converted from being an AL fan to being an NL fan, they cozied up to the idea of the pitcher hitting. Fans whose journey took them in the other direction did end up sliding toward the DH side of the dial, although not as strongly. Once you have a taste for what the game looks like with the pitcher hitting, you might see the allure. It means that baseball fans aren't as set in their ways as we might think. Maybe the difference between starting a fight in a bar and realizing that there's more than one way to look at the game is a little exposure to the "other" side.

In fact, I have my own theory that the designated hitter hung on as long as it did because of the expansion of cable television. When I was growing up, if you lived in an American League city, you likely only went to games that involved a DH and never saw your favorite team send a pitcher to bat unless they made the World Series. I was enough of a baseball junkie that I would sometimes watch the Saturday *Game of the Week* that was televised nationally, and sometimes I'd be rewarded with a game between the Dodgers and Cardinals.

Even if you weren't a baseball junkie, you still had a place to find pitchers batting. Ted Turner, owner of both Atlanta's baseball franchise and the local Atlanta TV station which broadcast their games, had the idea to syndicate Channel 17's feed across the emerging medium of cable in the 1980s. It was strange for people all over the country to be watching a something that was local to Georgia, but the idea worked. The channel was later re-cast as Turner Broadcasting System, and as more cable systems picked up the channel, even those outside the Southeastern United States, Turner's team turned into "America's Team." Now, the people of Poughkeepsie and Pensacola had a major league team who would visit their living room every night and it was a National League team. In the 1990s, when Atlanta made a run of World Series appearances, they had a following of fans in other cities who had become smitten by flipping through the dozens of new channels they had access to on cable.

Cable is a place where a lot of my generation tasted forbidden fruit for the first time. Our family's cable package also carried WGN in Chicago, which broadcast Cubs games and WOR out of New York, which had the rights to the Mets. Oddly, there didn't seem to be an American League team with a consistent national reach. Because of the magic of cable, I got to see a double switch playing right there on my television screen. For a 12-year-old, it was mind-blowing. Even though the old National League rule about pitchers batting is gone—and to lay my own cards on the table, I'm happy that it's gone—I still have an inexplicable soft spot in my heart for it. Maybe those late 1980s Mets and Cubs games on basic cable made someone else realize that things could be different too. The other drunk person in the bar might actually have a point. Maybe instead of starting a fight, late-night double switches saved someone's life.

IT WAS AMAZING that Ron Blomberg of the Yankees strode to the plate at Fenway Park on Opening Day of 1973, drew a bases-loaded walk off Luis Tiant, and then didn't grab a glove when the Yankees were finally put out. Blomberg's Yankees were up 3–0 after the top of that first inning, but eventually lost to the Red Sox 15–5. Everyone focuses on Blomberg's role in that game because he got to hit in a designated way first, but the box score has a bit of delicious irony in it. The Red Sox notched 20 hits, including at least one hit by eight of their nine starters. The exception was the one player in the lineup who had been designated to hit, Orlando Cepeda, who went 0-for-6.

April 6, 1973, was the day that the twins were separated and the

April 6, 1973—New York at Boston (Regular Season)

New York (A)	AB	R	H	RBI	Boston	AB	R	H	RBI
Clarke, 2b	5	0	1	0	Harper, lf	6	1	3	1
White, lf	5	0	0	0	Aparicio, ss	6	0	1	1
M. Alou, rf	5	2	2	0	Yastrzemski, 1b	4	2	2	2
Murcer, cf	3	1	0	0	Smith, cf	5	2	2	0
Nettles, 3b	2	2	1	2	Miller, pr-cf	0	0	0	0
Blomberg, dh	3	0	1	1	Cepeda, dh	6	0	0	0
F. Alou, 1b	4	0	3	0	Petrocelli, 3b	4	3	3	0
Munson, c	3	0	0	0	Fisk, c	4	4	3	6
Michael, ss	4	0	0	0	Griffin, 2b	5	2	4	2
					Evans, rf	5	1	2	1

New York (A) —   301 010 000   5 8 2
Boston —   143 403 00x   15 20 0

2B—M. Alou 2 (2), Fisk (1), Smith (1), Evans (1), Harper (1); HR—Nettles (1, off Tiant, 3rd inning, none on), Yastrzemski (1, off Stottlemyre, 1st inning, none on), Fisk 2 (2, off Stottlemyre, 2nd inning, 1 on; off McDaniel, 4th inning, 3 on); HBP—Fisk (1, by Cox); Smith (1, by Cox); SF—Yasstrzemski (1); SB—Griffin (1), Yastrzemski (1); CS—Clarke (1); DP—Boston 1 (Fisk-Aparicio); E- Nettles (1), Michael (1); LOB—New York 7, Boston 11; T—2:57; A—32,882

New York (A)	IP	H	R	ER	BB	SO
Stottlemyre, L (0–1)	2.2	8	8	6	0	1
McDaniel	2.1	7	4	4	1	2
Cox	3	5	3	2	1	0

Boston	IP	H	R	ER	BB	SO
Tiant, W (1–0)	9	8	5	5	5	2

longest experiment in MLB history began. Looking back, the designated hitter rule was one of the weirdest things about professional sports in the United States. The length of the football field doesn't change based on the home team, nor do some basketball courts have a five-point line. Part of the delightful quirkiness of baseball was that both the field dimensions and rules changed from place to place.

The early rules of baseball de-emphasized the role of the pitcher. The term "pitcher" itself is a relic of the 19th century. While the overhand throwing motion that we now think of has *become* the definition of "pitching," the word used to mean something different. It's an underhand motion that's meant to place the object in a specific landing spot, like with horseshoes or cornhole bags. In the 1845 Knickerbocker Rules, considered by many to be the first codified laws of baseball, "throwing" was explicitly forbidden and it wasn't until the 1870s that raising one's arm above the waist was permitted. The batter could also request where the ball should be thrown, whether above the belt or below. Since the batter knew where the ball was going, it made it easier to strike the ball into play so that the running part could begin. The game, after all, was called "base ball." It was supposed to be about the bases. The pitcher was mostly there to serve the ball up and get the process started.

Some pitchers became tricksters though, experimenting with changing speeds, adding spin to the ball, and using an overhand delivery, and eventually the rules were re-written to allow all of it. That changed literally everything about *the* game of baseball. Freed from its initial restrictions, pitching developed into its own art. It quickly became obvious that pitching was both the most specialized and most important skill set on the field. The pitcher was the only player who was guaranteed to touch the ball and if he was any good at his craft, it made the job of the other eight players on the field much easier.

The skills that translated into good pitching were different than those needed for hitting and fielding. There was a fair amount of athleticism and body coordination needed for both, but the pitcher was effectively in motion for most of the game, repeating the same actions over and over. Hitters spend most of their time sitting, and it might be half an hour between the times when an individual fielder has to do something. When hitters or fielders do react, they need quick, powerful movements, going from standstill to sprint in half a second. The pitcher most certainly needed arm strength, but also the ability to make precise finger and hand movements during the pitch to get the spin just right, something that position players didn't need to think about. The pitcher also needed to be able to figure out how to use all those spins and speeds to fool the batter on a few pitches in a row.

When baseball emerged in the 19th century, it was a game played by clubs, often clubs of "gentlemen," and clubs are supposed to be collections of equals. The language that we use to speak about baseball reflects that history. MLB teams are still commonly referred to as "ball clubs" and what are called "locker rooms" in other sports are "clubhouses" when baseball players are in them. Baseball was also a local game. A player athletic enough to be a good pitcher for the local "town ball" club was likely good enough based on raw athletic talent to be both a good hitter compared to his teammates and to play another position if someone else happened to be taking a turn on the mound. The pitcher was just one of the nine and everyone was supposed to contribute. The foundation of baseball's rules, and more importantly its culture, was forged in this environment. If everyone was an equal, the pitcher batting seemed natural and practical.

Even in the early days of what became known as the "major leagues," the line between specialized pitchers and specialized position players was still coming into focus. In what is widely acknowledged to be the first major league game, the Cleveland Forest Citys visited the Fort Wayne Kekiongas on May 4, 1871. The box score from the game lists Cleveland pitcher "Uncle" Al Pratt, who would lead the 1871 National Association recording a rousing 34 strikeouts in 224⅔ innings, batting in the sixth position. The pitcher for Fort Wayne, 19-year-old Bobby Mathews, hit second. Pratt played seven games in the field that year, when he was occasionally relieved by, and likely switched places with, outfielder Charlie Pabor. Mathews didn't play the field that year, primarily because he was busy pitching every single inning that the Kekiongas logged that year. Starting lineup data are hard to come by before the 1900s, but we do have data for 1871, 1872, and 1874. In those years, the pitcher hit somewhere other than ninth in the lineup 84, 78, and 70 percent of the time, respectively. Back then, the pitcher wasn't just considered an automatic out.

In 1871, there were a total of 11 players who pitched in at least five National Association games. Four of them (36 percent) also played at least five games in other non-pitching positions. The next year, it was 13 out of 18 (72 percent). As late as 1884, the number was 68 percent. Team rosters were smaller in the 1800s, but even in 1901, considered the beginning of the "modern era" with the formation of the American League to pair with the already 25-year-old National League, 14 percent of pitchers also did significant moonlighting on other parts of the diamond. The practice mostly dried up by 1910, but by that point, the game had spent nearly 40 years in which the idea of the pitcher as a specialist player hadn't fully flowered. Forty years is a long time.

As baseball grew in popularity and developed into a profession, more talent (and money) came into the game and teams signed players from further afield, looking for the best of the best to fill their rosters. While a player might have elite pitching skills and be "pretty good" with the lumber, being a major league hitter, even then, required elite skills. Still, the fact that a player had elite pitching skills proved to be enough of a reason to sign him. A good batter could only affect one of every nine plate appearances that the team took. A good pitcher could affect *all* of the plate appearances that the other team took. If you were any good at pitching, it didn't matter that you couldn't quite cut it as a hitter.

As the rift between pitchers and hitters developed, it was openly talked about. In 1891, the newspaper *The Sporting Life* complained that "[e]very patron of the game is conversant with the utter worthlessness of the average pitcher when he goes up to try and hit the ball. It is most invariably a trial, and an unsuccessful one at that." The quote is in a story reporting on a proposal that mirrored the present-day designated hitter rule. It was later voted on (and defeated) by the franchise owners of the National League. Had the vote gone a different way, the designated hitter would have been older than anyone reading this book. It would have been part of the old ballgame. Instead, the cement was left to harden and the pitcher batting became the norm, even if everyone knew it was a farce.

Faced with a choice between two arrows, teams had to make a decision about what to do with the pitcher. We know what decision they all made. Throughout major league history, teams were willing to punt an entire lineup spot to ensure that they had a quality pitcher on the mound. This was done without question. The fact that it produced a near-automatic out was something that they decided to live with. In theory, a team could have tried to find the best hitters who could still pitch "well enough" and "out-hit their mistakes" in the way that teams will sometime sign a sweet-swinging, but defensively suspect outfielder. No one tried that. The act of pitching is just too important and too hard to be good at.

WHEN THE AMERICAN League finally adopted the designated hitter rule, they did so to try to inject more offense into the game. In 1972, the average MLB team scored a mere 3.69 runs per game, which was one of the lowest offensive outputs in MLB history, higher than only a few years in the "dead ball" era and the 1968 "Year of the Pitcher." More than that, the American League had seen scoring fall to 3.47 runs per game among its teams, compared to the much more respectable 3.91 runs in the National League.

One way to spur some action would be to replace the automatic out at the bottom of the lineup with a trained hitter. The American League went for it. The National League stood pat. Ron Blomberg stepped to the plate, and the great experiment began in earnest. In Chapter 1, we talked about the question "What if things had been a little different?" This is the one case where we have decades of history (and data) to help us answer that question. It turns out that the designated hitter rule was a study in how one little change can affect things that no one would have ever expected.

Let's start with the obvious. Table 8a shows the number of runs scored per game in each league in the years before and after the implementation of the DH rule in 1973.

Table 8a. Average runs per game, AL vs. NL teams

Runs Scored per team	AL Teams	NL Teams
1970	4.17	4.52
1971	3.87	3.91
1972	3.47	3.91
1973	4.28	4.15
1974	4.10	4.15
1975	4.30	4.13
1976	4.01	3.98

Wait a minute. That chart shows that in 1973, the American League did feature higher scoring games, but in 1974, the National League surprisingly scored more, even without the designated hitter. Even in 1976, the AL barely topped the NL. Perhaps the designated hitter was a giant flop? Let's continue that chart.

Table 8b. Average runs per game, AL vs. NL teams

Runs Scored per team	AL Teams	NL Teams
1977	4.53	4.40
1978	4.20	3.99
1979	4.67	4.22
1980	4.51	4.03
1981	4.07	3.91
1982	4.48	4.09
1983	4.48	4.10

Sometimes it takes an effect a little while to show up in your data set. Were we to extend that chart farther, it would show that the American League opened up a steady and persistent gap of around three- or four-tenths of a run per game over the National League. It wasn't until 2020, a season which was significantly altered by the COVID-19 pandemic, that the National League outscored the American again. During that year, the National League adopted the designated hitter rule in what was supposed to be a temporary measure. It turned out that two years later, it became permanent.

Let's say an average National League team, fed up with their pitchers having a "triple slash" line (AVG/OBP/SLG) of .110/.150/.142—which was what they hit in 2021, the last year of pitchers batting—decided to release all of them and instead sign hitters who were around league average. In this way, they could always have nine professional hitters in the lineup, like the American League did. They'd likely have seen a gain of four-tenths of a run per game in their offensive output. That's good. The problem is that someone still has to pitch.

In 2021, MLB pitchers as a whole had an earned run average of 4.27. If you count unearned runs—and they do count—the average pitcher gave up 4.65 runs per nine innings. Among the pitchers who threw at least 100 innings in

2021, the worst ERA belonged to Rockies starter Chi Chi Gonzalez at 6.46. We have to assume that if our league-average hitters also had the ability to pitch better than a 6.46 ERA, more of them would have spent some time on the mound as well. The only one who did was the one-of-a-kind Shohei Ohtani. At the *very* least, the average team would be surrendering more than two extra runs per game if they let their position players pitch, and it would have probably been *a lot* worse than that. No one would trade a four-tenths run increase in scoring for a two-run increase in the number of runs given up. One of these arrows is clearly bigger than the other. If that meant playing with a lineup with only eight professional hitters in it, so be it.

The reality is that pitchers were awful hitters, even back to the infancy of the American and National Leagues, and the gap between pitchers and the rest of the league only became wider over time.

Figure 5. Pitcher on-base percentage (OBP) vs. league, 1950–2021 (2020 excluded)

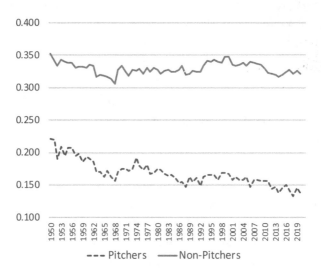

Pitchers hitting is the closest we'll ever get to answering the question of what would happen if an elite athlete from one sport decided to move to another sport full-time. In 1994, basketball legend Michael Jordan abruptly "retired" after his Chicago Bulls had won three consecutive NBA Championships. Instead of participating in the 1993–94 NBA season and most of the 1994–95 season, Jordan decided to play baseball. The Chicago

White Sox signed the locally discovered 30-year-old outfield prospect and Jordan was assigned to the team's AA club in Birmingham. In his lone season at AA, Jordan hit .202 with three home runs. Clearly there was no lack of athletic ability. Jordan returned to the NBA in 1995 and led the league in scoring for the next three seasons while the Bulls won three more NBA championships. You need to be more than just a good athlete to hit a baseball.

Pitchers are, by definition, professional athletes who are selected because they excel at a very specific set of skills. Just not *that* skill. In some parks, we asked them to try anyway. The results were predictable. During the DH's swan song year of 2021, pitchers struck out more than 40 percent of the time. There's no shame in that. Pitchers are surely better hitters than 99 percent of other adults, but they were tasked with going up against some of the finest pitching talent on earth: *themselves.*

The battle over the designated hitter reveals one of those not-so-hidden forces that shape the game. The fundamental question of baseball is: *What do we do about the pitcher?* A baseball club might have been conceived as a team of equals, but some players turned out to be more equal than others. If you want to understand *the* game, you have to understand the role of the most important person on the field, the pitcher.

WERE THERE EFFECTS of the designated hitter, other than the obvious? From 1973 through 2021, the two leagues drifted apart in other ways, many of which could be tied directly back to the DH. For starters, bullpen usage began to differ between the two leagues. In 2021, the average American League team used 3.33 relievers per game, compared to the average National League team, who used 3.54. That's a difference that persisted through the history of the designated hitter. The problem wasn't that National League relievers were worse and needed replacing more often. Starting in 1997, MLB was kind enough to provide a nice natural experiment when for the first time, interleague games took place between American and National League teams. The home league's rules applied, which gave us games in which American League teams played without a DH, and some where National League teams played with one. Looking at data from 2021 for visiting teams, it was clear why NL teams always seemed to have a few extra spare hurlers.

Table 9. Number of relievers used per game, 2021

	American League Park	National League Park
American League Team	3.30	3.69
National League Team	3.26	3.56

Baseball's one-way substitution policy meant that a National League manager, operating without the DH, sometimes had to choose between sending the pitcher to the plate, which would allow him to pitch in the next half-inning, or a pinch-hitter. Sometimes a manager had to lift a pitcher for a pinch-hitter before he may have wanted to. It meant that National League teams needed slightly deeper bullpens when putting together their rosters. By the end of the season, NL relievers, on average, had a few more days when they had to warm up and enter a game. Over time, that can wear a staff down.

Interleague play showed us something else about the designated hitter rule. Not only is there a home-field advantage in baseball, there was also a "home rules" advantage. In same-league games, between 1997 and 2021, the home team won 53.8 percent of the time. During that same period, American League teams won 56.2 percent of their interleague home games, while the National Leaguers won only 51.7 percent of theirs. Clearly, the American League had an advantage. When visiting the other league, the adjustments that teams had to make didn't just cancel out. In an American League park, the National League team was inserting a bench player into its lineup at DH, while the American League already had a DH specifically selected for his ability to hit. At a National League park, when a pinch-hitting situation arose, the American League team had someone who was good enough to be a starter, often one signed entirely for his ability to hit, waiting on its bench. The National League team had no such luxury. It was easier for American League teams to adapt to National League rules, and the results showed it.

In the most famous interleague series of all, the World Series, it hasn't always been clear what path the leagues would take in resolving the differences between their rules. From 1973 to 1975, American League teams had to leave their designated hitters at home in the Fall Classic, but in 1976, Dan Driessen of the Cincinnati Reds became the first designated hitter to appear in a National League park in a game that mattered. For a decade, the World Series alternated rules, with the entire series played under one set or the other. It wasn't until 1986 when the "home team rules" policy was adopted. From 1986 to 2021, home teams won 57.1 percent of World Series games, a stronger home-field advantage than in the Divisional Series (53.6 percent) and League Championship Series (55.5 percent) rounds that featured two teams from the same league.

Starting in 2018, home-field advantage in the World Series was awarded to the team that had the better record during the regular season. Because the American League had an edge in interleague games, the American League champion was more likely to have a better record than the National League representative, and was more likely to be facing a more tired bullpen. The advantage was slight, but the designated hitter rule indirectly made it more likely that an American League team would win the World Series.

I KNOW THAT this will get me in trouble, but I cheered the day that the designated hitter came to the National League. During the COVID-19 season of 2020, National League teams had used the DH and, other than a massive, worldwide pandemic, nothing awful happened as a result. In 2022, MLB made the inevitable official. A close look at the numbers shows that the game had simply evolved past the need for pitchers hitting anyway.

The word that comes up most often in pro-pitcher arguments is "strategy." Baseball is unique among the "major" sports in that it has both one-way substitution (a player removed may not return) and no game clock. A game could go on forever, and you only have a limited number of players to get you through the day. Removing a pitcher as a hitter also meant removing the pitcher *as a pitcher*. In the National League, there was always the question of what would happen if the pitcher was due up to hit in a key situation with runners on base and the score close, especially if he was pitching a good game so far.

We like watching people squirm in baseball, and this was a decision that managers in the National League had to make and AL skippers didn't, and so the thinking went, it meant that National League managers had to master "strategy." Or did it? Let's look—by inning—at what percentage of the time the pitcher's spot came up in NL rules games, and among those situations, how often he hit for himself.

Table 10. Pitcher hitting for self percentage, 2017–2021, NL Rules Games

Inning	Pitcher's spot came up	Pitcher hit for self
1	2.2%	100.0%
2	43.8%	99.0%
3	59.1%	97.9%
4	36.5%	91.2%
5	54.5%	75.7%
6	37.9%	42.7%
7	43.7%	15.8%
8	40.1%	8.1%
9	42.2%	5.7%

There was really only one inning where it could have gone either way, with the sixth inning being a toss-up. It means that we pretty much knew what a manager was going to do, mostly because they all did the same thing. Most of the time, managers didn't even have to make that decision. The pitcher's spot only came up a little more than a third of the time in the sixth inning. Even then, in an age of pitch counts, it was sometimes obvious what was going to happen anyway.

Ah, but there were those delicious situations where sometimes everything came together. A pitcher was cruising, but his spot in the lineup came up in a tight spot. Table 11 shows the percentage of games in which a manager faced some of those tough calls. The numbers in parentheses below are the rates at which the pitcher ended up hitting for himself.

Table 11. Frequency of "difficult situations" and pitcher hitting for self percentage, 2017–2021 (2020 excluded)

Situation	5th inning	6th inning	7th inning
Pitcher is due up, game is within 2 runs, the pitcher has given up 3 or fewer runs so far	34.6% (85.0%)	14.4% (46.7%)	18.3% (16.3%)
Pitcher is due up, game is within 2 runs *and his team is losing*, the pitcher has given up 3 or fewer runs so far	12.6% (78.6%)	4.2% (39.4%)	5.1% (3.1%)
Pitcher is due up, game is within 2 runs and his team is losing, *but there are runners in scoring position*, the pitcher has given up 3 or fewer runs so far	1.9% (71.0%)	0.6% (23.2%)	1.1% (1.9%)

The classic agonizing scenario where a pitcher is pitching well, but the situation calls for a trained hitter would happen a couple of times per year. Even then, it's really only in the sixth inning that we saw any sort of variability in what happened next.

Around the time the designated hitter rule was put in place, something else happened. The role of the pitcher changed. This is something we'll talk about in detail in Chapter 4, but slowly, starting pitchers began to pitch fewer innings. Teams began to use relievers for shorter bursts, often one inning at a time. In the National League, it meant that a manager could pinch-hit for the starter earlier and earlier, and because the relievers were mostly coming out of the game anyway after throwing an inning, they could also easily be pinch-hit for.

Figure 6. Percentage of all plate appearances taken by pitchers in NL rules games, 1973–2021 (2020 Excluded)

The National League solved the problem of pitchers hitting by pinch-hitting, while the American League used a designated one. There's a difference between "strategy" and "being handed a set of rules which requires pushing three buttons, rather than one."

The other argument against the DH that Ed from Lakewood would make on the local sports yakker was that National League rules promoted "small ball," which is the style of play that emphasizes things like bunting, stolen bases, and hitting and running. The reason why pitchers were often called on to bunt was not because they're somehow exceptionally good bunters. In fact, from 2017 to 2021, when pitchers laid down a bunt to advance a runner, they were successful 76.0 percent of the time, compared to trained hitters who succeeded 81.6 percent of the time. Even if the part of baseball that you love the most is seeing a good sacrifice bunt, you want a trained batter doing it.

The reason for the bunting was that since the pitcher was a near-automatic out anyway, teams might as well try to get something in return for that out. In situations (2017–2021 again) with either two outs or no runners on base, pitchers—who had no reason to bunt—struck out 46.4 percent of the time. When they did make contact, 64.1 percent of those balls were hit on the ground. Of those ground balls, 88.9 percent ended up in the glove of an infielder. The price of all that "strategy" was watching someone who was probably going to either strike out or hit a weak ground ball. It's not like bunting was a guarantee of success. In plate appearances where a pitcher tried to bunt at least once during his minute in the sun, he *still* struck out 25.8 percent of the time. Pitchers bunted because it's the one batting skill that they got a C– in, rather than an F.

National League rules also didn't actually encourage bunting from anyone other than the pitcher. Again, during the period of 2017 to 2021, in situations where there was a runner on first with no one out and someone other than a pitcher up, the batter bunted 4.3 percent of the time in games played under NL rules. Under American League rules, the rate was 4.6 percent. If you already have one batter in your lineup who's an automatic out, you probably don't want to give away even more outs.

Were there more steals with the designated hitter in place? Looking at situations where there was a runner on first with second base clear, the runner attempted to steal 6.2 percent of the time under NL rules and 6.3 percent of the time under AL rules. Did Ed from Lakewood get to see more hit-and-run in NL games? No. Looking at situations where runners were on (and excluding 3–2 counts), in games played under NL rules, teams put both the runners into motion and the ball into play 0.7 percent of the time. In the AL it was 0.8 percent. The evidence suggests that if Ed really likes small ball, he should welcome the designated hitter.

About the only piece of in-game strategy that the lack of a designated hitter produced was the occasional intentional walk ahead of the pitcher. In a key situation, especially with two outs and first base open, teams would walk the scheduled trained hitter to face the pitcher instead. They did this 668 times from 2017–2021. As a point of reference, pitchers got 416 extra-base hits (of any sort) during that time. While pitchers would occasionally have a moment of glory, the real thing that the lack of a designated hitter brought was more intentional walks which were designed to kill off rallies.

Finally, there was the argument that took aim at the role the designated hitter played in the game. Fans who were disappointed that the pitcher didn't have to hit were also disappointed that there was a batter who didn't need to contribute in the field. The stereotype of the designated hitter has always been of a lumbering oaf who may not have even owned a glove. The numbers tell us a different story.

In 2021, I found the 15 players who logged the most time at the designated hitter spot. These would have been the "regular" DHs for their respective American League teams. It turns out that on average, they had 170 plate appearances at positions *other than designated hitter*. It means teams had aready moved away from having a regular designated hitter who only did one thing. The DH role has become less of an identity and more of an assignment that someone does each day.

THE DESIGNATED HITTER debate shows us two things. One is that when you look back and ask the question "What if things had been a little different?" it's easy to reach for a simple answer. The American League thought that they were doing something that would make the games more interesting and higher scoring. Over time, we can see things no one would have anticipated happening as a result. I don't know that we'll ever have another natural experiment in sports like that again. For nearly 50 years, two mostly isolated and otherwise equal leagues played with one small variation in their rules. We all got to watch it develop over time. And argue about it.

It turns out that the designated hitter did bring more offense into the American League game, but baseball is a complex system. In a complex system, small changes can end up having effects on things that you never expected them to. If you want to understand the not-so-hidden forces that shape the game, you have to be willing to look for those sorts of downstream effects. It's an exercise in thinking a problem all the way through before you jump to the simple answer.

The second thing that the designated hitter debate teaches us is that baseball revolves around and must first be understood from the pitcher's mound. That seems an odd thing to say given that we're supposed to be discussing the designated *hitter*. It was never about the hitter who filled that slot. It was about who *wasn't* batting. The point of the designated hitter was to answer the question "What do we do about the pitcher?"

The reason that we now have the designated hitter in the National League is that most of the arguments against it either weren't true to begin with or were becoming less and less true. Pitchers hitting didn't actually produce more small ball. It was mostly just pitchers bunting. Whatever "strategy" there once was had been replaced by a parade of pinch-hitters and relievers. The reality of pitchers hitting was mostly strikeouts and weak ground balls, risking injury to do something for which they were not trained and weren't good at. About the only argument left was that pitchers hitting was a tradition, but it was a tradition that was based on a lie. A baseball club is not nine players of equal standing. A baseball team consists of one very specialized player and eight friends.

Teams were willing to torpedo their own lineups, dedicate half their rosters to one of the nine positions, and even rewrite the rules of the game to work around a level of batting ineptitude that would never be tolerated from any other position. Pitching is *that* important in *the* game of baseball. As we go forward to understand the new ballgame, we need to understand the role of the most important player on the field: the pitcher.

Chapter 4

The Evolution of an Octopus

My wife was born in Moscow. When the Soviet Union collapsed in the early 1990s, her parents, both virologists, decided that it was an opportune time to leave. My wife was 10 when that happened, so she came with them to the United States. All relationships have an improbable origin story. Mine just happens to involve the end of the Cold War. While my wife had no choice in changing continents, she had a brother 11 years her senior who stayed behind to make a life for himself in Moscow. Petr eventually wrote his own five facts, becoming a professor of music and the father of three of my nieces. From what I understand, he's a celebrity in the field of contemporary Russian compositions for orchestra. I sometimes wonder what it's like to be that deep into such a weirdly specific niche.

I don't get to see Petr very often, but he and his family make summertime visits to the United States, and I enjoy talking to him. He's an intelligent and thoughtful person. One day, during one of those visits, he wanted to know more about this game that I spent so much time thinking and writing about. Baseball is largely unknown in Russia, and he was curious. Then he asked me *that* question: How exactly is baseball played?

It's a terrifying question. Baseball isn't a race. It's not a distance sport where you throw yourself or some object as high or far as you can. It's not a bucket sport where you try to get the ball into a goal and stop your opponent from doing the same. There just aren't a lot of reference points for baseball.

Undaunted, I grabbed a piece of paper and drew a rough representation of a baseball field, and then made a dot near home plate (in the right-handed batter's box). I started my explanation with: "Here's where the batter stands." I talked about how the batter must face off against the evil pitcher, who is throwing the ball toward him, and how the batter's objective is to hit the ball between these two lines and not have it be caught. Then, he tries to run from base to base and not have the ball beat him there. Eventually, the goal is to re-touch home. If he does, his team gets a run and the team with the most runs wins.

I noticed something about how I told the story. It was entirely about the batter's brave adventure. It's a strange decision, given that the batter is only half of the equation. It's understandable that I framed it that way. When trying to explain any game, it's a good idea to start with the more universal features of competitive games. Baseball is a "points game," so I naturally described the way in which baseball's points are scored. You can't score if your team is pitching.

Sports (and their fans) are products of the culture that produce them, and the batter is the "hero on a quest." There our brave hero stands, alone in the right-handed batter's box with a simple wooden weapon, and he must face 98 mph fastballs and elude nine different monsters in an attempt to both hit the ball and make it to the next station unscathed. The "hero's journey" is the storyline to every non-sports video game I played and every movie that I saw growing up. After talking to Petr, I realized that I instinctively viewed the game of baseball from the batter's box, because the batter always feels like the hero in the story. Sometimes, you have to take yourself out of your own cultural fish tank to see the water that surrounds you.

From 2018 to 2022, it was 11 times more likely for a game to end on a strikeout (34.4 percent of games) than a home run (3.1 percent), and yet just about every fictional baseball game ends with the batter doing something to win the game. No one writes baseball poetry about the pitcher ending a game on a strikeout, unless it's to moralize about arrogance *on the part of the batter*. We use heroic, warrior words to talk about batters. They "battle" against the pitcher. When they make a noble out, giving up their turn to drop down a bunt in service of moving the runner over, we hail their "sacrifice." Aren't there nine other players on the field? Instead of defaulting to the batter as the focal point, what if we took a slightly different viewpoint in explaining baseball?

YOU SEE, PETR, there are nine players out here. They need to work as a team to prevent this guy with the bat (in the right-handed batter's box) from scoring. They can do that in a couple of different ways. In this middle circle here is the most important one of the nine, the "pitcher." The pitcher starts with the ball and tries to throw the ball past the batter, although he can't throw it too far away from the batter. If he does that too many times, the batter gets to go to the first base over here for free. The pitcher tries to fool the batter into swinging at the ball with his bat and missing. He can also fool the batter into not swinging, but pitching the ball into an area where the batter probably could have made contact if he swung. If the pitcher fools the batter three times, then the batter is "struck out" and outs are the most important part of the game.

The entire point of the game is for the defense to collect three outs before one of the other team's players makes it all the way around the bases. Once a team has collected three of these "outs," the game resets itself. Any runners that the other team has on base are erased and the team has to start over in the next half inning.

A strikeout isn't the only way to get an out. The batter is trying to swing the bat and hit the ball away from these defenders so that he can run to first base before the ball gets there. However, if one of your defenders catches the ball before it hits the ground, it's an out. Even if it hits the ground, if your defenders either touch the batter with the ball or get the ball to a defender standing on this first base before the batter gets there, that's also an out.

The problem is that the field is a big place and these nine guys aren't going to be able to cover all of it, so you have to think about where you put them. The pitcher has to stand here in this circle, and the catcher has to be behind the batter to catch the pitch. It used to be that the other seven fielders could stand where they wanted, but now there are some regulations about that. Teams set up in a 4-3 formation, with four fielders in the inner part of the field, and three in the outer part. They're best off trying to locate themselves where they think the ball is going to go, because the quicker you get the ball, the more likely you are to get an out.

Once a batter reaches first base, he can stay there (but no one else from his team can), and then move to the next base, as long as he doesn't get caught, until he reaches the original "home" base. When he does that, it's a run, and more than anything, it's what you want to stop from happening. It's the penalty for not collecting three outs fast enough. The team that is best at preventing runs wins.

The batters that you have to worry about are the ones that can hit the ball over the fence. If they do that, the batter gets an automatic run, so the pitcher has to be careful not to allow that. Other than that, there's always a chance to make an out and outs move the game forward.

I bet that as you read those last few paragraphs, you felt a little uneasy. Baseball as a game of getting *outs* and *preventing* runs, rather than getting *hits* and *scoring* runs, just doesn't feel right. It sounds like I'm describing a different game altogether, even though you can recognize all the rules. We usually talk about baseball as the quest for runs, with outs being the penalty that the offense pays for not being good at hitting the ball. What if we looked at baseball the other way around as a primarily defensive game? I have to wonder how much of baseball strategy would have been different if Player 1 in the story of baseball had been the nine-member defense on a mission to suppress the batter, rather than our weird cultural quirk to prefer the lone man, battling against an army that he must conquer.

I FIRST READ Charles Darwin's *On the Origin of Species* in college. For a book that's as famous as it is taboo in certain circles, it surprised me by being rather dull. Whether I fully appreciated it at 18 or not, there's no denying Darwin's place in the history of ideas. His observations started one of the largest scientific revolutions in history.

Darwin observed that finches on different islands within the Galapagos archipelago had different styles of beak. Some were longer, seemingly made for getting to food that was inside trees. Others had more compact, tougher beaks which were best suited for cracking nuts and seeds. All of them seemed to be ideally suited to the food that was available on each island. Because we now live in the world of evolutionary biology, our minds immediately fill in the rest. The birds were likely descended from a common ancestor. Among those original finches, some would have had slightly longer beaks than others, just by chance. The birds with the longest beaks would be more likely to eat, more likely to survive, and more likely to reproduce. Their baby birds would have inherited inherit those long beak genes. The process would repeat itself.

Darwin reasoned that over a longer period of time and two different sets of circumstances, two groups of finches might develop to be very different from one another, each suited to the conditions on their home island. At some point, they would be different enough to be considered separate species. It was a leap of faith for Darwin to propose this theory of natural selection. At the time, there was not yet direct evidence for the modern understanding of genetic inheritance. That discovery came soon after and paired with Darwin's work, it gave rise to the theory of organic evolution, which supposed that even humans developed in the same manner, slowly moving toward the form that we now know with legs and arms and a duodenum, ready to play baseball.

Baseball has evolved too, and in this chapter, I want to tell the story of one particular finch that has driven more changes in the game than just about anything else: the one-inning reliever. There has always existed in baseball a species of player known as "the pitcher." As modern baseball fans, we instinctively know that are two kinds: starters and relievers, and that for the most part, they are mutually exclusive. It wasn't always that way. What was once a single species has diverged into two.

Consider a baseball fan at the turn of the 20th century who is asked to describe the job of a pitcher. The rules of the game were largely the same then as now, and so their description of gameplay would be recognizable. Our fan of 1901 will make a critical assumption that you won't. In 1901, there were eight teams each in the already established (and still-running) National League and the newly chartered American League, and between them they featured 139 pitchers, which is fewer than nine per team. In 1,109 games played, there were 327 relief appearances for the entire season among those 16 teams. Total. Across both leagues. How things have changed. In 2022, there were 534 relief appearances *per team* in MLB.

The idea of relief pitching eventually did take hold. By 1922, more than half of starts ended before the game did, but most pitchers played a little bit in both roles. In Figure 7 below, we can see the percentage of pitchers who threw at least 50 innings in relief who also had at least one start within that same season (2020 was naturally excluded because in the shortened season, no one threw 50 innings of relief).

Figure 7. Percentage of relievers who also started, 1950–2022

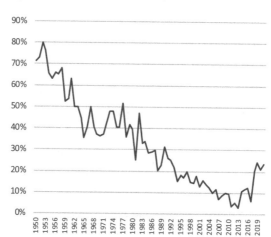

There was a time in baseball history where there weren't "starters" or "relievers." There were pitchers, and they were either pitching as the starter or in relief that day. As a pitcher, you were expected to face the other team's entire lineup and make it through a couple of innings, even if you weren't the first pitcher of the day. Teams would usually have their best four or five pitchers start games and the rest relieve. Somewhere along the line, things changed, at least among the relievers. Figure 8 shows the percentage of relief appearances in MLB that lasted more than three outs, the percentage lasting fewer than three outs, and the percentage lasting *exactly* three outs.

Figure 8. Percentage of relief appearances, by outs recorded, 1950–2022

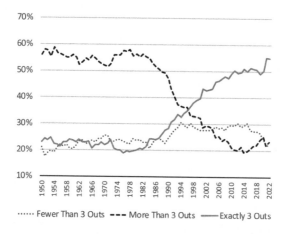

······ Fewer Than 3 Outs --- More Than 3 Outs ——Exactly 3 Outs

The majority of relief appearances now last exactly three outs. In 2022, they accounted for 55 percent of appearances, and most of those were three outs gathered in the same inning. The new ballgame has seventh-inning specialists, and the language is telling. We now talk about pitchers by what inning they are assigned to. How did we end up here?

Around the mid-1970s, relieving as a *distinct style* of pitching began to emerge. This was the first era of relief specialists. There was still an expectation of innings (plural), but maybe only two or three. As the expectations of what a relief outing looked like grew shorter, relievers were able to "let it rip" a little more. The results show it. Figure 9 shows that around that time, the percentage of batters that relievers struck out began to pull away from starters.

Figure 9. Strikeout percentage by pitching role, 1950–2022

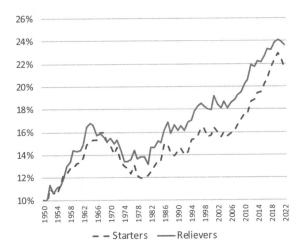

One of the most remembered features of the 1970s was the "ironman fireman" reliever, someone who came into a close game and pitched multiple innings in pursuit of the newly coined "save," a statistic which was formally adopted by MLB in 1969. Because the fireman was the first truly defined relief role of the modern era, it has acquired a certain legendary status. There are plenty of fans who wonder why MLB teams don't bring it back. The top practitioners of the art, including Goose Gossage and Rollie Fingers, are spoken of in hushed, reverential terms. There's no question that they were gifted pitchers, but the role that they filled evolved mostly out of necessity.

In 1969, MLB added four new expansion teams to its ranks, growing from 20 to 24 clubs. In Chapter 2, we talked about how it's important to think about the ratio of the quality of the talent pool to the number of roster spots in MLB. When you increase the size of a league by 20 percent, you have to find players to fill the new rosters who, by definition, wouldn't have been good enough to make it last year. The new teams would need 20 new starters and the logical place to look for them would be the best of the "failed" starters who had been banished to the bullpen. They weren't great options, but sometimes you have to live with "best available." In addition, each new team needed a few relievers, meaning that what reliever talent was out there was being stretched even thinner than it had been.

Figure 10. Percentage of relievers with strikeout rates greater than starter average, 1950–2022

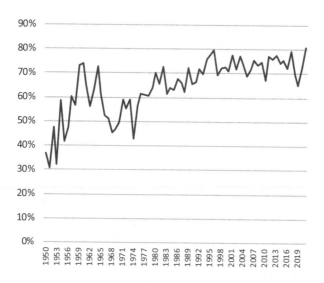

We can see that through the 1950s and 1960s, relievers grew more likely to log strikeouts than their starting teammates. But in the 1970s, after expansion left teams raiding the bullpen cupboards for extra warm bodies to put in the rotation, there was a valley that MLB didn't climb out of until the 1980s. The 1970s have acquired a certain mythology as the era of not only the fireman, but also of elite starters who went deep into ballgames. In fact, there *was* a small surge in the complete game rate in the 1970s, which evaporated quickly in the 1980s and has been in free-fall ever since. Most people have interpreted this as evidence that pitchers in the 1970s were somehow more rugged and durable. I have a different hypothesis. When a manager in the 1970s looked out to the bullpen in the seventh inning of a close game, there weren't a lot of good choices out there. You basically had to squeeze what you could out of the relievers who were decent and sometimes, just leaving the starter in was your best option.

By the late 1980s and 1990s, the talent pool had caught up to the needs of teams, and even as there were more expansions (in 1977, 1993, and 1998), the talent pool kept pace. The 1980s were also the time when the three-out outing began its ascent, and I don't think that's a coincidence. There were now enough decent relievers around that teams didn't have to hang all their hopes on one pitcher. They could divide up the work. As teams began to experiment with the short-burst format, some interesting things happened. Pitchers saw their pitches "play up." Research shows that when a pitcher moves from the rotation to the bullpen, their average velocity goes up by a couple of miles per hour. The one-inning format also meant that a pitcher wouldn't see the same batter twice in the same game. In the cat-and-mouse game of pitchers against batters, starters, who will likely face the same hitters three times over, generally need to have three or four good pitches in their toolbelt in order to get those hitters out three separate times. A pitcher might get away with throwing gas for one at-bat, but once the hitter figures out how the pitch moves and times it up, they'll eventually be able to tee off. With the one-inning format, a reliever who had two good pitches, but not a well-developed third, suddenly found an island where he didn't need one.

For a starter who had "failed" in a specific way, the new role was a burst of opportunity. Now, there was an entirely new way to be a finch. Pitchers without that third pitch or the stamina to carry a workload of even 100 innings over a season—ones who may have never been considered for a major league roster—suddenly had a place on a baseball team. This wasn't a pitcher who could handle a start or even three innings, but he would also never be asked to do that. He wasn't just "a failed starter" anymore. This was a reliever. Baseball expanded its talent pool by welcoming new types of players into the game.

Let's stop here. Whether the one-inning reliever was a creation or an evolution, a species only survives if it can find a role that it fills in the environment. At certain points in baseball history, teams have experimented with a designated pinch-runner on their rosters. These were players who would rarely (or never) take an at-bat or play in the field, but they were fast. The most famous were the Oakland A's designated runners of the 1970s, including Herb Washington and Don Hopkins. Some teams will still do this during the playoffs, rostering a speedy player with the intention of only using him to pinch-run, but the concept never stuck during the regular season. It's not that pinch-running is worthless, but it wasn't worth enough to justify the roster spot.

How did one-inning relievers survive and thrive? First, it turned out that there were a lot of them out there, some hiding in plain sight. Prospects who could throw hard but were having trouble with their breaking stuff might focus on refining just the slider. Starters who flunked out of that role could always try their arm at relieving, and for some of them, it worked. When relievers were just the pitchers who weren't good enough to be in the rotation, it meant that when a manager called to the bullpen, the pitcher who came in was almost always worse than the starter he was replacing.

Because relievers were now working in an entirely new style of pitching, many of them were better on a batter-to-batter basis. What an individual short-burst reliever lacked in durability could be made up for by quantity. It might take three pitchers each pitching one inning to do what Goose Gossage used to do, but there were so few Geese to go around. Short-burst relievers became plentiful and so the model was available to all teams.

If a team had multiple good relievers, they could mix-and-match them in the later innings of a game, grab platoon advantages where they could, and the pitchers might still be available the next night to do it again. There was another perk of the new format. Teams relying on relief aces to pitch for two and three innings in close games ran the risk of injury to their ace. Even if their ace wasn't injured, after two or three innings, he might need the next day or two off. Having a bullpen full of short-burst relievers meant that teams could diversify that risk. One of the three best relievers might be injured, but two would still be left. It also meant that teams could begin to tailor pitching assignments to the situation. If the team went to its "good" relievers in the seventh inning with the game close, but then exploded for five runs in the top of the eighth, they could move to lesser arms to finish out the game and save the wear and tear on the good ones. The strategy allowed for better results and more flexibility. It became the dominant model in MLB because it worked.

We saw earlier that in the 1950s, most relievers started games in the same season, suggesting that the two roles were effectively still fused. As specialist relievers developed, most of them had grown up as starters, but had been "converted." In Figure 11, we can see what percentage of relievers (minimum 50 innings in relief) had *ever* started a game at the MLB level, either before or during that season.

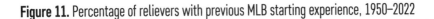

Figure 11. Percentage of relievers with previous MLB starting experience, 1950–2022

Up until 2007, more than half of relievers had at least some starting experience. By 2017, that number had fallen to 39 percent (the slight rebound at the end is the effect of the "opener.") It's possible that today's MLB relievers were starters in the minors (some were), but we see that teams are pushing that role specialization earlier and earlier in the developmental process. It's a testament to how the MLB talent pool expanded and diversified through the re-definition of a role. There are still plenty of "failed starters" in bullpens, but now there are amateur pitchers who are developed specifically as relievers.

We have been witness to the reliever evolution. More than just a new style of pitching, this was a new philosophy in how teams thought about pitching roles. Through much of baseball history, the limiting factor in how long a pitcher was allowed to stay in the game had been either fatigue or ineffectiveness. With the three-out model, there's an understanding that once the inning is over, the pitcher will be lifted from the game, *even if he could go further*. Relievers have become tactical assets.

IT DOESN'T LOOK like the downfall of civilization at first. It's a regular-season game from May 2018 between the Rays and Angels. We can see the Angels valiantly trying to come back from a five-run deficit in the eighth and ninth innings, but falling short 5–3. Rays shortstop Daniel Robertson tagged Angels starter Andrew Heaney for a grand slam, accounting for the four runs that Heaney gave up. Notably, none of them were earned, as Angels first baseman Jefry Marte made an error with two outs in the second inning, which allowed Mallex Smith to reach first. Two batters later, Robertson got hold of one and put it in the left-center-field seats.

Heaney walked five and Tampa Bay left seven runners on base, so perhaps the game should have been a little more lopsided going into the ninth. Mike Trout's two-run home run off Ryne Stanek turned the game into a "save situation" for which Jesús Colomé was called upon to enter the game and restore order. If you didn't read all the way down or didn't know the backstory, you might have missed the final step in the reliever evolution.

When you see it, it looks like a misprint. Perhaps while relaying the final numbers along the newswires, someone got confused and shuffled things out of order. Maybe there was a mix-up between Rays reliever Chaz Roe, who

May 19, 2018—Tampa Bay at Los Angeles (Regular Season)

Tampa Bay	AB	R	H	RBI	Los Angeles (A)	AB	R	H	RBI
Robertson, ss	4	2	1	4	Cozart, 3b	4	1	1	0
Cron, 1b	4	0	1	0	Trout, cf	4	1	2	2
Duffy, 3b	3	0	0	0	Upton, lf	4	0	0	0
Ramos, dh	4	0	1	1	Pujols, dh	3	0	1	0
Arroyo, 2b	2	0	0	0	Simmons, ss	4	0	0	0
Wendle, ph–2b	1	0	0	0	Kinsler, 2b	3	1	1	0
Refsnyder, lf	4	0	0	0	Marte, 1b	3	0	1	1
Field, rf	3	1	1	0	Calhoun, rf	2	0	0	0
Smith, cf	4	1	1	0	Young, ph-rf	1	0	0	0
Sucre, c	3	1	0	0	Maldonado, c	3	0	0	0

Tampa Bay — 040 000 100   5 5 1
Los Angeles (A) — 000 000 012   3 6 2

2B—Trout (9); HR—Robertson (5, off Heaney, 2nd inning, 3 on), Trout (14, off Stanek, 9th inning, 1 on); IBB—Duffy (1); DP—Tampa Bay 2 (Duffy-Wendle-Cron; Yarbrough-Arroyo-Cron), Los Angeles 1 (Kinsler-Simmons-Marte); E- Robertson (3), Anderson (1), Marte (2); LOB—Tampa Bay 7, Los Angeles 2; T—3:00; A—37,232

Tampa Bay	IP	H	R	ER	BB	SO
Romo	1	0	0	0	0	3
Yarbrough, W (4–2)	6.1	4	1	1	1	4
Roe	0.2	0	0	0	0	0
Stanek	0	2	2	2	0	0
Colomé, S (10)	1	0	0	0	0	1

Los Angeles (A)	IP	H	R	ER	BB	SO
Heaney, L (2–3)	6	3	4	0	5	7
Ramirez	0.2	1	1	1	2	0
Anderson	1.1	1	0	0	0	2
Johnson	1	0	0	0	0	1

finished off the last two outs of the eighth inning and Sergio Ro-mo. But no, this was the day that Romo, a 35-year-old pitcher who had to that point had never started an MLB game, made trivia. Romo took to the mound for Tampa Bay in the first inning of their game and struck out the side in order. In the second inning, Ryan Yarbrough emerged from the Rays' bullpen and proceeded to throw $6^{1/3}$ innings, scattering four hits and a walk, giving up one run. For some reason, the relievers were now starting. As if the Rays wanted to punctuate that this was not a mistake, Romo "started" again *the next day*. This gambit now has a name coined by researcher and Rays fan Bryan Grosnick. Romo was baseball's first declared "opener." Why did the Rays do it backwards?

WE BEGIN OUR journey in Las Vegas, a city that shines bright as a testament to the fact that people are bad at math. Slot machines are programmed to "give back" some percentage (less than 100) of the money they take in. Games like craps and roulette have payouts that don't match the odds of the events that win them. If you played any of those games over and over again, you would eventually go broke. Over a short period of time, an individual player might beat the house, but there will be more losers than winners. What happens in Vegas might stay in Vegas, but what's brought to Vegas usually stays there too.

The one exception is blackjack. There's a way to play where the odds are in your favor. The problem is that it involves a technique called "card counting," which isn't illegal, but for which casinos can kick you out anyway. The math is complicated, but it involves finding specific tables at specific times, based on how many "face cards" (jack, queen, king) have been dealt so far. To pull it off, you have to monitor the tables for these "hot" times and then insert yourself at the table, bet heavily, and walk away when the odds are no longer in your favor. Part of the operation is doing this in a way that you don't get noticed by casino security. If you play in a statistically sound manner and no one catches you, you can come out ahead. It's a long way to go for a bit of an edge, but if you bet hard on it, you can beat the house and take home some money. Perhaps Tampa Bay was trying to use some math to play the house out of its money too?

Before that day in May 2018, the Rays had already been experimenting with short-stint starters, limiting certain pitchers to facing around 18 batters. A quick look at the numbers shows us why they were so consumed with the number 18. There's something known as the "Third Time Through the Order Penalty." As the lineup merry-go-round spins a second and third time, starters' performance gets progressively worse.

Table 12. Batting outcomes against starting pitchers, by time through the order, 2022 and 1972

Time Through Order (2022)	AVG	OBP	SLG	Time Through Order (1972)	AVG	OBP	SLG
1st Time	.238	.303	.384	1st Time	.235	.302	.335
2nd Time	.248	.309	.410	2nd Time	.239	.298	.351
3rd Time	.264	.325	.445	3rd Time	.250	.310	.374
Average Reliever	.236	.314	.378	Average Reliever	.244	.325	.347

It's not entirely clear why the third time through the order penalty happens. Obviously, by that point the pitcher has thrown more pitches and is more tired, but there's also evidence that by the third matchup, batters might have become more familiar with the pitcher's repertoire. It's likely that both are true. Whatever the cause, it speaks to another of our not-so-hidden forces in baseball: *Pitchers get tired and lose effectiveness far earlier in the game than we might think.*

The average starter in 2022, by the third time around the lineup, had a performance that was below the league average for relievers. The good starters may fall to somewhere around merely average, but the awful starters are probably hanging on to their horses trying not to be spun off the ride. In 2022, the average reliever allowed a "triple slash" line of a .236 batting average, .314 on-base percentage, and a .378 slugging percentage. For a manager who has a full bullpen and is thinking about winning today's game, there are probably a couple of relievers who are going to get better results than the starter will.

Lest you think the "third time" effect is a modern problem, I've included the data from 1972 as well. We see that as pitchers moved into their third time through the order back then, they also lost some of their effectiveness. The problem in 1972 was that relievers allowed a combined batting line of .244/.325/.347. On average, the relievers weren't any better than what might be expected of the starters, even starters on their third time around. The starter might not have been as fresh as in the first inning, but he might have been the best option available. The reason that modern-day pitchers don't seem to go as deep into games as they once did isn't a fault in our starters. It's a tribute to the development of the relief pitcher. Back then, there just weren't as many good relievers, and so the starters stayed in.

The workload of the starter has been getting smaller. In 2022, the average starter recorded 15.62 outs, just north of five innings. It was once considered an insult to call a pitcher a "five-and-dive." Now it's the norm. That average is pulled down a tiny bit by the use of the opener, who gets formal credit for a game started, even though it's clearly meant to be an oddball relief appearance, but even if we take the average of the pitchers who recorded the most outs that day for their teams, we get 15.92 outs. Five-and-dive is the new seven.

Pitching has evolved to a model of shared responsibility. In 2022, teams used an average of 4.30 pitchers to get through the day, up from 3.15 in 1992 and 2.55 in 1962, but there's a limit to how much bullpenning a team can do. You can't sustain a baseball team over a season using an all-bullpen approach, or at least, an all short-burst reliever approach. There will always have to be a group of pitchers who can provide bulk innings, although that job description has gotten a little less bulky. Teams have begun to realize that some of their bulk pitchers aren't very good to start with, that they get worse as the game goes on, and they have better options available in the bullpen, especially in a close game. There comes a point where it makes sense to call to the 'pen. In an eight-member bullpen, you can probably find three pitchers who are better on a per-batter basis than a bad bulk. They make the most sense to handle the seventh, eighth, and ninth innings. As the influx of good relief pitchers has continued, it's pushed that balance point farther forward in the game. In fact, it pushed that point forward to a place where sometimes, teams can plan in advance to keep a dodgy starter away from the third time around the lineup and absorb the extra workload that comes with that decision.

As Tampa Bay (and others) experimented with these short-stint starters, they had to reckon with a cost. Research has shown that if a pitcher throws more than 115 pitches in a single outing, he bears an increased chance of an injury. Still, most starters can comfortably throw 100 or so pitches in a game and have no ill effects. Over 18 batters, a pitcher might only throw 60 or 70 of those pitches, but will still need four days of rest to recover before his next outing. Using a short-stint starter "wastes" 30 pitches that someone else will have to pick up. What if we could somehow reclaim those 30 pitches?

What if it's been one of *those* days and your team is already up 9–2 by the time your starter faces batter number 18? A manager might be tempted to say "We're already up by seven. Why waste a good resource on a game that's looking like a blowout? Why not just let the starter keep going?"

Returning to the Sergio Romo game, we can see the pieces of the puzzle come together. Ryan Yarbrough was a rookie in 2018, and in April and early May, the Rays had been "stretching him out" into longer outings. His previous appearances had lasted 12, 26, 48, 58, 79, and 83 pitches. Going into the game, Tampa probably had a quick hook waiting for their young hurler. Rays' manager Kevin Cash knew that several relievers would be getting a call that day. Looking back at the box score, we can see that of the nine Angels who started, only Kole Calhoun was a left-handed hitter and Romo had made career out of being tough on righties. Cash was probably already warming Romo up in his head.

If Yarbrough was only going to pitch to 18 batters, then it would make sense that Romo the righty might be the first reliever out of the bullpen to face the decidedly right-handed top of the Angels lineup. If Romo was going to face those three or four hitters anyway, and Yarbrough was going to face everyone twice, it didn't really matter what order they did it in. They would both end up facing the same hitters the same number of times. Outs are outs.

There's a small bit of value that the Rays could gain by letting Yarbrough "relieve." After Yarbrough's 18th batter, Cash would still have the option to leave Yarbrough in. With Romo starting, Yarbrough's 18th batter would come later, and the game would have had more of a chance to reveal itself. As it happened, Yarbrough had made it into the seventh inning by the time he faced his 18th batter, a strikeout of Justin Upton. Had Yarbrough started, Kevin Cash would have had to make a decision on whether Yarbrough could stay up past his bedtime in the sixth inning. In the sixth, the Rays were up four runs, but in the top of the seventh inning, the Rays had scored a run, pushing their advantage to five. It's possible that Cash would have gone to the bullpen with a four-run lead, but with the benefit of the extra time to make the decision and an extra run of cushion, he could feel better about keeping Yarbrough on the mound and hopefully save his bullpen a little.

In addition, as Yarbrough entered the "third time through the order" zone, he was going up against Jefry Marte and Andrelton Simmons, rather than Justin Upton and Mike Trout. The point of the opener wasn't what Romo did in the first inning. It's what Kevin Cash was able to do in the seventh. The box score shows us that Cash left Yarbrough in. Yarbrough pitched an extra inning that someone else didn't have to. It's a long way to go for a little bit of value, but every little bit helps.

IN GAME 3 of the 2021 World Series, Atlanta starter Ian Anderson threw five innings of no-hit ball and didn't return for the sixth inning. Anderson faced exactly 18 Houston Astros that night, leaving before seeing the top of the Astros lineup for the third time. Predictably, there were plenty of people demanding an explanation. How could Atlanta manager Brian Snitker pull someone from a no-hitter, and in the World Series at that? Part of the answer is that research tells us that even if a pitcher is "cruising," there's no evidence that he'll continue to do so. He'll likely revert back to whatever his seasonal average is, meaning that Ian Anderson was still Ian Anderson and not a reincarnation of Greg Maddux. Not that anyone wanted to hear about the numbers.

The full reason that Ian Anderson left the game was quietly profound. Starters hold a different place in the game than they have before. In years past, Game 3 would have been framed as Ian Anderson, lone hero, against the Houston Astros. In the new ballgame, the game was really Atlanta's pitching staff against the Astros. That's a very small shift in words, but a huge difference in baseball culture. I don't think baseball culture has caught up.

Recall that most relief appearances now last exactly three outs, and mostly three outs within the same inning. Most readers will focus on the fact that one inning is a short burst of effort. That's important to understanding the new ballgame, but there's something else hidden in there. The reliever is no longer on the mound "until he's tired." He has a specific job, and that job has a predetermined endpoint. Once he's done, he leaves. With pitchers being judged not by how long they could last, but by how well they could complete a specific mission, they didn't have to worry about "saving a little bit." You can let the tank run empty, *because* there's an endpoint.

I'd argue that it's the endpoint, even more so than the short-burst format, that has allowed the reliever evolution to flourish. Pitchers were allowed to focus on what they did best and to throw everything into it. Even as specialist relievers developed, there was, at first, still an assumption that the mark of a good starter was "length." The bullpen was seen as a supplement to whatever the starter couldn't finish. Slowly, that model has been flipped.

We are entering the world of the "bulk pitcher," who may or may not even start the game, and whose job is to provide coverage for enough innings to get the game safely to the bullpen. That word "enough" means that, like a reliever, a starter might have a predefined point at which his day will end. It might be 100 pitches or 18 batters or six innings, but there's an endpoint. It means that he too can reach back for a little extra in the third inning, *because* he doesn't have to worry about the seventh. That's going to have an effect on how good starters can be on a batter-to-batter basis.

In modern baseball, you need to remember seven words: *Everyone is a reliever. Even the starters.* In the old framing of "Ian Anderson against the Astros," it was Anderson's job to keep going until he couldn't anymore. Now, Anderson is just another pitcher in a line. Culturally, we still hold on to the idea of the starter as the lone hero on the mound, rather than as a member of a committee. The game just isn't played like that anymore.

IF YOU WANT to understand the new ballgame, you have to understand the new roles that pitchers play in it. Most importantly, you have to understand the evolution of the relief pitcher as its own separate species. Sometimes within a habitat, a new finch migrates to the area and it ends up as a disaster for the ecosystem. The new species takes over, slowly at first, but eventually displaces many of the old animals and plants and changes all the rules. That's called an invasive species. Relievers are a lot like that. They've evolved over the past few decades and become the dominant force in baseball. There are a lot of people who worry about the reliever evolution because of what it's done to the time-honored place of the starting pitcher in the game. If we're not careful, it's going to have other, much more devastating effects.

Figure 12 below shows games from 1980 onward in which a team went into their batting half of the seventh inning losing, but only by a run or two. That's not a great situation to be in. Chances are good that you're going to lose, but at the same time, there's still hope, and it's that hope that keeps you watching the game. That's why this chart is so concerning. The line shows what percentage of those games teams ended up winning through the years.

Figure 12. Expected win percentage, losing by one or two in seventh inning, 1980–2022

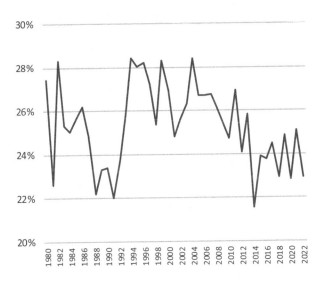

That graph does track somewhat to the overall scoring environment in baseball. When the ball started flying out of the park in the mid-1990s, it became easier to put together a rally. When scoring started to fall in the late 2000s, it got harder to pull off a late-inning comeback. But when scoring rebounded in the late 2010s, the comeback rate didn't jump. Teams had too many good relievers who could more effectively close the door on those small leads. Comebacks do still happen, but not as often. It means that some of the dramatic tension that used to come from saying, "It ain't over until it's over" is gone. You can't blame teams for using a model that works. If you're cheering for the team that's ahead, you love this graph, but as a fan of the game, you don't want this graph to fall too far. If it becomes known that a team behind by one in the seventh inning really only has a 5 percent chance of winning, people will start tuning out when they get to that point.

Late in a game where the pitching team is holding on to a one-run lead, even in a game where I don't have a rooting interest, it's fun to just watch the gears turn. Close games are interesting, even in other sports. I once ended up watching the second half of an Australian Rules Football game at 1:00 AM, even though I had no idea what was going on, because Sydney and Brisbane were tied!

There's a silly idea floating around that, left to its own devices, baseball will always fix itself. Things don't work that way. There's no divine blessing on the game. The reliever evolution is a fundamental change in the way that the game is played, because it deals with the most important player on the field, the pitcher, and makes him better by making more of him. The once verdant meadow of the baseball field has been invaded by a new species, and baseball needs to figure out what it's going to do about that.

Chapter 5

The Right-Hand Rule

My younger brother is left-handed. I'm right-handed. We both played rec center and church league softball over the summers when we were kids. He was the better athlete, though neither of us was particularly good at the game. Like countless eight-year-olds, we mostly just enjoyed the fun of getting to take a few at-bats and run around the bases before downing some orange slices. On defense, we both wanted to be infielders. That's where the action was. You not only got to field the ball, but throw it too, and sometimes you even got to make an out. The outfield wasn't any fun. Few kids had the ability to hit the ball out there and when one kid had the freakish strength to do it, it was probably a home run anyway. If you played the outfield, you mostly just stood there in an aqua t-shirt.

Once we got to the age where the fielding positions weren't assigned on a "let's give everyone a turn" basis, I got moved to the outfield because I was a terrible fielder. My brother, on the other hand, got moved there because he was left-handed. At the major league level, it's difficult for a left-handed thrower to play on the infield, and I guess his coach took himself a little too seriously. They're eight. This is the local park. It's okay if a lefty plays short. It's odd how profound a difference something so trivial can make.

Then again, most of my five facts can trace their way back to things even more random. My wife ended up at a tiny liberal arts school in the middle of nowhere Ohio because the college guidance counselor at her high school in Atlanta had a son who had gone there. I live in Atlanta because my wife's parents got jobs at the Centers for Disease Control when they emigrated from Russia. The CDC is an oddity for the fact that it's the only major federal agency in the United States that is not headquartered in the Washington, DC, area. It's there because there was a malaria outbreak in the Southeastern U.S. in the 1940s. Thanks, mosquitoes.

Baseball, on the other hand, was always in the air throughout my life. While my parents would say goodnight to me and tuck me under my covers, it was Cleveland broadcaster Herb Score who would sing me to sleep. When my dad would take me to get my hair cut, Don the barber would have the Saturday *Game of the Week* on. When we'd go to visit my grandparents, Grandma would be sure to have the TV tuned to Channel 43 when Cleveland was playing. Family was important, but so was baseball.

Of my five facts, the two that seem the most inevitable are being born in Cleveland, something I had literally no choice in, and my love for baseball. It means that a good chunk of my life was tied up in Cleveland baseball. When I was a kid, Cleveland was my team. The thing about growing up is that sometimes you look back and you realize that not everything was what it seemed. In the late 1980s, Joe Carter was the undisputed best player in Cleveland. He hit home runs. He stole bases. He drove in 100 runs every year. He even played center field. I was convinced that even if he wasn't the best player in MLB, he was one of them. After he left Cleveland, Carter made an indelible mark on MLB history. The box score for Game 6 of the 1993 World Series only notes "HR—Carter (2, off Williams, 9th inning, 2 on)" but it was the last play of that World Series.

Sometimes though, your five facts bump into each other in ways you don't expect. Years later, the researcher in me realized that Carter's gaudy stat line hid some uncomfortable truths. He wasn't a very good defensive player. He didn't take walks like other power hitters did and his career on-base percentage was just a touch above .300. The RBIs were mostly the fortune of hitting behind on-base savants like Brett Butler and Julio Franco in Cleveland and Roberto Alomar, Paul Molitor, and Carlos Delgado in Toronto. During a stop-over in San Diego, Carter got to bat behind some guy named Tony Gwynn. Carter was a good player and had a career that anyone would be proud to have, but he wasn't the all-time great that the Cleveland kid in me thought he was.

Then there was the team that I cheered for. I was told growing up that they were called "Indians" for a noble reason, to honor the first Native American to play in the majors, Louis Sockalexis. While Sockalexis was member of the Penobscot Nation and played for the then-Cleveland Spiders, the rest of the story was anything but honorable. A bit of a phenom in his rookie year, Sockalexis got off to a good start in 1897 and then was injured in July. He partially recovered and hobbled through the rest of the season. That year, the Spiders became informally known as "Indians" mostly because fans, both in Cleveland and in other cities, came out to the ballpark to yell racist slurs at Sockalexis. In 1898, he lost his starting job and then was released after seven games in 1899. Neither Sockalexis nor the Spiders, who finished 20–134 in 1899, appeared in the majors again.

In 1915, the Cleveland Naps, a different franchise, needed a new moniker. Their star player and namesake, Napoleon Lajoie, had his contract sold to the Philadelphia Athletics in a cost-cutting move to help Cleveland owner Charles Somers's balance sheet. Somers, a businessman whose other investments were faltering, needed cash badly and had even experimented with changing the team's official name to the Cleveland Molly Maguires in 1912, in an attempt to market to the blue-collar workers of Cleveland. The real Molly Maguires were a pro-labor organization who didn't shy away from violence when they agitated for workers' rights against coal magnates like… Charles Somers. Somers wasn't beyond cheap gimmicks with the team's name to try to draw a crowd.

Despite the legend about honoring Sockalexis, newspaper coverage of the name change barely mentioned him at all, though it did include a few cartoonish, oafish depictions of Native Americans. Honor had nothing to do with it, nor did Sockalexis make sense as someone to honor. By 1915, he was dead and had no connection to Cleveland after being released. Had the team wanted to honor a former player, Hall of Famers Addie Joss and Cy Young had more recently played for the team. In fact, Joss had tragically died in 1911 and was so beloved by fans and players alike that the best players in baseball honored him posthumously by staging what unofficially became the first All-Star Game. Reaching back to a player who'd had a couple of good months nearly 20 years earlier doesn't make sense, unless of course it wasn't honor that they had in mind.

Sometimes you find that pieces of your life were determined by things you wouldn't have expected. Sometimes they hide some truths that you'd rather not face. In the therapy room, sometimes you have to help a person to face things that aren't comfortable. Sometimes that person is you. The truth is that I grew up cheering for a team that had taken its name as a desperate publicity stunt from the memory of a man whom fans taunted because of his race.

BASEBALL IS A GAME that looks orderly on the surface. Nine players play nine innings and the four bases are all ninety feet apart, arranged in a diamond shape. A line running from home plate through second base and to the edge of the infield dirt would produce a mirrored image on either side. As long as we don't look beyond second base, everything looks in balance. The oddity is that baseball is alone among major sports (and most of the minor ones) in not only allowing its playing surfaces to differ from each other, but also to be asymmetrical. The left- and right-field walls don't have to be the same distance away from home plate as any other park, or even as each other in the same park. No one bats an eye about that.

We think of the players symmetrically too: four infielders, placed neatly two to a side, and three outfielders, spread out equidistant from each other, with a center fielder lined up in the middle. The 4-3 infield-outfield split was known even in the nineteenth century, and it makes sense when you look at the geography of the game. The runners are trying to get to the bases, and someone needs to be on duty to receive a throw at each base. The catcher can cover home, and we'll need three "base men" somewhere within spitting distance of those bags, but why did a fourth infielder come to be?

If a ground ball reaches the outfield, it's assumed to be a base hit. The outfielder's job is to hold the batter to a single. Outfielders are instead most concerned with fly balls. While the outfield is a much bigger place than the infield, the infielders are closer to the batter, which means the ball gets to them more quickly *and* there's a second part to what they need to accomplish in order to record an out. Outfielders have more time to react and only just need to "get there." It made sense to allocate an extra hand to the infield to help with the more difficult task, and with the 4-3 formation established, teams naturally spread out their fielders to cover as much ground as possible.

For a game that looks symmetrical before the pitcher winds up, it is anything but that once the ball is in play. There's a not-so-hidden force that shapes the game that's woven so deeply into its fabric that it's rarely questioned. *When you hit the ball, you run to the right.* Even when children play pick-up games on grassy fields and sandlots that don't have proper markings or bases, they know to establish first base to the right of the batter and that the bases are run counter-clockwise. There's no agreed upon reason for when and why baseball started running to the right, but the most commonly cited one is that roughly 90 percent of humans are right-handed (and no one knows exactly why!) and a right-handed batter is already turned sideways and looking that way while standing in the batter's box. It made sense to run forward. Whatever the reason, that simple rule influences so much about the game.

It's hard to know what would have happened if things had been a little different. In the other globally popular bat-and-ball game, cricket, batters strike the ball and then run straight ahead toward the other team's bowler (effectively, their pitcher). There's the game of pesäpallo, often called "Finnish baseball," in which players run to the left to the first base after striking the ball, and then in a zig-zag pattern across the field to touch the other bases. Maybe handedness wouldn't have been such a big deal in the game if the batter charged the mound after every ball in play, but the path of the right-handed batter has been beset by inequities and the tyranny of evil men.

On the infield, plays on defense—mostly ground balls—naturally flow toward first base. In our batter-centric world view, we call that the "right side of the infield" (and what's behind it, we call "right field") despite the fact that for the defenders, who are the majority of the people on the field, first base is to their left. By prioritizing one side of the field over the other, it meant that the third baseman had longer throws to make than the shortstop who had a longer throw than the second baseman. Since there was always a force at first, soft hands for catching throws were important to a first baseman. The diamond shape of the field meant that our two "up the middle" infielders had a bit more time before a groundball got to them, and so were expected to cover more ground. The ability to range over and snag the ball became something that was quite useful. The corner infielders needed to have quicker reaction times. Shortstop, in particular needed a very broad set of athletic capabilities, pairing good range with an arm capable of making a throw from the "left" side of the diamond to first base. We might go so far as to say that the "run to the right" rule invented the very positions that we know.

Some of those talent combinations were easier to find than others. In Chapter 3, we saw that if a player was any good at pitching, they were basically excused from having anything resembling a competent MLB-level bat. As baseball became a game of specialized defensive positions, teams would be a little more forgiving of a weaker bat if a player could fill one of the harder spots. We instinctively know this. A first baseman who hits like an average first baseman is an average player. A shortstop who hits like an average first baseman is an All-Star.

The right-hand rule also creates an uneven playing field for aspiring left-handed baseball players. Three infield positions are effectively off-limits. Because plays on the infield flow to the fielder's left side, a right-handed thrower can field a ground ball and in the same motion, orient themselves toward first base and assume a natural throwing position. A left-handed thrower must first step across his body and then make the throw. Batters normally get down the line in a little more than four seconds, so there's not a lot of room for extra steps. There's also a fourth position, catcher, which doesn't normally see a southpaw. There's no specific reason why a left-hander couldn't catch, but the last left-handed throwing player whose primary position was catcher was Jiggs Donahue in 1902.

If you're a left-handed thrower, you are effectively restricted to four of the eight non-pitching positions on the field, and three of those (first base, left field, and right field) are spots that have the highest levels of offensive production when batting. To make it on a roster, a left-handed thrower not only has to be a good hitter, but a good enough hitter to stick at a high-offense position. Or a pitcher.

Despite the rules being written for the benefit of right-handers, baseball sure has a lot of left-handed players. In 2022, 40 percent of all plate appearances were taken by a batter standing in the left-handed batter's box and 27 percent of pitches were thrown by someone using their left arm. How did it happen that 10 percent of the population took up a third of baseball's playing time?

We saw in Chapter 1 that the platoon effect gives a left-handed batter has a natural advantage against right-handed pitching, and righties do throw more than 70 percent of all pitches, so teams have an incentive to look for an extra lefty bat where they can find it. What's interesting is that among plate appearances taken by second basemen in 2022, 46 percent were taken left-handed. How did a position that's off-limits to left-handed throwers end up that way? Some of those batters were switch hitters, but baseball has a little secret. Of the hitters who came to the plate hitting exclusively left-handed in 2022, two-thirds of them were right-handed throwers. Handedness matters a lot in baseball, but baseball still finds a way. If there's an indicator of how truly athletically gifted baseball players are, it might be the sheer number of them that can play the game on both sides of their bodies.

IF YOU LOOK at box scores from the late 1800s, they have the familiar positional abbreviations next to each of the players. We've been using the same nine words to describe what players have been doing on defense since nearly the beginning of the game. Everyone recognized that a third baseman was something different from a second baseman and a left fielder, but the idea of that *particular* formation of fielders went unquestioned for more than a century. Then in the 2010s, something happened.

Table 13. Percentage of pitches thrown with shifted infield

Year	All Pitches	Vs. Left-Handed Hitters	Vs. Right-Handed Hitters
2015	10%	18%	4%
2016	14%	24%	7%
2017	12%	22%	6%
2018	18%	30%	10%
2019	26%	42%	16%
2020	35%	50%	23%
2021	31%	52%	17%
2022	34%	54%	21%

The infield shift represented the first widespread tinkering with the "standard" positioning of fielders in a century, but it quickly overtook the game. By 2020, the shifted "3-1" infield had become the default defensive formation against left-handed hitters. There was a long tradition in baseball of fielders moving a bit to the left or right to "shade" a hitter, but it seemed as though there was an invisible fence separating the left and right sides of the diamond most of the time. Eventually, teams noticed there were some left-handed hitters who pulled almost all of their ground balls. If a batter isn't likely to hit a ball near the third-base line, why station a fielder there?

We also see that shifting wasn't quite as popular against right-handed hitters. Baseball's faux symmetry strikes again. Against a left-handed batter who likes to pull, teams would station a "third infielder" in short right field, between the first and second basemen. That left the extra fielder far enough back to not run into the other two, but if a ground ball came that way, our shifted fielder was close enough to first to pick it up and throw over for the out. It was also a good place to catch soft line drives that might have otherwise gone through the "three/four hole" and fallen in front of the right fielder.

Against a right-handed batter, a team could have put a fielder out in short left, but by the time a ground ball rolled all the way out there, it's too long of a throw to reliably make to first. That meant that the third infielder needed to play closer in, by the infield dirt, and there wasn't as much space that he could cover that the other two weren't already covering. There wasn't as much profit in shifting a right-handed batter.

In 2018, I published a book called *The Shift: The Next Evolution in Baseball Thinking*. When I did sports talk radio appearances to promote the book, I found myself re-assuring Ed from Lakewood that it was not 300 pages about where to play your infielders, but it did have a chapter called "Why Didn't David Ortiz Just Bunt" which talked about the infield shift and what we knew about it at the time. When I wrote the book, data on the shift were surprisingly hard to come by, at least publicly. The data that were available only reported on plate appearances which ended with a ball "in play." Any shifted plate appearances that ended in a walk, strikeout, hit batsman, or home run—all of the outcomes where the defense doesn't touch the ball— weren't recorded. The assumption was that since a strikeout or a walk didn't involve the fielders, the shift wouldn't have impact on those outcomes. But *everything* in baseball is connected. Pitchers can count the infielders just as well as the batter, and maybe they changed the way they pitch as a result. In fact, that's exactly what happened.

After I had released *The Shift*, MLB Advanced Media (MLBAM), the arm of MLB that produces the StatCast graphics that are sometimes included in broadcasts, published data for all pitches from 2015 onward, including whether the infield had been shifted when the pitch was made. It allowed for a much more detailed examination of the strategy, including whether the infield shift had an effect on things like strikeouts and walks.

We need to be very careful when we analyze the infield shift. It's a specific subset of hitters who were more likely to be shifted. If we see that more home runs were hit in front of the shift, we want to make sure that it's not because we're looking at a sample of sluggers. Fortunately, we have a way around this. We can look at how the same players performed with and without the shift on. If a player had a .300 on-base percentage while the shift *wasn't* on, and the shift made no difference whatsoever, we would expect to see a .300 OBP with the shift on. If the shift had an effect, we would expect to see either an increase or decrease. For an individual hitter, there can be a lot of random variation in that sort of analysis, but if we sum across the entire league, the randomness in individual cases tends to cancel out, and we can get an idea of the effects of the infield shift more generally.

Table 14. Effects of the infield shift, same-player comparison model, 2022

Outcome	Change from Expected
Strikeout	+1.1%
Walk	+0.6%
HBP	−0.1%
Single	−1.1%
Double/Triple	−0.2%
Home run	−0.2%
Out in Play	−0.1%
OBP	−.010
BABIP	−.014
BABIP on grounders	−.021

In the table, a positive number means that something happens more often in front of the shift. For example, hitters overall struck out in 1.1 percent more of their plate appearances than we would have expected. Something else that quickly jumps out of the data is that batters also *walked* more in front of the infield shift than we would expect. The shift did a good job in reducing the number of singles, as well as Batting Average on Balls in Play (BABIP). It was designed to take away ground ball singles on the pull side of the infield, so that makes sense. The problem is that the additional walks wiped out some of the effect of the singles saved. It turns out that one of the best ways to beat the shift was to let the pitcher walk you. After all, you can't throw out a runner who gets to walk to first base.

Further research using that same MLBAM data shows us why the walks happened. The data set has pitch locations, and we can look to see whether pitchers changed where they threw the ball in front of a 3-1 defense. Sure enough, with the shift on, especially against left-handed hitters, pitchers stayed away from the outer third of the plate in the strike zone. A ball on the outer third is an invitation for the hitter to poke it to the side where there was only one fielder on duty. Because pitchers became shyer about part of the strike zone, they ended up nibbling, and that naturally led to falling behind hitters and sometimes walking them. The infield shift changed the shape of the game that the batter and pitcher were playing. If we just look at BABIP and the balls that are struck into play, we see that the shift had a modest effect, but it did tilt in the defense's favor. When we look at all the possible outcomes of a plate appearance though, the shift was ever-so-slightly positive for the defense, although not by much.

But handedness matters so much in baseball, and we just discussed how it was much harder to shift on right-handed batters than lefties. Perhaps that makes a difference? Using the same method as above, we can look at how the shift affected right-handed and left-handed hitters differently.

Table 15. Effects of the infield shift, same player comparison model, 2022, by handedness

Outcome	Right-handed hitters	Left-handed hitters
Strikeout	−1.9%	+3.5%
Walk	+0.3%	+0.8%
HBP	+0.0%	−0.3%
Single	+0.3%	−2.2%
Double/Triple	−0.4%	−0.0%
Home run	−0.0%	−0.2%
Out in Play	+1.6%	−1.5%
OBP	−.002	−.020
BABIP	−.009	−.018
BABIP on grounders	−.013	−.027

It turns out that a couple of surprises are lurking. The infield shift was much more effective against left-handed hitters than against righties. Left-handed hitters were also much more likely to walk or strikeout in front of the shift. They knew that there was a trap waiting for them if they put the ball in play and so they become more reluctant to make contact. Right-handed batters struck out a lot less. Strangely enough, one of the main effects of the shift had nothing to do with balls in play. It was in how it made left-handed hitters strike out more often. That's what drove most of the benefit that teams got from moving an infielder over.

NEAR THE END of the 2022 season, MLB announced that it was banning the infield shift, starting in 2023. It was a bold move on the part of the league, but there was a recognition that the shift was beginning to move the game in a direction that the league didn't like, and there was no countermove to the shift other than banning the strategy outright. A little bit of math shows us why. We usually think of the infield shift being used against hitters who pull the ball "a lot," but where is the line that separates the ones that pull enough to justify the shift and those for whom the standard 2-2 defense is a better idea?

Table 16. BABIP on ground balls, left-handed hitters, by shift, 2022

	No Shift	Shift	Difference
BABIP if pulled	.169	.120	−.049
BABIP if oppo/center	.307	.310	+.003

By pulling a third defender to the right side of the infield against a left-handed hitter, a team's defense became better by 49 points of BABIP on pulled ground balls. When the batter hit the ball either the opposite way or up the middle on a ground ball, the defense gave back only 3 points, compared to a 2-2 defense. If a batter were to pull exactly half of his ground balls, the defensive team would still do well to shift, because on the ones that the batter did pull, the defensive team would gain more in BABIP than they would lose on the ones he didn't. In fact, because of that imbalance, a team could expect fewer than half of the opposing batter's ground balls to be pulled, and it would still make sense.

A little algebra tells us that the break-even point is a five percent "pull rate" on ground balls. In 2022, the average left-handed hitter pulled 52.3 percent of their ground balls. In other words, against a left-handed batter, the numbers say that the familiar 2-2 defense should be the oddity that people marvel at, not the 3-1 infield shift, but that's not the way people think about baseball.

For a while, bunting against the shift looked like it might be a good response. If a team was going to leave the left side of the infield unguarded, a batter only needed to push a bunt past the mound to pick up a free single. The batter gave up the chance for an extra-base hit, but for a while, the chances of getting a hit were good enough to make it worth trying. The problem was that teams recognized this too and came up with defensive strategies that didn't work every time but cut down the chances of a bunt hit enough that the batter would be better off swinging away. Some fans wondered why batters didn't just hit the ball the other way. While that's much more easily said than done, even if the batter could hit the ball the other way, doing so comes with a cost. Batted balls to the opposite field tend not to be hit as hard, and the best predictor of whether a ball will become a base hit is how hard it comes off the bat. That loss of exit velocity from hitting the ball to the opposite field canceled out the benefit of aiming toward a lightly guarded section of the field and batters weren't going to change their entire approach if they would just get the same results.

If left alone, baseball would have developed to where almost all left-handed batters were shifted, and I want to stop there for a moment and talk about that. The question of whether or not to ban the infield shift is a loaded one. When I worked as a therapist (fact three), I had a supervisor who liked to say, "Most of the time, an argument isn't about what it's about." It sounds like something St. Yogi of the Bronx might have said, but it describes human relationships all too well. If there's a disagreement between two people who have a solid relationship, they usually calmly sit down and figure it out like adults. When there's a deeper rift between them, they argue. As a therapist, sometimes my job was to get them to acknowledge that deeper rift.

It seems a little weird that people get so passionate about where the shortstop stands until you realize that they aren't really arguing about where the shortstop stands. For some fans, baseball is about symmetry. It might just be the illusion of symmetry, but they expect the game to look a certain way. There should be two infielders on either side, and a ground ball up the middle *should* be a single. While the rules have never actually said that, it still feels fundamental. The infield shift affected the flow and cadence of the game in some very real ways. Had baseball been born in the age of computers and spray charts and advanced statistical modeling, teams might have realized early on that a 2-2 formation wasn't the best idea and played a 3-1 formation from the beginning of the game. It didn't happen that way though and history is sticky.

On the other side of the argument, by banning the infield shift MLB is saying, "Pretend you didn't do any of that hard work to figure out the tendencies of the hitters." Within sporting culture, we usually applaud the people who come up with a new strategic idea. What does it mean when MLB can clamp down on innovation?

There were also those who disliked the infield shift because they believed that it led batters to try to hit the ball *over* the shift (and ideally, the fence). The issue of symmetry is a matter of taste, but we've already seen that the shift produced an increase in strikeouts, at least for left-handed batters. Could banning the shift be the answer to runaway strikeout rates?

MLB's anti-shifting rule requires teams to station four fielders on the infield dirt, with two on either side of second base. The "four on the dirt" rule prohibits teams from putting a fielder in short right anyway and saying "It's not a shift. We're playing a four-outfielder formation!" The next best (legal) defense for most shift-able left-handed hitters is to station a fielder as close to second base as they can. There are some hitters where teams were already doing that. Fortunately, for us, the MLBAM data set tracks these "partial" shifts too.

Using the same method we used a bit ago, focusing on left-handed hitters, and comparing players to themselves, we can look at how hitter outcomes change in front of these *partial* shifts, and look at them compared to the changes associated with the *full* infield shift.

Table 17. Effects of full and partial shifts compared to 2-2 defense, left-handed batters, same player comparison model, 2022

Outcome	Changes (Full Shift)	Changes (Partial Shift)
Strikeout	+3.5%	+3.2%
Walk	+0.8%	+1.3%
HBP	−0.3%	+0.2%
Single	−2.2%	−1.4%
Double/Triple	−0.0%	−0.1%
Home run	−0.2%	−0.7%
Out in Play	−1.5%	−2.5%
OBP	−.020	−.007
BABIP	−.018	−.005
BABIP on grounders	−.027	−.011

Against left-handed batters, the barely-not-a-shift doesn't get quite the same results that the full 3-1 shift does. It ended up looking like a junior varsity version, with one exception: the strikeouts are still there. If MLB wants to inject more action into the game by banning the infield shift, they might not get as much by squeezing this lemon as they had thought. In 2022, MLB began experimenting in the minor leagues with the "pie slice" at second base, drawing a zone of exclusion behind the second base bag which defenders could not enter before the pitch. The strategy effectively pushes defenders off the second base bag and forces them into a more traditional positioning, presumably in the hope of more traditional results. The initial shift ban itself was tested in the minor leagues in this way, and if banning the infield shift doesn't bring about the desired results, the pie slice might be called up from the minors to take its place.

THE OUTFIELD NEVER gets mentioned when people talk about the shift. As teams studied data to figure out where to put their infielders and discovered that they should move one across the mid-line of the diamond, they were studying positioning data for their outfielders too. It had an effect. We can see that BABIP on fly balls and line drives to the outfield has fallen significantly since the mid-2000s.

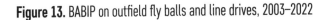

Figure 13. BABIP on outfield fly balls and line drives, 2003–2022

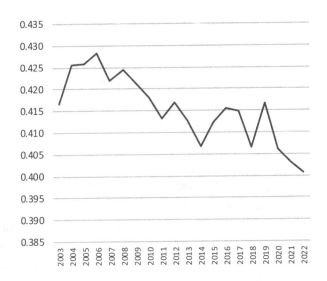

Better outfield positioning has reduced BABIP on fly balls around 15–20 points. A little earlier, we saw that the infield shift had a similarly sized effect on ground balls. It's just that no one noticed what was happening in the outfield because it didn't look obvious when teams were moving fielders around out there. In 2022, there were signs that MLB teams were starting to get a little bolder with their outfield tinkering. About half a percent of pitches were thrown with four players roaming the outfield. The 2-2 balance on the infield had already been upset, and it looked like the 4-and-3 taboo was the next to be broken.

What did a team gain if they played a fourth outfielder? Again, MLB Advanced Media comes to our rescue. Whether or not an "air ball," either fly ball or a line drive, is caught depends largely on two things. One is how far the fielder has to run to get to the ball and the other is how long the ball hangs in the air, both of which are easily measured using StatCast technology. MLB has published data on catch percentages given different combinations of those two factors. Not surprisingly, balls that hang in the air for a few seconds or are hit nearby to a fielder are almost always caught.

An "average" MLB runner can go from home to first (90 feet) in 4.3 seconds when they run at full speed. That's roughly 21 feet per second. Players can hit top speeds greater than that, but everyone needs some reaction time, and they have to accelerate from a standstill. That brings down their overall average. Outfielders don't have to run full speed after every ball, but we'll use 21 feet per second as our guidepost. With a little help from our 10th grade geometry class, we can estimate that the area each outfielder can cover is a circle with a radius of 21 feet for each second of hangtime.

Eventually, we do have to worry about the outfielders running into each other. To take an extreme example, if a fly ball stayed in the air for a full minute, all three outfielders could run to the proper spot, have a moment to play rock-paper-scissors to figure out who would catch it, and still have time to move under and glove it. The nice thing about 10th grade geometry is that there's a formula to account for that overlap in range too.

Using more of that fancy math, we can figure that with a fourth outfielder, the chances that a fly ball will be caught go up by about 4.3 percentage points. That might not sound like much, but 4.3 percent is the same as 43 points of batting average. What if we took one of the infielders, maybe one from the opposite field side that doesn't get a lot of traffic, and had them patrol the outfield sometimes?

Clearly, we have to account for what happens when there's only a three-member infield on duty. If only we had a data set that tells us what happened when teams removed an infielder from the opposite-field side. Hey, wait a minute!

Table 18. BABIP of opposite field/middle grounders and soft line drives, 2022

Situation	With Shift	Without Shift	Difference
RHH, ground ball, opposite field	.469	.387	.082
RHH, ground ball, middle	.255	.244	.011
RHH, soft line drive, opposite field	.883	.828	.055
RHH, soft line drive, middle	.632	.690	−.058

Let's focus on right-handed batters for a moment. The numbers for lefties were basically the same, but the effect of the 3-1 infield shift is greater. For right-handed batters, the infield shift wasn't a great idea, but perhaps teams hadn't quite yet realized the strategic opportunity beyond the infield dirt. We can see that by shifting an infielder away from the opposite field for right-handed batters (the first-base side), ground balls hit to that area get a boost of 82 points of batting average. Soft line drives, which are sometimes catchable by infielders, get a boost of 55 points. It seems silly to trade 82 points of BABIP for 43, until you realize that the entire reason that the shift was born was that batters don't hit opposite field ground balls very often. In the same way that five quarters are worth more than one dollar bill, giving up 82 points of BABIP on something that a batter doesn't do often in trade for 43 points on something he does quite commonly, hit a fly ball to the outfield, can make sense if the ratio is right. How big does that ratio between outfield flies and opposite field grounders have to be before the fourth outfielder makes sense? It's roughly 2-to-1.

From 2018 to 2022, 41 percent of all balls in play hit by right-handed batters were either fly balls or line drives that were hit into the outfield. In that same time period, only about 5.3 percent of balls in play were opposite field grounders and 3.6 were soft or medium hit line drives to the opposite field, for a total of 8.9 percent of balls in play that would have been actionable by an oppo-side infielder. The ratio of outfield fly balls to opposite field infield balls is over 4.5-to-1. There would have been exceptions. Some pitchers tend to give up more grounders and some more fly balls and that changes the calculus, but banishing an infielder to the outer-lands would make sense a good chunk of the time. Except that now, it's illegal to do that too.

This was the uncomfortable point that MLB had come to. According to the math, most left-handed batters should see an infield shift. Against right-handed batters, the evidence points toward teams being better off if they play a three-in, four-out formation. It was probably only a matter of time before the fourth outfielder began creeping into baseball the way that the shifted infielder did. Teams would have to think about how those formations would be affected by baserunners and sometimes the traditionally spaced four-member infield would have been a better play, but teams might have eventually been shifting back and forth between three or four different formations throughout a game. The infield shift was only the beginning.

May 15, 2022—Toronto at Tampa Bay (Regular Season)

Toronto	AB	R	H	RBI	Tampa Bay	AB	R	H	RBI
Springer, dh	4	0	0	0	Lowe, dh	4	1	1	0
Guerrero Jr., r	4	0	1	0	Franco, lmi	4	1	1	0
Hernández, rf/scf	4	0	0	0	Ramírez, rf	3	1	0	0
Bichette, lmi	4	0	0	0	Kiermaier, cf	1	0	1	0
Espinal, rmi/s/f	3	0	1	0	Choi, r	4	0	1	1
Chapman, 3b/lsg	2	0	0	0	Arozarena, lf	4	0	1	1
Gurriel Jr., lf	3	0	1	0	Mejía, c	3	0	0	0
Kirk, c	3	0	1	0	Bruján, rmi/f/scf	3	0	1	0
Tapia, cf	2	0	1	0	Phillips, cf-rf	2	0	0	0
Jansen, ph	1	0	0	0	Walls, 3b	3	0	0	0
Zimmer, cf	0	0	0	0					

Toronto — 000 000 000   0 5 2
Tampa Bay — 000 003 00x   3 6 0

2B—Kirk (3), Bruján (2); HBP—Phillips (1; by Manoah); SH—Lemke (1); SB—Kiermaier (3); CS—Espinal (1), Arozarena (3); DP—Tampa Bay 1 (Bruján-Franco-Choi); E- Chapman 2 (2); LOB—Toronto 4, Tampa Bay 5; WP—Manoah (1); T—2:47; A—20,986

Toronto	IP	H	R	ER	BB	SO
Manoah, L (4–1)	6	5	3	1	0	4
Richards	1	0	0	0	0	1
Borucki	0.2	1	0	0	0	2
Phelps	0.1	0	0	0	0	1

Tampa Bay	IP	H	R	ER	BB	SO
Springs	4.2	4	0	0	0	2
Wisler, W (2–1)	1.1	0	0	0	0	1
Feyereisen, H (4)	1	0	0	0	1	3
Poche, H (7)	1	0	0	0	0	0
Kittredge, S (5)	1	1	0	0	0	0

THIS ISN'T THE way that the papers printed this box score the next day, but it's more accurate, and it's a good example of where baseball would probably have headed if things had been a little different. In the first inning, with the right-handed batting George Springer leading off the game, the Rays shifted their infield to the left. Starting pitcher Jeffrey Springs was a ground ball pitcher, and so nominal second baseman Vidal Bruján opened the game playing on the "wrong" side of second, drifting over to his right to make a small barrier of humans with shortstop Wander Franco and third baseman Taylor Walls. Bruján was on the move quite a bit during the game. In the sixth inning, this time with fly ball pitcher Matt Wisler on the mound, the Rays deployed a four-member outfield against Springer. Bruján went out to right-center field, while starting center fielder Brett Phillips moved to play in the left-center-field alley. The regular box score reports that Bruján stayed at second base the whole game, but that's not really what happened.

The Blue Jays weren't to be outdone. On two occasions, with Brandon Lowe up, "second baseman" Santiago Espinal went out to right field, while right fielder Teoscar Hernández scooted over into the power alley, forming a midfield tandem with Raimel Tapia. With the left-handed hitting Lowe up, shortstop Bo Bichette slid over to Espinal's second-base position, while third baseman Matt Chapman effectively played shortstop and third at the same time. In addition to his occasional outfielding duties, Espinal played the role of the short right fielder when the Blue Jays put an infield shift on a left-handed batter, again with Bichette moving over to join the right side of the infield to play something more akin to a traditional second base and Chapman being left home alone. At other times, Espinal would cross second base and play on the left side of the infield. Bichette was always to the right of Espinal (though to the batter and the television audience, Bichette was always to the left).

It seems like we should have had a different name for the player who was playing in that shifted short right-field position. It wasn't even the same player from team to team. Some teams sent their third baseman over there. Some shifted the second baseman there and had the shortstop come over to the dark side. Some left the shortstop to guard the left side of the infield. Some teams, if you watched them closely, flip-flopped who went where in the middle of an at-bat.

There was a lacuna. A gap in our baseball language. An unspoken word. It was clearly a defined role to play in that particular spot. Even though more than a third of MLB plate appearances in 2022 took place with a shifted defense in place, we never had a name for what *that* fielder was doing. We've had the same nine names for the positions on a baseball diamond for more than a century. MLB was so shocked when someone invented a 10th position (and perhaps an 11th) that they literally outlawed it. Maybe Bud Abbott and Lou Costello were preparing us all along, though it turned out that when they asked, "Who's on third?" he actually was near first base some of the time. Maybe if there had been a name for it, it wouldn't have felt so strange.

What should it have been called when the third baseman was shifted into short right field, fielded a ground ball, and threw the batter out? I don't think anyone ever knew and our scorecards didn't give a darn. They still said G5–3. In baseball, we cling to the numbers 1 through 9 as though they hold some secret code to the universe.

One of the not-so-hidden forces in the game is that *baseball is a game with more than nine positions*. There are only nine defenders allowed on the field, but what if, for a moment, we set aside the old suite of nine words and asked what we'd call each fielder if we had never heard the word "shortstop?" We can at least save the names "pitcher" and "catcher." The rules still define where they stand (or squat), but now we need words for the other seven. We have a word that means "an infielder who moves around to different spots," but "utility infielder" doesn't seem quite right for what we're trying to say.

I've seen scorecards that tried to solve the problem of the ground ball to the third baseman in short right field with a notation of G5s–3. The batter grounded out to the fielder who was playing "third base," but who was playing in a shifted role at that moment. I'd nominate that when a player was in that spot, they should have been known as "the shifter." Then there's the player who would have seen some time on the infield and some time as the fourth outfielder. I recommend we call that player the "floater." We probably won't get to hear baseball's versions of the "s" word and the "f" word, but if things had been different, we might have. We can now see Santiago Espinal's line in the box score, which reads "Espinal, rmi/s/f." Espinal was so much more than a second baseman that day. He played in both the shifter role and the floater role, and among the middle infielders, was the one that was always to the batter's right, even if it wasn't always to the right of second base.

We would have needed some other words too. In a four-outfielder formation, the center fielder often played in either right-center or left-center field, with either the floater or one of the corner outfielders moving over to play a more central role. Perhaps this guest in the middle could have been the "semi-center fielder." Vidal Briján, whose line reads "Briján, rmi/f/scf" played the traditional second base/right middle infield role some of the time, but was also the Rays' floater and semi-center fielder. The Blue Jays, on the other hand asked Teoscar Hernández to be their rf/scf.

There are some other words we would have needed. In a shift against a left-handed batter, there was always one infielder who stayed behind between second and third. That role could have been given the title "left-side guardian" and we see the notation "lsg" by Matt Chapman's name who did that job for the Blue Jays. (On a day in which eight of the nine Toronto hitters were right-handed, Raimel Tapia being the only exception, Tampa Bay didn't use a left-handed infield shift, and so no shifter or left-side guardian were needed.)

Finally, we come to Vladimir Guerrero Jr. and Ji-Man Choi, both of whom played "first base" for their teams that day. Choi, in particular, had previous experience roaming the outfield, and while Briján also had an outfielder's passport, neither Taylor Walls nor Wander Franco had played the outfield at the major league level. With a different second baseman, Tampa Bay might have preferred an experienced hand as their fourth outfielder, with perhaps one of the other infielders standing nearby to first to receive throws on a ground ball while Choi was out of the office. It might have all eventually led to a ground ball fielded by the second baseman playing on the left side of the infield and thrown to the third baseman who was handling put outs at the bag at first. At that point, scorecards everywhere would all have spontaneously caught fire.

BEFORE WE BURY the infield shift, there's one piece of it that was never explicitly in the discussion of its demise. In Chapter 4, we talked about the cultural preference to see everything in baseball from the perspective of the batter. It happened here too, without anyone ever acknowledging it. When fans would talk about the infield shift, they would instinctively talk about how it took hits *away from the batter*, as if the batter was entitled to those hits and the defense was doing him some grave injustice. Banning the infield shift is taking away from the defense's ability to gather outs.

It's not clear that banning the shift (and the fourth outfielder) will bring more action into the game. MLB might eventually end up getting what they want, but while the infield is now forbidden from shifting, MLB has certainly undergone a philosophical shift. Competitive innovation will only be tolerated up to a certain point. Baseball is a game, but MLB is a business. When innovation takes away from the enjoyability—and to be frank, the profitability—of the game, MLB has to decide whether that's going to be okay. Like it or not, the new ballgame will be shaped by that not-so-hidden force. Navigating that argument is now one of the fundamental questions in baseball. In the new ballgame, MLB will carry a big stick.

I also don't think we've seen the last of the infield shift. While the rules now mandate four infielders, one of whom doesn't actually figure to do much, what happens if a team experiments with shortening up their right fielder to play in the "shifter" role, having their third baseman play as far back on the dirt as possible to give some coverage to left field and having the two remaining outfielders try to cover as much ground as possible? Maybe it wouldn't work, but if it did and it "took hits away from the batter," would MLB wield its stick again and bat down the new strategy? The infield shift ban isn't the end of the story. It's the beginning of a fight that MLB has picked with the power of big data, and the new ballgame will see some interesting confrontations between those two in the coming years.

Chapter 6

Wait, Who's in Left Field Now?

I had a feeling I wasn't in Kansas anymore. This was Sheremetyevo Airport in Moscow, and there were four guys just standing there holding Kalashnikovs, looking at me. In Russia, the airport secures you. I had grown up in the 1980s, and every piece of popular media that I consumed had a go-to trick for pointing out the villain in the story. You made him Russian and gave him a nuclear weapon. Or gave him a Russian accent and a gun. Even after the fall of the Soviet Union, you made him "Slevetikan" and gave him an overdue library book. As a storyteller, you didn't have to waste any valuable time developing Boris's character. Simply coding him as Russian was enough. It was as if the very mouth of hell was located in Moscow and once in a while, someone walked out of it with a plan for world domination. And then someone in the United States made a movie about foiling it. I felt completely unprepared to be the plucky American who had to save humanity.

My wife, Tanya, asked Boris something, and taking his hand off his gun for a moment, he smiled and pointed to the right. She took my arm and led me that way. "What did you ask him?" I wanted to know. Apparently, she had just asked which way to customs. This was going to be an interesting couple of weeks.

I was in Moscow for the twin reasons that my wife was presenting at the 2006 European Bioenergetics Conference and that I finally got to meet our 11-month-old niece. My brother-in-law Petr picked us up at the airport and after a night at his apartment, we went to Lomonosov University for the conference. The original plan was that the conference goers would be housed in a dormitory on campus, but due to a clerical mishap (I assume directly planted by the Kremlin itself to increase the dramatic tension) we were moved to another property, two subway stops away from the university. I would have known that if I had been able to read any of the subway signs. I was a stranger in a strange land. From that day forward, I never again looked down on anyone who came to the United States from another country. I'm a reasonably functional human, and here I was reduced to not being able to read even the shampoo bottle in the shower. At least I think it was shampoo. My hair did feel a little weird after that shower, but then everything felt weird on that trip.

We settled into the dorm, and found out that to get in and out we were required to present a paper entry pass. Each room was issued only one, and we needed to show it to a Russian guy in a security guard uniform, who may or may not have had a nuclear weapon under his desk. I found myself terrified of him and I couldn't figure out why until about a week later. Even someone trained in clinical psychology (fact three) sometimes has trouble figuring out what's going on in his own mind. You never realize how deeply some of those messages were drilled into you as a kid.

After two days being locked in a Russian tower with a few books that I had brought for entertainment, my wife suggested that perhaps I should instead sneak into the conference with her. All of the top mitochondrial scientists from all over Europe were there. Strangely, all of the presentations were held in English, and for a few moments, it was nice to hear the word "the," but the rest of it might as well have been in Russian. I'm still not entirely sure what an organelle is.

The only part that I truly understood was when some scientists from Florence bragged about how efficient Italian mitochondria were in winning the recently completed 2006 World Cup. What they didn't expect was that it would lead to a shouting match, as scientists from France and Germany (whom Italy had defeated in their final two games) took exception to the bragging. I don't know a whole lot about soccer, but I understood sports trash talking and for a moment the very confusing world of Moscow made sense. You never realize how much even the little cues of home make a difference until they're all taken away.

IT'S THE NINTH inning. You're down 3–2 with two outs and your light-hitting third baseman is due up. Time for a pinch-hitter! Well, not so fast. The bench is a little thin right now and there's no one left who's ever played third before. Your fourth outfielder is available to hit and has a decent bat, but even if things go well and you keep the game going, you face the prospect of someone standing at third who's only ever been there as a runner. It's probably not going to be pretty.

It's rare for a manager to pinch-hit so aggressively that he might end up with a player in a strange defensive role. At first blush, it's weird that it's weird. If a team enters the ninth inning trailing, they can't win unless they score some runs. Why aren't they doing everything they can to score, even if it means having to face the music later? If you don't score, the music won't play at all. Baseball writer Kevin Goldstein, who has spent several years in the Houston and Minnesota front offices, calls these oddball events with players in strange positions #WeirdBaseball. Baseball is a game of resource management played under uncertainty, and sometimes you run out of resources, especially when you get to the 12th inning. He's coined what might be termed the Goldstein Rule: once a game passes midnight local time, the chances of #WeirdBaseball go up exponentially. You're supposed to eat ice cream when it happens.

I REMEMBER THIS game specifically because Travis Fryman and I both ended up a little out of place. I went to the game with my younger brother and a couple of his friends. In 2000, tickets to Jacobs Field were still a hot commodity, as Cleveland was nearing the end of what would become a 455-game streak of consecutive sell-outs. My brother's friends had somehow come into these tickets, but as they were all

June 11, 2000—Cincinnati at Cleveland (Regular Season)

Cincinnati	AB	R	H	RBI	Cleveland	AB	R	H	RBI
Reese, 2b	6	1	0	0	Lofton, cf	4	0	3	1
Larkin, dh-ss	6	1	1	0	Vizquel, ss	7	0	0	0
Griffey Jr., cf	5	2	2	3	Fryman, 3b-1b	5	1	1	0
Bichette, rf	2	0	1	0	Justice, rf	7	0	1	0
Tucker, rf	4	1	2	0	Sexson, 1b-lf	6	2	2	1
Young, 1b	5	0	0	0	S. Alomar Jr., c	5	2	2	0
Boone, 3b	5	1	2	2	Thome, dh	5	0	1	1
Stynes, lf	5	1	1	0	Ramirez, lf	4	0	2	0
Santiago, c	2	0	0	0	Cabrera, pr-lf	0	0	0	0
Taubensee, c	2	0	0	0	Branyan, ph	0	0	0	0
Castro, ss	3	0	0	1	R. Alomar, pr-2b	1	0	0	0
Casey, ph	1	0	0	0	Wilson, 2b-3b	4	0	2	1
Aybar, p	0	0	0	0					

Cincinnati — 000 000 050 000 2   7 9 1
Cleveland — 021 001 100 000 0   5 14 1

2B—Boone (13), Ramirez (3); HR—Sexson (13, off Dessens, 7th inning, none on), Griffey Jr. (18, off Speier, 8th inning, 2 on); SF—Castro (1), Wilson (1); SH—Stynes (2), Wilson (1); SB—Wilson (2); DP—Cincinnati 3 (Young-Castro; Graves-Taubensee-Young, Boone-Reese-Young), Cleveland 1 (Alomar-Vizquel-Fryman); E- Boone (6), R. Alomar (6); PB—S. Alomar Jr. (3); WP—Villone 2 (3), Finley (6); LOB—Cincinnati 8, Cleveland 14; T—4:38; A—43,036

Cincinnati	IP	H	R	ER	BB	SO
Villone	6	8	4	4	5	3
Dessens	1	2	1	1	0	0
Graves	3	3	0	0	2	1
Williamson	1	0	0	0	0	1
Aybar, W (1–2)	2	1	0	0	1	2

Cleveland	IP	H	R	ER	BB	SO
Finley	7	3	3	3	2	2
Reed, H (3)	0.2	1	1	1	0	0
Speier, BS (5)	1.1	1	1	1	0	0
Brewington	2	1	0	0	1	2
Karnieniecki, L (1–3)	2	3	2	2	3	0

Finley faced three batters in the eighth.

15, they needed someone to drive them downtown. I hadn't planned on a baseball game that day, but I wasn't going to turn one down, even if it meant having to be the "responsible adult." Years later, I was able to find this box score because it was the only time Travis Fryman played first base in his big-league career. I remember sympathizing with him. I wasn't quite sure what I was doing either.

The game was billed as "The Battle of Ohio," even though Cincinnati is four hours away from Cleveland by car and their airport is in Kentucky. The box score tells us that the game took longer than the drive. Cleveland built a 5–0 lead and looked poised to take the game easily, as Cleveland starter Chuck Finley had carried a one-hitter through the seventh inning. The box score notes that he faced three batters in the eighth: an Aaron Boone double, a Chris Stynes single, and a seven-pitch walk to Benito Santiago, with two of the pitches eluding catcher Sandy Alomar Jr. Finley was done. Side-winding right-hander Steve Reed came in and held Juan Castro and Pokey Reese to a sacrifice fly and a fielder's choice that should have been an inning-ending double play that locked the score at 5–2 in favor of Cleveland. Seizing on the turn of fortune, Barry Larkin singled, which put runners at first and second with two outs for Ken Griffey Jr., who came to the plate representing the potential tying run.

Cleveland manager Charlie Manuel had a team battling a rash of injuries and didn't have a left-handed reliever available to face the left-handed hitting Griffey and so Justin Speier was summoned to face what was now a surprisingly tense situation. I remember hoping that Griffey wouldn't hit a home run to tie the game, not because I wanted Cleveland to win, but because it would set us on course for extra innings. Before the game, I had spoken to the parents of my brother's friends about that possibility. There was another family event later in the day, and they had asked me to have everyone home by about 6:00. Speier fell behind Griffey 2–0, and the box score tells the rest of the story. The game was tied. They ended up playing 13 innings.

Fryman found himself at first base by accident. In the 10th inning, Manuel pinch-hit Russell Branyan for Jolbert Cabrera. Branyan drew a walk and scooted into second on Enrique Wilson's single, but ended up injured in the process. Roberto Alomar, who had been kept out of the starting lineup because he too was nursing a nagging injury, rose from the bench to pinch-run for Branyan. Had Branyan stayed in the game, he would have been the obvious choice to assume left-field duties once Omar Vizquel hit into a 1–2–3 double play to end the inning. Instead, Manuel had to do some shuffling. Alomar went to second base, where he won 10 Gold Gloves over his career, and utility infielder Wilson moved to third. Someone had to play left field, and first baseman Richie Sexson had played there before. That left first base vacant.

Fryman, for his part, did what he could. He regularly handled a more difficult position, third base, and at the end of that 2000 season, Fryman would be honored with the Gold Glove Award for his work there. Surely, he could handle first base for a couple of innings. As I nervously glanced at my watch and did some mental math around exiting Jacobs Field, getting to the car, driving home, and still dropping everyone off by 6:00, Barry Larkin led off the Cincinnati 11th with a ground ball to short and Fryman received the throw from Vizquel without incident. In the 12th, he did similarly, receiving a throw from Alomar on a ground ball by Eddie Taubensee.

It was in the 13th inning that things went sideways. Griffey Jr. grounded a single through the right side, between the injured Alomar and the neophyte Fryman. I wasn't there to see that one because I had to tell three very disappointed teenagers that we were leaving early. I don't know whether it was the sort of ball that a more experienced first baseman or a second baseman not battling an injury would have gotten to. Maybe it was. It's hard to pick out the play that goes un-made. Michael Tucker then bunted the ball to Alomar, who threw it past Fryman, allowing Griffey Jr. to go to third and Tucker to second. Two batters later, Aaron Boone knocked both of them in with a single, and Cincinnati won the game 7–5. Was Cleveland's fate sealed when they had to play #WeirdBaseball?

JUST ABOUT ANY major league player wearing a glove can field a ground ball hit directly to him and turn it into an out. The dirty secret of baseball is how thin the margins are between greatness and garbage. The difference between a good hitter and a bad one is one hit over the course of a week. Baseball teams usually play six games a week, and if you start all of them, you'll get 25 or so at-bats over that time. The batter who gets six hits in those 25 at-bats is hitting .240. The batter who finds a seventh is hitting .280. The same goes principle applies to fielding. There are plenty of balls that no human being would be able to field. There are plenty of the two-hopper, no-drama balls. Hidden in there are the ones that good fielders will get to that the bad ones don't.

We normally think about baseball players primarily for their athletic gifts. We don't often recognize how much the extensive amount of practice they do matters. #WeirdBaseball offers us a chance to ask that question. What would happen if a gifted athlete played a position that he had not studied?

Using data from 2003 to 2022, I found all of the "emergency" first basemen, like Travis Fryman had been that day. I picked the ones who had regular playing time at other positions, but who had also filled in at first base for fewer than 18 innings that season. I looked to see what happened during those emergency shifts. It turns out that emergency first basemen (70.5 percent success) were slightly better than regular first basemen (69.3 percent) at fielding ground balls hit their way. First base is usually the spot on the field where mobility matters the least, so our guest star who usually plays another position probably moves a bit better, and that mobility transfers over. Unfortunately, that's where the good news ends for our fake fielders.

The problem is that the most common time for a first baseman to touch the ball is when it's thrown to him on the "3" end of a 4–3 or 5–3 or 6–3 ground ball. Using play-by-play data, I looked to see how often real first basemen had a throw from an infielder clank off their glove. When receiving a throw, a real first basemen made an error about 0.1 percent of the time and the impostors did so 0.3 percent of the time. That would add up over time. First basemen receive a *lot* of throws.

Errors aren't always the best way to measure defense either. It's easy to see the catch that the first baseman didn't make, but what about the catch that he could have made better? Sometimes mistakes are made in ways that aren't entirely obvious. For example, on a ground ball in the hole, the shortstop may range over, grab the ball, and make a throw that will require a good scoop by the first baseman. A trained first baseman is not only going to be familiar with how to make that scoop, but also the little tricks that might make all the difference on a "bang-bang" play. Our fake first baseman might not know those tricks and the ball might take an extra tenth of a second to find the pocket of his glove. No official scorer would ever give him an error because he didn't drop it, but a more experienced fielder would have done it better and more importantly, gotten the out.

I looked at all ground balls that were hit to an infielder, and 12.1 percent of them ended up as hits or reached-on-errors when a regular first baseman was patrolling the bag. When a fake first baseman was on duty, there was a 14.2 percent reach rate. It might not seem like much, but in 2022, the average team had 1,166 balls hit to its second baseman, third baseman, or shortstop. If 2.1 percent of them were to be changed from outs to hits, that's 24 extra runners reaching base. Chances are, within a single game, the replacement first baseman would get it right, but if someone played first base like that all the time, they'd bleed away a lot of value over the course of a season.

We can do the same sort of analysis for the other three infielders. First, we can look at how many ground balls the fielder gloved before they skipped through the infield for our "emergency" second basemen or shortstops or third basemen, compared to the rest of the league.

Table 19. Percentage of ground balls fielded

Position	"Emergency" group	Everyone else	Difference
Second Base	78.0%	79.0%	1.0%
Third Base	75.4%	75.8%	0.4%
Shortstop	78.6%	79.8%	1.2%

Infielders who are faking it are much worse than the regularly scheduled ones, and that remained true *even if they were above-average regulars at another infield position.* Over the course of 162 games, those differences would add up to about 4.5 extra plays *not* made by a second baseman, 1.7 extra plays *not* made by a third baseman, and a whopping 6.4 plays at shortstop. That's just from extra ground balls that get through the infield.

Once the ball is in the infielder's glove, how often does that result in an out being made?

Table 20. Percentage of fielded ground balls turned into outs

Position	"Emergency" group	Everyone else	Difference
Second Base	97.8%	97.9%	0.1%
Third Base	91.4%	95.0%	3.6%
Shortstop	94.1%	96.6%	2.5%

Over 162 games, that would be 0.4 additional non-plays for a second baseman, 13.1 plays for the third baseman, and 11.0 plays for the shortstop. The difference between an average infielder and a cringe-worthy one is around 25 plays per year, and so far, we've only looked at ground balls. When put into a new position, our lost fielder will likely play like one of the worst fielders in the league at that spot.

We also need to think about who ends up in these emergency roles to begin with. If a manager needs an emergency shortstop, he's not going to just pick someone at random. It's probably going to be the second or third baseman, perhaps the one who played short at some point along the way in college or the minors but eventually had to move off the position. Even the players who are the closest match to a shortstop without being a regular shortstop are awful at the job.

The same thing happens, but to a lesser extent, in the outfield. Newbie outfielders let more fly balls drop than do experienced ones. On a percentage basis, it's not a lot, but over the course of a season and a lot of fly balls, a small percentage can add up.

Table 21. Percentage of fly balls caught

Position	"Emergency" group	Everyone else	Difference
Left Field	81.3%	85.9%	4.6%
Center Field	84.6%	86.2%	1.6%
Right Field	82.7%	86.2%	3.5%

The emergency group still gets to more than 80 percent of the fly balls, but they are significantly worse than league average. In 2022, the average team had 250 fly balls that were eventually fielded by a left fielder. A difference of 4.6 percent over that many fly balls is 11.5 extra balls that fall in. Again, this is before we think about line drives, being able to cut the ball off in the gap, and throwing out (or holding) runners on the basepaths. The numbers in center (5.2 plays) and right field (10.0 plays) are similarly bad.

In Chapter 3, we considered the case of pitchers, gifted athletes in their own right, but who weren't picked for the team for their hitting skills. Back in the dark ages before the universal designated hitter and despite that athleticism, pitchers were terrible hitters. Fielding follows the same rules. You can't just plunk a player down into a position that they've never been in before and expect that athletic talent will do the rest. It is really hard to master a fielding position in baseball. We come again to one of our not-so-hidden forces in baseball: *Baseball is a game that is about much more than athletic talent. It's a game of skill.*

Experience and learning matter. You might think that it would be easy for a shortstop to move to second base, but now for a ball up the middle, he'd have to range to his right, rather than his left and angle his body in a different way toward first to make the throw. It's not that players don't know how to do that, but months and years of repetition can teach little ways to do it a little quicker. Sometimes, that's the difference between "safe" and "out." Fans of baseball often look down on utility players, because they're not good enough to be starters. Utility players have a superpower of their own. It's a skill to be able to play multiple positions well or even just well enough.

FOR THOSE OF us who collected baseball cards as kids, we were used to seeing a position listed next to a player's name. Rickey Henderson was a left fielder. Ryne Sandberg played second base. For many years, MLB teams operated under the starter-backup model of positions. A team had a starter at a position, who would get most of the playing time there, and someone who filled in when needed. The starter owned that piece of real estate, whether it was second base or left field. More sneakily, that piece of real estate was intimately connected to that player. In the new ballgame, things have changed. We saw in Chapter 4 that teams are moving toward a model of sharing the workload among their pitchers and, as a result, teams use many more pitchers per game than they once did.

Figure 14. Pitchers used per team per game, 1950–2022

We see an inflection point in the late 1980s, as the modern relief pitcher was emerging. With more pitchers needed on a daily basis, more spots on the roster were needed for those pitchers. The short-burst reliever fundamentally changed how teams thought about pitching, but it turns out that the reliever has made teams think differently about the other half of their roster. As the bench has gotten smaller, it's put pressure on the few that do ride the pines to have more gloves in their locker. That's not the only way that teams have adapted.

Teams have begun actively developing multi-positionality, not only among their utility and bench players, but among their regulars. In the minors, where the games don't actually count, it's common for teams to identify players who might be able to carry several gloves and intentionally have them wander around the field to get a feel for several spots. Research that I've done shows that it takes about half a season of experience for a player to get fully comfortable with a position. If teams let a player do that in the minors, then it's not #WeirdBaseball if he happens to end up at third base one night in an MLB game. Once a player has a few different spots mastered, a team might as well use that ability to their advantage. The data show that's exactly what has happened. Figure 15 below shows the percentage from among players who appeared in at least 81 games in a season who played in at least five games at four or more positions.

Shortened seasons in 1981 (strike), 1994 (strike), and 2020 (COVID-19 pandemic) are excluded.

Figure 15. Percentage of regular players playing four or more positions, 1950–2022

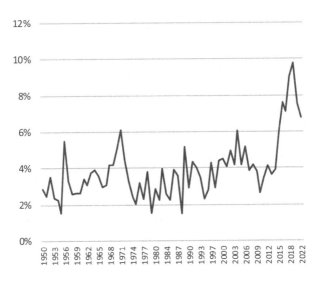

There have always been a few players who moved back and forth in the field, but teams leaned more forcefully into the strategy in the 2010s. There's the obvious benefit that teams can add more pitchers onto their rosters, but with more players who are able to play in more places, it also leaves a little bit of room for managers to get creative with their lineups. You can squeeze someone in who's a better fit against that day's pitcher and move two players around to compensate. Later in the game, you can pinch-hit in a key situation and still keep the defense solvent. It's another not-so-hidden force that is shaping baseball: *The new ballgame is multi-positional.*

Even the divide between infielders and outfielders is starting to break down. Traditionally, bench players would specialize as either "utility infielders" or "fourth outfielders" and if regular players were multi-positionalists, they tended to stick to one section of the field. There were the occasional outfielders who spent time at first base, but now we see something even more than that. Figure 16 shows the percentage from among players who appeared in more than 81 games who spent at least five games at either second, short, or third *and* at least five games at an outfield position in the same year.

Figure 16. Percentage of regular players playing both infield and outfield, 1950–2022

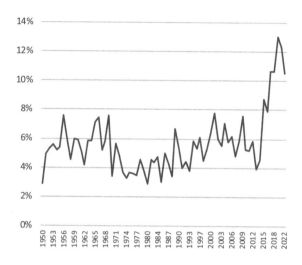

Players don't stay in one place like they used to. It's what enables teams to carry the short benches that free up spots for the eighth reliever in the bullpen. But it's more than just a way to squeeze more pitchers onto the roster. What's interesting is that while, in theory, the increased roster flexibility might allow managers to grab strategic advantages by increasing the amount of platooning they are able to do, that's *not* what happens. Figure 17 shows the percentage of plate appearances in which the batter had the handedness advantage.

Figure 17. Percentage of batters with handedness advantage, 1950–2022

From the 1950s through the 1980s, platooning increased steadily, but then fell as teams started to eliminate some of the spots for bench bats and at the same time began rostering more relievers who could match handedness for one or two hitters. Around 2000, when the one-inning relief model reached dominance, we see an equilibrium and then even a small drop off in platoon advantages when our multi-positionalists began appearing.

If managers aren't using the positional flexibility on their rosters to grab a strategic advantage, what are they doing? The answer is the same as it was on the pitching half of the roster. The expansion of the MLB talent pool has brought an influx of talent to both the pitcher's mound and the batter's box. On the mound, given three good options rather than one, managers have spread out the pitching workload. Fresher pitchers are better. We see the same thing happen on the lineup card.

I looked to see how much playing time the "starters" for each team have accounted for through time. For each year, I took eight multiplied by the number of teams (so, in 2022, eight times 30, which is 240) and found the players from one to that number on the list of most plate appearances taken. I then looked to see what percentage of all plate appearances they accounted for that year.

Figure 18. Percentage of plate appearances taken by "starters," 1950–2022

As multi-positionality has become a force in the game, teams have used this as a way to get their regulars a breather. That should tell us something about what teams value. Over a long season, where position players play most nights, "the grind" can get you. Even if you can fight the mental grind, constant high-level physical effort takes its toll after a while. In the same way that teams have found that spreading out the effort on their pitching staffs was a good idea, teams are inching toward a similar model with their position players. In the new ballgame, rest might be the biggest strategic advantage of all.

The idea that rest is a luxury, or worse a sign of weakness, is deeply woven into the fabric of United States culture. Baseball has long associated "always showing up for work" with virtue. Like so many other "market inefficiencies" that we've found over the years, what if that attitude was just another toxic aspect of the culture that everyone assumed was true until someone did a little math and realized that it wasn't? It turns out that players are more effective when given occasional rest. What if we built our baseball teams— and since I'm here, the rest of our culture—in ways that permitted people to take a breather now and then and not feel guilty about it?

ON AUGUST 19, 2009, one of my five facts changed. In fact, I still celebrate August 19 as a personal holiday, because it was the day that I saw my last therapy patient. Ever. The last requirement of a doctoral program in clinical psychology is a year-long internship at which you work 40 hours per week as a therapist, and I did mine just down the street from Jacobs Field in Cleveland. There was even a day where Cleveland was playing a noon getaway game, and lacking any patients on my schedule at that hour, I took advantage of their "lunch and three innings" promotion. My patients that afternoon never knew the difference.

My third fact now is that I am a mental health *researcher*. While I'm thankful for the time that I spent working with patients, I discovered during my internship that clinical work is a very good and noble profession, and it is also the wrong profession for me. As of my last patient that day, I was officially "Doctor Carleton." That night, I met my friend "Omar" (we'll call him that because that's his name) to celebrate the end of my life as a therapist in the best possible way. He and I had been friends since high school and if sitting around and talking about baseball were an Olympic sport, we would have won gold medals in the doubles event. Cleveland was playing the Los Angeles, California Angels of Anaheim, California, which is near Los Angeles in California, and I didn't even have to go too far after I finished work.

That night, Omar and I puzzled over a curious decision by Cleveland manager Eric Wedge. Batting second that night was Jamey Carroll. That wasn't weird, as the 35-year-old Carroll had forged a career as a utility infielder out of a knack for getting on base, even if he rarely hit for power. But when the Jacobs Field public address announcer read out the night's lineups, Carroll was listed in left field. Why was the utility infielder in left field? We were stumped.

Carroll acquitted himself decently in the outfield that night, catching three fly balls and making a pretty good play on a sinking line drive off the bat of Bob Abreu to end the third inning. It turned out that I was seeing the front end of a baseball trend. Left field has long been a refuge for players with big bats and no gloves. It's the position on the field that gets the least action during a game, so if you need to hide a fielder somewhere, it might as well be there.

A moment ago, we saw that the percentage of playing time accounted for by "starters" in general has been in decline. There's no place where this is more obvious than in left. In 2022, the 30 primary left fielders in MLB accounted for only 55 percent of the playing time at the position, the lowest of the eight non-pitching spots. That percentage has been falling fast. What's interesting about the remaining 45 percent of playing time is who's taking it. If the top 30 on the playing time list are our "regular" left fielders, then the next 30 are our primary backups. They only accounted for 21 percent of the playing time in 2022, and everyone else who occasionally guested in left field took 24 percent. Other than the mound, left field is the spot on the field that sees the largest number of players standing there over the course of a season.

In Chapter 3, we saw that most primary designated hitters spent some time in the field and that the designated hitter role wasn't so much an identity as an assignment. It's become a way to get a batter into the lineup without having to worry about defensive duties. Left field has similarly become a "slush spot." Some teams do have a regular presence there and perhaps a proper "fourth outfielder," but league-wide, MLB teams have become more willing to simply move someone into left field out of convenience. It's not just players coming over from right field. That does happen, but we can see that second and third basemen, the Jameys Carroll of the world, are trying their hand in the seven spot. Or at least they're being told to go out there and do the best that they can. It turns out that Who might really be in left field today.

In the new ballgame, the starter-backup model of roster management is breaking down. When everyone's a multi-positionalist, the replacement for the starting second baseman who needs a day off might be playing in right field, with the right fielder moving to third and the regular third baseman moving to second. There's always been a little bit of this in baseball, though the pace is accelerating, and again, we can see it in the data. Figure 19 finds all situations in which a team's "regular" at a position (defined as someone who made more than half the starts at a position for the team in that season) needed a day off. They were on duty in the game before. They were on duty in the game after, but that one day, they took a break. We can look to see who started in their place. The two options would be a backup player (someone who didn't start in half of his team's games) or a regular from another position sliding over.

Figure 19. Percentage of days off covered by regulars from other positions

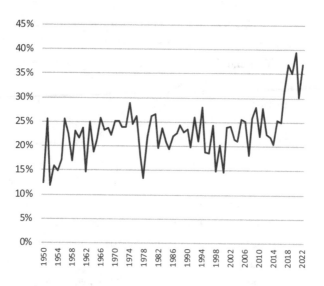

We can see that the rate of "sliding over" has jumped in recent years. In 2022, 37 percent of days off were covered by "sliders." It used to be a sign of "making it" in baseball if a player had a regular position that they could count on playing every day. What we're seeing is that even those everyday players are expected to move around the field like they're utility players.

The next time you're watching a game, and you notice that someone is playing in a spot where you didn't expect them to be, I'd invite you for a moment to consider all of the forces that led to that moment. The reliever evolution led teams to dedicate more of their roster spaces to pitchers. With benches shortened, it became more important for players to be able to play in several places. It meant that teams had to make changes in their entire player developmental process, because learning to play a position well takes practice. Teams have adapted, but the old model of positions in the game is slowly being replaced. In the new ballgame, the mark of a good player is growing to include not only what he does on the field, but also how versatile he is, because that allows managers more flexibility in getting other players onto the field who will help the team win.

Chapter 7

The Batter Strikes Back... and Out

Even as a kid I knew that Nolan Ryan was special. In July of 1989, the 42-year-old future Hall of Fame flamethrower came to Cleveland with the Texas Rangers. It was Ryan's first time back in the American League in a decade, and that night, Muni was filled with people who wanted one last peek at greatness. And nine-year-old me. A funny thing happened on the way to Ryan's farewell tour though. In 1989, Ryan led the American League in strikeouts with 301 and finished fifth in Cy Young voting. The next year, he led the league in strikeouts *again* and threw the sixth no hitter of his career. In 1991, at the age of 44, he threw a seventh.

The box score from the little slice of greatness that I saw on that particular night at Muni doesn't smile kindly on Ryan. He gave up seven runs in five-and-a-third innings. He did record seven strikeouts, but more importantly, he walked six. His opponent for the night, Cleveland's Greg Swindell, fared better, completing the game for Cleveland, giving up one run and striking out 10. But when Ryan left the game in sixth inning, something odd happened. The crowd gave him a standing ovation, and for the first time in my life, I cheered for the visiting team. My father pointed to Ryan as he walked toward the Texas dugout for the final time that night and said, "Now you can say you saw a Hall of Famer."

Ryan became MLB's all-time strikeout leader—and also, its all-time walks allowed leader—by virtue of his other claim to fame: he pitched a lot of innings. After being traded by the New York Mets to the California Angels before the 1972 season, Ryan logged some impressive miles on his right arm, averaging 272 innings per season from 1972 to 1979. In a baseball world where the average start now lasts five innings, there are those who long for the days of "pitchers like Nolan Ryan." During that eight-year span, he completed more than half of his starts. The thing is that there weren't a lot of pitchers like Nolan Ryan. In Chapter 4, we saw that much of how pitchers were used in the 1970s had more to do with the fact that there just weren't a lot of good options in the bullpen. Relievers were still largely expected to pitch the same way that starters did, and if they were any good at it, they quickly became starters in their own right. Nolan Ryan at 75 percent might still have been better than whatever relievers the Angels had at the time.

Nolan Ryan was a master of a very particular style of pitching at a very specific time in baseball history. He was durable (or perhaps lucky), which allowed him to pitch for 26 years with little interruption. He is legendary for having thrown seven career no-hitters, and also 12 one-hitters, although in retrospect, that legend benefits from the fact that baseball has always considered walks a non-event and is willing to overlook Ryan's somewhat questionable control. (Ryan's third no hitter in 1974 against the Minnesota Twins included *eight* walks!) He's a Hall of Famer by any measure, and I can say I saw him pitch, even if it was on a night where he was felled by such Cleveland legends as Brad Komminsk, Paul Zuvella, and Félix Fermín.

Nine years later, in May of 1998, I remember another Texas-born right-hander having a game so enchanted that despite the fact that I lived in Cleveland, the local radio station broke into its regular programming to carry the last inning of a game being played by the Chicago Cubs. That day, I listened as 20-year-old Kerry Wood struck out the last of 20 batters in his fifth major league start. Indeed, Wood was a hit and a hit batsman away from perfection in that game. It felt like Nolan Ryan was back, but this time things turned out a little differently. Kerry Wood didn't pitch in 1999, as he tore his ulnar collateral ligament and needed Tommy John surgery. He did return in 2000, and in 2003—by which time I lived on the North Side of Chicago—Wood led the league in strikeouts for the Cubs. It was also the last year that he topped 200 innings pitched. By 2005, Wood had become a reliever and never fulfilled the promise of his youth. Maybe becoming Nolan Ryan wasn't so easy.

One of the things I've found about getting older is that the way I approach fandom has changed. When I was younger, Cleveland was *my* team, mostly because Cleveland was my place of birth (fact one). As you grow up, you hopefully realize that there's more to life and baseball than just geography. I got my first taste of that cheering on Ryan as he walked off the mound in Cleveland, respectfully doffing his cap to the fans who had come to see *him*. I felt it again when I realized that I was emotionally invested in a game that meant nothing to my favorite team because part of me knew that the Kerry Wood Game was special. There's a line that you cross from being a fan of a team to a fan of the game. I think that line might be called "adulthood."

Years later, when I downloaded the MLB app onto my phone, it asked me to declare an allegiance to my favorite team. It's a weird question now. I still picked Cleveland, even though I hadn't lived there in a long time. This time, it wasn't about the team itself. I miss Cleveland and it's a way to keep a little bit of the city in my life. My fandom now stems from that nostalgic longing, mixed with the knowledge that it would make my grandmother happy to see the Guardians win a World Series. Atlanta means something to me too and when I go to games at Truist Park, I cheer for the very team that broke my heart in the 1995 World Series, something I couldn't have imagined doing when I was younger. I now realize that there's nothing wrong with both cities and both teams meaning something to me. What I'm really in love with is *the* game of baseball.

Being in love with the game comes with a burden. You stop thinking about the game in terms of whether your favorite team is winning or losing. The reason that those Ryan and Wood games stuck out in my memory is that they were special at the time. When Nolan Ryan mowed down a quarter of the hitters he faced in his career, it was something to celebrate. Now the whole league pitches like Nolan Ryan. It's a problem. In 2022, 22.4 percent of all hitters walked back to the dugout holding the letter K in their hands and among starters who threw more than 100 innings, Ryan's career strikeout percentage of 25.3 percent would have been good enough for 34th place. In the new ballgame, Nolan Ryan would have been a little better than average at striking hitters out, but nothing special.

A force has taken hold of the game, and even if my favorite team might benefit from it, the adult in me needs to ask whether we need to do something about it. If we're going to talk about the new ballgame, we need to talk about strikeouts.

Figure 20. Percentage of batters striking out, 1871–2022

This graph literally begins in the Ulysses S. Grant administration, with the now-defunct National Association, and continues through 2022. It's true that strikeouts have been going up for literally a century and a half, and so we might be tempted to minimize what has happened since the turn of the millennium. That spike at the end is the problem. In 2000, one in six batters (16.6 percent) struck out, but by 2022, that number had jumped by 5.8 percentage points. That's the same amount of increase that took place from the early 1950s to 2000. So, while strikeout rates have gone up over time for a long time, the change is accelerating. How did we get here?

We saw in Chapter 2 that the speed of the average fastball has been steadily increasing since 2002 (other pitches have followed suit), and that faster pitches are harder to make contact with. The talent pool is expanding. Physical training methods and nutritional knowledge are becoming better refined. Pitchers are being used strategically in ways that allow them to throw at "max effort" more often, but velocity alone doesn't explain the strikeout surge.

While pitchers are capable of throwing faster than ever, there's been a *decrease* in the number of fastballs thrown. In 2022, less than half (49.1 percent) of pitches were heaters, down from 64.4 percent in 2002. The biggest beneficiary of that shift has been the slider (up from 12.1 percent of all pitches in 2002 to 21.8 percent in 2022), and the change isn't caused by a parade of two-trick relievers who get by on a fastball and a slider. We see the same pattern among starters.

It turns out that the slider is a very effective pitch, particularly against same-handed hitters. It mimics a fastball most of the way through its flight until it darts to the side at the last moment. It's also a swing-and-miss pitch. From 2015 to 2022, it generated a whiff 16 percent of the time, twice the rate of a four-seam fastball. Fastballs get strikes too, but they're more likely to come in the form of a foul ball or a called strike. That makes off-speed pitches riskier. Fastballs are... erm, fast, and they might simply overpower the batter's neurological ability to react quickly. If the slider doesn't break, it's mostly just a meatball that stays out over the plate, but if a pitcher can throw a good slider, that movement will have the batter swinging at a spot where the ball isn't.

Over time, we *haven't* seen that sliders are getting more electric. Instead, we've seen that more pitchers are more comfortable with throwing the pitch. The reason why is important. In the 2007, MLB quietly installed what became known as the "Pitch F/X" system in its ballparks. The system was able to log not only the velocity of each pitch, but also how much it moved (down to the fraction of an inch!), how much it spun, and where it landed in the strike zone. The data themselves were interesting, but the technology that they represented was more so. While radar guns have tracked velocity for years, there were companies that began producing portable devices that could make these same measurements on spin and movement in real time, and *that* was the game changer.

The difference between a good slider or curve and a bad one is a couple of inches of break. The trained eye—a good pitching coach, for example—can usually pick up on that difference. The cameras offered something else though. As someone who is both trained as a child psychologist (fact three) and a dad (fact four), I spend a lot of time thinking about the ways in which children learn and develop. The camera offered pitchers (and pitching coaches) a chance to engage in what's known as "scaffolding." You don't just show a child algebra and expect them to figure it out. You have to build each level as you climb, introducing new skills as you go. The job of a teacher is to present the material, but also to provide feedback and guidance at each step of the way. Sometimes that feedback is "Yes, you did it!" Sometimes you need to go back to the chalkboard.

Shaping a pitch from an achy breaking ball into a major league quality one is a slow, multi-step process. You have to get the grip just right and the mechanics have to fall in line, and sometimes you want to play around with little changes to see if they work. The payoff might only be a tenth of an inch of break, but that's worth something, and it's something that even the trained naked eye might not be able to see live.

Pitchers can now perform little experiments with their deliveries and get instant feedback on whether or not it worked. They don't have to wait for video later on, when they are removed from the moment. While the muscles are still recovering from the effort, the brain can process that "it worked!" and the pitcher can do more repetitions to start laying down muscle memory. String enough of those incremental gains together, and you can consciously build a pitch that you feel good about because you know not only that it works, but also how it was built.

What's more is that access to these types of cameras is fairly widespread. While MLB teams were the obvious first investors in the technology, some college programs have followed, and there are businesses, chief among them Driveline Baseball, which specialize in providing data-driven coaching and training, with access to those same cameras and methods. Scouts can now go back to their front offices with not just a glowing review of an amateur pitcher's crackerjack curve, but telemetry to prove it.

At first, the rise of the breaking pitch might not seem like it would be such a big deal, but it presents a pretty big problem for the batters. For a long time, there was an unwritten rule that pitchers should "establish the fastball" early in the count. It was one part tradition and one part necessity. Because fastballs are easier to control and less risky if they end up in the strike zone, they were an ideal pitch with which to start an at-bat. Breaking pitches were more likely to end up as a ball if the batter didn't swing, and the pitcher didn't want to fall behind. It wasn't until pitchers had some leeway to give that they might mess around with the breaking stuff.

With more pitchers having faith in their hook, it means that even from the first pitch, batters can't just guess fastball. In fact, while most people think of the strikeout surge as a problem of strike three, I'd argue that the problem comes earlier than that. There's an old adage in baseball that *the most important pitch in the game is strike one*. It's one of the not-so-hidden forces in the game. To understand why, let's look at Figure 21.

Figure 21. Strikeout rate, by result of first pitch, 1993–2022

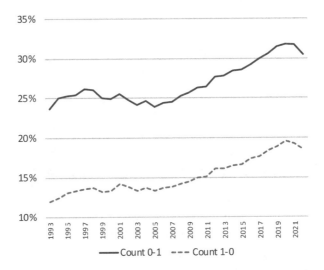

We only have data back to 1993, but there has consistently been a 12 percentage point gap in strikeout rates between plate appearances that start with a strike and those that start with a ball. A good chunk of the increase in strikeout rate can be tied back to strike one, which makes the next graph so concerning. Figure 22 shows the percentage of plate appearances in each year that began with a strike. We can see that there was an inflection point in the early 2000s and then again in the 2010s when all of a sudden, pitchers started getting ahead of hitters more often.

Figure 22. Percentage of plate appearances starting 0–1, 1993–2022

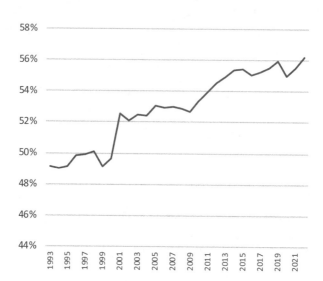

In the early and mid-2000s, it was common to hear about teams telling batters to "work the count." This was the era of *Moneyball*, where walks were finally getting their due as something other than a strange non-event that for some reason didn't count toward your batting average. It was also the era where teams began realizing that high pitch counts for starters were an injury risk. "Working the count" was a not-so-subtle code for taking more pitches, which would drive up a starter's pitch count. Since teams were becoming more protective of their starters, they'd have to leave earlier and the bullpen would have to cover more of the game. The hope was that a team might get to the "soft underbelly" of the bullpen. If the starter could be forced out by the sixth inning, the other team would probably have to use their fourth-best reliever.

We can see that period of time very clearly in Figure 23. In the early 2000s, swing rates on the first pitch (and in general) began falling, hitting a low in 2010. By being more passive, hitters could run up the pitch count, and if the pitcher was wild, could work a favorable count and perhaps a walk.

Figure 23. Swing percentage on first pitch, 1993–2022

The thing about games is that two can play them. Pitchers recognized that hitters were being more passive on the first pitch, effectively saying that they weren't going to swing until the pitcher threw them a strike. Pitchers responded with a resounding "Well, if you insist." By the middle of the 2010s, swing rates were back up, but that didn't fix the problem. Strikeout rates continued to climb.

This time there was a different culprit. Batters were swinging more, but they were also *missing* more. Figure 24 shows not only contact rates on the first pitch of an at-bat, but also on two-strike pitches. It's one thing to be aggressive on the first pitch. If a batter swings at it, it probably means that he was looking for one specific pitch and got it and decided to take a cut. If you swing and miss, you still have two more chances. On a two-strike pitch, the incentives are different. If you're going to swing, you should be prioritizing contact. If you foul the ball off, you've effectively wasted a pitch, but if you miss… well, if you're reading this book, you should probably know what happens next.

Figure 24. Contact rate on first pitch and two-strike pitches, 1993–2022

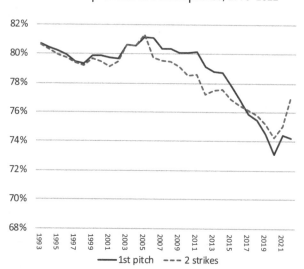

It's obvious why strikeout rates went up. Batters were swinging and missing more often on the first pitch and getting behind in the count more often as a result. They also weren't "protecting the plate" when they had two strikes. Why were hitters acting like they'd never heard the song where it explains that it's one, two, three strikes you're out? The answer is in Figure 25.

Figure 25. SLGCon on first pitch and two-strike pitches, 1993–2022

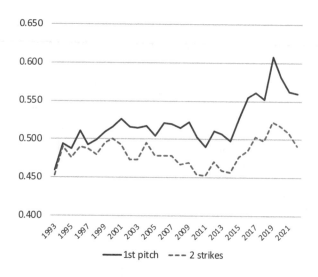

SLGCon sounds like a gathering of mollusk enthusiasts, but it's short for "slugging on contact." Slugging percentage is well-established stat within the game. While batting average divides hits over at-bats and counts all hits as equals, be they singles or home runs, slugging percentage weights events by the number of bases that they produce (singles are one, doubles are two, outs are still zero). The graph only looks at the outcomes on balls that are hit into the field of play, so strikeouts are all removed. What's left is a measure of how good that contact was, especially in terms of producing extra-base hits.

As hitters began to swing more and hit the ball less, it wasn't for naught. When they did make contact, they were more likely to get an extra-base hit. This is a strategy unofficially known as "swing real hard in case you hit it." Not everyone was doing it, but the league as a whole was trending that way, and they were even doing it on two-strike counts. Batters were making a collective decision to trade contact for power, even in situations where it meant risking a strikeout.

WE'VE DIAGNOSED WHAT happened, but "why?" is always more important. There are several arrows all pointing the same way, and it's away from contact. We've already talked about some of them. Pitchers throw harder, making the task of the batter more difficult. Pitchers are more likely to throw breaking balls, which means that batters can't default to "fastball" without risking a silly-looking swing. If you're only going to get one or two shots in an at-bat, you might as well swing hard.

Some of it had to do with advances in defensive positioning. The infield shift punished players for a more contact-oriented approach. One effect seems to have been batters trying to hit the ball to the one place where the defense couldn't catch it: over the fence. There was a sneaky effect of the shift too. With teams better able to position their players before the pitch, fielders were able to rely more on positioning than athleticism to track down a ball. On top of that, more outs kept coming via the strikeout, meaning there were fewer balls that needed fielding. It meant that teams were able to squeeze more "big guys" into the lineup, who might not be defensively gifted, but had the power potential to hit a few more home runs if they accepted a larger risk of a strikeout. During the late 2010s, those who did swing hard and swing up found a ball that was willing to cooperate with them. A lot of these effects fed back on themselves.

Some of the strikeout surge has to do with understanding how poker is played. Sometimes in poker, you end up deep into a bad hand, but you continue to bet on it, not because you believe you've got a great chance to win, but because the math works out. You might have a 10 percent chance of winning, but if asked to make a $100 bet to stay in for a chance to win $5,000, it makes sense for you to place that bet. If you make 10 of those bets over time, you'll lose nine of them and you're out $1,000, but the one that you win brings in five times more than that.

Hitters have been facing two-strike counts for a century and a half, and traditionally, they've changed their entire approach at that point by "shortening up" or "expanding the zone" to avoid striking out. This sounds like a silly question, but what's so bad about striking out? There's the obvious problem, which is that outs are bad, but there's no glory in grounding out to second either. In 2022, 42.0 percent of plate appearances that went to two strikes ended in a K, but once you're in that two-strike count, there's nothing you can do to take those two strikes off the scoreboard. You have to play the hand you're holding.

You might alter your approach to cut down on the chances of striking out, but at what cost? With the bases empty and/or two outs, if you make an out, it doesn't matter what type of out you make. In 2022, that described 74.7 percent of all plate appearances. If you cut down your chances of striking out by 5 percent, but increase your chances of making a field out by 6 percent, what have you really gained? The standard answer is that you can at least move up a runner, but the data tell us that doesn't happen very often. In situations where advancing a runner was possible in 2022, field outs only moved them up 32.2 percent of the time. Base hits, on the other hand, moved them 100 percent of the time, and extra-base hits moved them farther still. What if you could trade an increased chance of a strikeout for an increased chance of an extra-base hit?

Part of the problem is that strikeouts have always been framed in the language of failure. People use the phrase "struck out" in other areas of life. "I tried to find concert tickets, but I flied out to left," doesn't have the same power as an expression. While a strikeout is the worst possible outcome for a plate appearance, most of the time it is just another out. As hitters have accepted more risk of striking out by taking lower contact swings, even with two strikes, they've increased their chances of getting a high-value, extra-base hit. It's high-risk, high-reward bet, but sometimes those bets are worth it. Teams are beginning to think differently about strikeouts. In the new ballgame, *strikeouts aren't a moral failing.* They're just a cost of doing business, and sometimes they're worth the cost.

I HAVE A fondness for post-apocalyptic survivalist fiction. I remember reading a particularly good one in high school called *Alas, Babylon*, which, like all other pieces of post-apocalyptic fiction from the 1950s, was set in the aftermath of a nuclear exchange between the United States and Russia. It focuses on a small, fictional town in Florida that has to learn to live in the nuclear wasteland. Toward the end of the book, the war ends, but the main characters are left with the realization that the nuclear wasteland is their world now.

I feel that way sometimes when I think about strikeouts in MLB. There are plenty of factors that have led to the increase, and it's hard to pin down which one is responsible because the answer is "all of the above." The data are right there in front of us. Even if strikeout rates plateau, the pitchers aren't going to get any worse. In fact, as the game grows around the world, there will be more kids who take up baseball and a larger pool of talent from which to draw. MLB can't outlaw pitchers working on their craft, nor batters from taking big swings if it makes sense to do so.

On top of all that, there's one more graph that we need to reckon with. All of the swinging and missing has produced another side effect.

Figure 26. Average number of pitches per plate appearance, 1993–2022

The number of pitches that each hitter sees has gone up, meaning that individual plate appearances take longer. In addition to all the strikeouts, it means longer periods of silence between the balls that do go into play. It means games that last longer. That's not a great combination. For a long time, I told myself that either these trends would counter-balance themselves, or alternately that the game was meant to evolve, and if this is the way it evolves, so be it.

My fifth fact is that I love baseball, but that means I'm not the fan that MLB needs to attract. You may be in love with the sport as it is, but the corporate conglomerate that brings it to you is in love with people spending money on it. Strikeouts are a hard sell to the casual fan. It might take changing *the* game of baseball, and by that, I mean changing fundamental things about the game, in order to bring strikeouts under control.

For several decades, baseball had taken a rather *laissez-faire* approach to its rules, mostly letting the game evolve with little interference. The NFL, on the other hand, has a reputation for constantly tinkering with its rules to generate a more pass-oriented, crowd-pleasing style of play. Are we perhaps entering an era where MLB takes a page from the NFL's playbook?

MLB has already experimented, through its partnership with the independent Atlantic League, with moving the pitcher's mound back by a foot. The thought was that it would make the act of pitching harder. The ball naturally slows down as it meets air resistance on its way to the batter's box. It may start out as a 95-mph fastball out of the pitcher's hand (and that's what gets reported), but it's traveling a little slower when it gets to the plate. The longer distance also gives the batter a few more milliseconds to pick up on spin and break and to make decisions about swinging. The pitcher has to put in a little extra effort on each pitch. It's the sort of thing that feels like a small step and a massive change all at once, and it also feels a little icky. Baseball's dimensions are part of its identity.

Maybe there are other ways that MLB could slowly ease the strikeout rate back down? In the 2019–2020 off-season, MLB enacted a rule that teams could "only" have 13 pitchers on their 26-member roster, though the rule was scrapped when the 2020 season (and 2020 in general) was overrun by the COVID-19 pandemic. A thirteen-pitcher limit still allows teams to carry five starters and, as we discussed in Chapter 4, an octopus bullpen. Maybe we need to kill the octopus.

If one of the root causes of the strikeout surge is an abundance of relievers, the solution might be to take away some of that abundance by limiting teams to 10 pitchers on their active roster. Teams would still work the edges of the rules, but it would force managers to have individual pitchers work more innings in each outing. Not surprisingly, when we look at the data, relievers are less effective (and they record fewer strikeouts) in their second inning of relief, and a limit on pitchers on the roster would require some of them to step away from that single-inning-burst model and into a second frame. Starters would also have to work deeper into games, as there simply wouldn't be as many relievers on the roster, and the starters too would throw more pitches while they were more tired.

FANS OF A certain age will know this box score by the notation, E—Buckner (1). The replay of Mookie Wilson's roller up the first-base line going between Bill Buckner's legs as a jubilant Ray Knight rushed home to score the winning run in Game 6 of the 1986 World Series is a highlight that's hard to escape, even for those of us who were six years old at the time. The Red Sox had been up three games to two, and took a 5–3 lead into the bottom of the 10th inning, but the Mets scored three in the bottom of the inning to win the game and then eventually won Game 7.

I don't want to talk about Bill Buckner. I want to talk about Calvin Schiraldi. It was a different ballgame in 1986. Being in the playoffs will shorten up the list of who's allowed to enter a game from the bullpen, but 1986 was just before the era of the one-inning relief pitcher, and the Red Sox and Mets that year *combined* to use a total of 31 pitchers for the entirety of the regular season. In 2022, the average team used 29.

October 25, 1986—Boston at New York (Game 6, 1986 World Series)

Boston	AB	R	H	RBI	New York (N)	AB	R	H	RBI
Boggs, 3b	5	2	3	0	Dykstra, cf	4	0	0	0
Barrett, 2b	4	1	3	2	Backman, 2b	4	0	1	0
Buckner, 1b	5	0	0	0	Hernandez, 1b	4	0	1	0
Rice, lf	5	0	0	0	Carter, c	4	1	1	1
Evans, rf	4	0	1	2	Strawberry, rf	2	1	0	0
Gedman, c	5	0	1	0	Aguilera, p	0	0	0	0
Henderson, cf	5	1	2	1	Mitchell, ph	1	1	1	0
Owen, ss	4	1	3	0	Knight, 3b	4	2	2	2
Clemens, p	3	0	0	0	Wilson, lf	5	0	1	0
Greenwell, ph	1	0	0	0	Santana, ss	1	0	0	0
Schiraldi, p	1	0	0	0	Heep, ph	1	0	0	0
Stanley, p	0	0	0	0	Elster, ss	1	0	0	0
					Johnson, ph-ss	1	0	0	0
					Ojeda, p	2	0	0	0
					McDowell, p	0	0	0	0
					Orosco, p	0	0	0	0
					Mazzilli, ph-rf	2	1	1	0

Boston — 110 000 100 2 5 13 3
New York (N) — 000 020 010 3 6 8 2

2B—Evans (2), Boggs (4); HR—Henderson (3, off Aguilera, 10th inning, 0 on); SH—Owen (2), Dykstra (2), Backman (2); SF—Carter (1); IBB—Boggs (1), Hernandez (4); HBP—Buckner (1, by Aguilera); SB—Strawberry 2 (4); DP—Boston 1 (Barrett-Owen-Buckner), New York 1 (Backman-Elster-Hernandez); E- Buckner (1), Gedman (2), Evans (1), Elster (1), Knight (1); WP—Stanley (1); LOB—Boston 14, New York 8; T—4:02; A—55,078

Boston	IP	H	R	ER	BB	SO
Clemens	7	4	2	1	2	8
Schiraldi BS (2), L (0–2)	2.2	4	4	3	2	1
Stanley	0	0	0	0	0	0

New York (N)	IP	H	R	ER	BB	SO
Ojeda	6	8	2	2	2	3
McDowell	1.2	2	1	0	3	1
Orosco	0.1	0	0	0	0	0
Aguilera	2	3	2	2	0	3

Stanley faced one batter in the 10th. Two outs when the winning run scored.

Both the Red Sox and Mets were effectively functioning with a five- or six-member bullpen throughout 1986.

Schiraldi came to the Boston bullpen mid-season after a first half spent at AAA Pawtucket, but had quickly become a favorite of manager John McNamara in high-leverage situations because he was a high strikeout pitcher. Schiraldi struck out 28 percent of the batters he faced in the majors in 1986, a rate which outpaced the man whom he relieved, noted K artist Roger Clemens (24 percent). It's telling that Schiraldi was on the mound for three innings that night and faced 16 batters, striking out only one of them. He had come into the game in the eighth inning with the Red Sox up 3–2, but given up the tying run. Still, McNamara stayed with him. In the ninth, he survived a two-on, no-out jam to keep the game going.

In the top of the 10th, after Dave Henderson hit a home run to put the Red Sox ahead, McNamara had Schiraldi hit for himself(!) choosing to go with Schiraldi for a third inning over anyone else in the bullpen. Schiraldi looked poised to close out the game and the World Series after getting both Wally Backman and Keith Hernandez to fly out, but then three consecutive singles forced McNamara to call for Bob Stanley, whom the box score tersely recounts faced one batter in the 10th. Stanley had already logged outings of three, two, and one inning in Games 2, 3, and 4. It was Stanley's wild pitch that allowed Kevin Mitchell to score the tying run, though Stanley did induce Mookie Wilson to hit a weak ground ball that should have gotten the Red Sox out of the inning and into the 11th.

In the new ballgame, Schiraldi would have never been sent out for the 10th inning. He may not have even seen the ninth, because Boston would have had a small phalanx of one-inning specialists ready to go. The lesson to be learned here isn't that Boston may have won if they had embraced modern bullpen theory. We'll never know that one. We do know that with a shortened bullpen, pitchers are effectively forced into longer roles where you can't just rear back and try to strike everyone out. Pitchers would have to pitch to contact, and the ones who are good at getting weak contact would be in much higher demand. There would be more balls in play, even if some them are just dribblers up the first-base line. Once the ball is in play, you never quite know what's going to happen, and I think that's part of what fans have been missing in the era of strikeouts.

There are ways by which MLB could artificially encourage more contact and fewer strikeouts in baseball, but they would come at a philosophical cost. MLB would have to make changes to *the* game of baseball. Teams would have to be told that while there are ways in which they might play the game more efficiently, they can't do those anymore. It's not because it gives someone an unfair advantage, but because it makes the game less interesting.

One of the most important aspects of the place that baseball holds in United States culture is (the illusion of) continuity. The game has changed plenty over the years and will continue to change, but rarely were the changes the result of top-down commandments. When there were top-down commandments—the designated hitter rule comes to mind—fans have felt rather passionate about those changes, but MLB is going to face the collision of two arrows that normally don't point against each other. Should MLB preserve the continuity of the game, leave the framework of the game as it has been, and let the game evolve as it will, or should it tinker with that framework in a way that promotes a more "entertaining" game?

MLB will likely try to find ways in which they can get the most entertainment value for the least intrusive changes that they can make, but what happens if it becomes obvious that some major piece of the framework needs to be changed? Eventually, MLB is going to have to answer one of *those* questions.

Chapter 8

Did Analytics Ruin Baseball?

I was a really bad therapist. Maybe I should be gentler with myself and reframe to say that, during my graduate training, I was a beginning therapist who might have eventually become decent at the craft. The truth was that I didn't love the work enough to put in the time to improve my therapy skills. As a result, I never got beyond being a bad one.

Back then, I was required to check in on a regular basis with a supervisor, who was an experienced counselor. We would talk about my cases and she would mentor me on different ideas I might use. In one training rotation, I was working with a patient in her late twenties who was feeling depressed because of some relationship troubles. As someone who specialized in child and adolescent psychology, this was a little out of my comfort zone, but I thought I had a good handle on the case. During our supervision session, I talked about the disagreements that the woman had been having with her boyfriend, and how I had planned out a course of treatment to get her to "cured."

After I'd been talking about the case for three or four minutes straight, my supervisor stopped me, gave me a rather disapproving look, and said, "Are you always so linear about *everything*?" It was a question that I wasn't ready for at the time. I stammered and asked her what she meant. She told me that therapy wasn't a game that you won. The point wasn't to get the client to *my* preordained endpoint. It was supposed to be a place where there was room for clients to process what was going on in their lives. There was a general direction that we all wanted to go, but I was being entirely too controlling of the route. Sometimes the best thing to do is sit back and let the client lead. Therapists can have control issues too.

The treatment model that I trained in is known as cognitive-behavioral therapy or CBT. The idea behind CBT is that psychological problems are caused by dysfunctional thought patterns. In a CBT framework, people feel depressed because when something goes wrong, they immediately jump to thinking things like, "It's all my fault," and "Things will always be this way." If that were true, then there would be reason to be depressed, but thankfully it usually isn't. As a CBT therapist, I would teach the patient to recognize these types of thoughts and then challenge them. Is this really going to last forever or is it a temporary inconvenience? By reframing the thought, the patient could find some relief. It's all perfectly logical.

Research shows that CBT is a very good way to treat things like depression and anxiety. People who have a CBT therapist recover more quickly and maintain that recovery longer, but there's a dark side to CBT if you're not careful. Some patients already know logically that what they're feeling doesn't make sense. It doesn't change the fact that they feel it. Sometimes the best thing that you can do is to validate that emotion and sit there in the room with it. Sometimes they just need someone to listen to their story. The danger of CBT is that it can become very transactional. Like a mechanic, my job is to fix your leaky thought patterns and send you on your way. If you don't get better, I did what I could. You're not being logical enough. Next patient.

Looking back, that was the hurdle that I never got over. My patients didn't always need logic. They needed something else entirely. Maybe age and experience would have taught me that, but I didn't stick around long enough to find out.

SO, LET'S HAVE at it. Analytics has unquestionably been the most visible force in the game since the start of the millennium. It certainly makes for an easy scapegoat for members of the Domestic Horticultural Anti-Trespassing Brigade. Did analytics ruin baseball? Yes. Yes it did, but probably not in the way that you're thinking.

We've already cataloged a few of the ways in which the game has changed. Some of those changes had entirely logical explanations, but even fans who would call themselves hardcore analysts will quietly admit that many of them have made the game less fun to watch, even if they are "efficient." Let's dive into some common complaints about the game and see whether the clues point to Professor Plum in the computer room with the spreadsheet.

Figure 27. Game length in minutes, 1950–2022

Whether the games are now "too long," they certainly became *longer* over time. There hasn't been a corresponding jump in the number of plate appearances. The average team has sent between 37 and 39 hitters to the plate per game over those years, certainly not enough to explain 40 minutes of extra time. Plate appearances take longer now than they once did. When we look at Figure 27, we can see a couple of eras of MLB game times. From the 1950s into the late 1970s, the average game took about two and a half hours. Then there was a 20-minute jump during the 1980s and early 1990s. This was hardly the most analytics-friendly era, so we can't pin that on number-crunching. The likely culprit is the increase in the number of televised games during this era, which required a little more between-inning time to sell ads. There's a second period of increase starting around 2000, which brought us to the era of the three-plus hour game.

We've already seen one of the reasons why. The number of pitches per plate appearance has gone up, mostly a result of all the swinging-and-missing that's has become part of the new ballgame. There's another contributor. Between 2007, when data were first kept on the matter and 2022, the amount of time *between* pitches has increased by about a second and a half. An average game has about 300 pitches in it, and an extra second and a half between each is enough to drive up the time of a game by seven or eight minutes.

The reason that long game times are such a big deal in baseball—after all, doesn't a football or a basketball game take just as long to play, start to finish?—is that baseball is a daily game. Fans of a particular football team need only invest three hours per week. Baseball asks a lot more. There's also the problem of uncertainty. Basketball and football have clocks, and while they stop for timeouts and commercial breaks, games tend to be fairly predictable in how much actual time they take. Sometimes baseball games go four hours for no good reason.

Why the dawdling? Until the 2023 season, there was no clock to stop it. If taking a few extra moments provided an edge, the analyst would say to take it. Frankly, I'd want a couple extra seconds to gather my final thoughts before climbing in to face a pitcher who throws 98 mph. There's also evidence that if pitchers take a little extra time, they get a tiny bit more zip on their fastballs. Every little bit helps. That leads us to our next problem in baseball.

The strikeouts really are out of control. We just spent an entire chapter on it how that happened. An individual strikeout has its own charm, but in bunches they get boring and translate to fans seeing fewer running, leaping, diving catches by fielders, or any sort of motion from them at all. It means a lot more waiting around for *something* to happen.

Figure 28. Minutes per ball in play, 1950–2022

The 21st century tail is concerning, and it's certainly not walks that are driving it. In 2002, the average team drew 3.35 free passes per game. In 2022, it had fallen to 3.06. Walks aren't the problem. The time of game problem and the *pace* of game problem both trace their origins back to the increase in strikeouts.

There's a great deal of athleticism and gamesmanship in the pitcher/batter matchup, but it's hard to see that from the upper deck. Fans usually say that they want to see multiple players (and the ball) moving around the field. I doubt that anyone is really wanting to see more routine 5–3 ground outs, but even those have their allure. He's probably out, but for a moment, you have the suspense of not knowing whether the batter will make it. Maybe the first baseman will drop the ball. There's joy in the process of coming to know the outcome of a single story. A play, if I may use a double *entendre*.

There's also a fear that baseball is evolving into a one-dimensional game. Strategies like the sacrifice bunt, the stolen base, and "moving the runners along" seem to be drying up as well. There's a reason that the Home Run Derby is a sideshow that takes place only at the All-Star break. Baseball as a game of cavemen bludgeoning the ball just doesn't seem right. What happens when the regular season games start to feel like that?

In Chapter 1, we talked about the disappearance of sacrifice bunting, which only accelerated with the universal DH rule. It's a skill to be an effective bunter, but it turns out that the sacrifice play just isn't worth it. In the classic sacrifice situation, with a runner on first and no outs, teams have traditionally bunted in the hope that they will reach a situation where they have a runner on second and one out. The problem is that teams score less often and score fewer runs when they do.

Table 22. Run expectancy, bunting situations, 2018–2022

Situation	Average runs scored	Percentage with 1+ runs
Runner at 1st, none out	0.91	42.1%
Runner at 2nd, one out	0.70	40.4%

On top of that, defenses have gotten better about foiling the bunts that do happen. Figure 29 shows that the percentage of bunts that successfully advanced a runner over time and that rate has fallen notably since the turn of the century. It means that even if managers do decide to bunt a runner over, the chances of it working have gotten worse.

Figure 29. Percentage of bunts successfully advancing a runner, 1950–2022

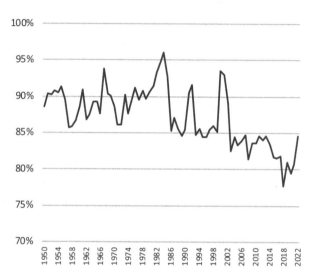

No matter how interesting bunting might be to the fan, you can't ask teams to bunt if it goes against their own interests. The same can be said for stolen bases. On a stolen base attempt, to gain 90 feet of real estate, a team must wager an out *and* the loss of the runner from the basepaths. That's a pretty big cost if you lose, and so mathematically, teams need to be a little more than 70 percent sure that they're going to make it.

Figure 30 and Figure 31 below show what has become of the stolen base over time. First, we see the rate at which teams have attempted a steal with a runner on first and none on second, and then the percentage of those attempts that have been successful.

Figure 30. Stolen base attempt rate, 1950–2022

Figure 31. Stolen base success rate, 1950–2022

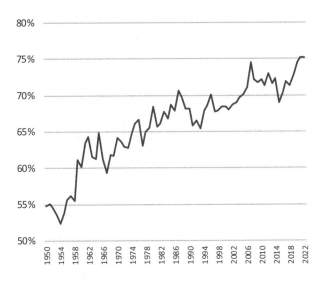

When we look at those graphs in tandem, we see a few interesting patterns. Certainly, stolen base attempt rates have declined, but in the broader view, we see that in the 1970s, they sharply *increased* and have gradually fallen off since. In the 1950s, *success* rates were low and relatively few attempts were made. If runners aren't good at stealing, then why run yourself out of an inning? There was a jump in success rates in the 1960s and into the 1970s, and more runners decided to give it a whirl. What's interesting is that, even as attempt rates have gone down, success rates have continued to inch upwards, eventually surpassing that 70 percent break-even mark. What we've seen is that teams are being more judicious about whom they flash the steal sign. You might have a 50/50 chance of being safe, but 50 percent success isn't enough to justify the risk. The increase in success has come mostly from teams weeding out the bad attempts. The opposite of a stolen base is no longer the caught stealing; it's a runner who doesn't try.

What we're finding is that the plays that fans considered "fun" because they were "strategic" turned out to be bad ideas most of the time. I suppose we can blame analytics for identifying them as bad ideas, but once we have that knowledge, what exactly should we expect teams to do with it? You can't simultaneously give people a mandate to figure out the best way to win a baseball game and then complain when they do exactly that.

June 2, 2021—Miami at Toronto (Regular Season)

Miami	AB	R	H	RBI	Toronto	AB	R	H	RBI
Chisholm, ss	5	1	1	2	Semien, 2b	3	2	1	0
Marte, cf	4	1	1	1	Bichette, ss	4	0	1	2
Aguilar, 1b	5	1	1	1	Guerrero Jr., dh	4	1	1	0
Cooper, dh	4	0	0	0	Hernández, rf	4	0	0	0
Dickerson, lf	4	1	2	1	Grichuk, cf	5	2	2	2
Duvall, rf	4	0	0	0	Panik, 3b	4	0	0	1
Diaz, 3b	2	0	0	0	Gurriel Jr., lf	4	0	2	0
Alfaro, c	2	0	0	0	Tellez, 1b	3	0	1	0
Devers, 2b	2	0	0	0	McGuire, c	4	0	1	0
					Davis, pr	0	1	0	0

Miami —   013 000 100   5 6 2
Toronto —   010 100 103   6 9 0

2B—Tellez (3); 3B—Guerrero Jr. (1), Bichette (1); HR—Dickerson (2, off Manoah, 2nd inning, 0 on), Chisholm (6, off Manoah, 3rd inning, 1 on), Aguilar (10, off Manoah, 3rd inning, 0 on), Marte (3, off Thornton, 7th inning, 0 on), Grichuk 2 (11, off Lopez, 2nd inning, 0 on; off Lopez, 4th inning, 0 on); SF—Panik (1); IBB—Marte (1), Guerrero Jr. (5), Hernández (1); HBP—Alfaro 2 (2, by Manoah, Castro); E- Marte (1), Chisholm (5); WP—Bender (1); LOB—Miami 7, Toronto 11; T—3:41; A—5,385

Miami	IP	H	R	ER	BB	SO
López	4	5	2	2	1	9
Bender	1.1	0	0	0	1	3
Bleier, H (7)	0.2	1	0	0	0	1
Bass, H (7)	1	0	1	0	2	1
Floro, H (7)	1	0	0	0	0	0
García, BS (2), L (3–4)	0.1	3	3	3	2	0

Toronto	IP	H	R	ER	BB	SO
Manoah	3.1	4	4	4	3	5
Payamps	2	0	0	0	0	1
Mayza	0.2	0	0	0	0	2
Thornton	1	1	1	1	0	2
Edwards Jr.	1	1	0	0	0	0
Castro, W (1–1)	1	0	0	0	0	1

One out when the winning run scored

IF THERE IS a post-apocalyptic box score filled with all of the horrors of the new ballgame, this might be it. Fans (all 5,385 of them) spent three hours and 41 minutes of their lives on a rainy Wednesday night to see 25 batters strike out, nine of them walk, and poor Jorge Alfaro get plunked twice. Of the 81 hitters who came to the plate, nearly half of them didn't put the ball in play. Both starters faced exactly 18 batters and were followed by a small parade of short-burst relievers. There were no bunts and no stolen base attempts. Four of Miami's six hits were home runs, accounting for all of their scoring.

Despite all that, we see that the Blue Jays provided some late-inning drama and heroics for the home fans, erasing a two-run deficit in the ninth. We see that Toronto managed two triples (one of which knocked in the tying runs) and a sacrifice fly by Joe Panik (which drove in the winning run). Even if baseball has some warts that need addressing, there are still beautiful little sparks that happen. Don't give up on it yet.

HOW DID ANALYTICS ruin baseball? It goes deeper than just how the game has changed on the field. No one set out to shape the new ballgame into this particular form. Much of it was organic change that would have happened even if *Baseball Prospectus* had never been founded. Analysts really only cataloged what was happening.

Many of the not-so-hidden forces that have shaped baseball since the turn of the century can be boiled down to one word: *efficiency*. The analytics movement in baseball has created a sport within a sport of finding ways to scrape little bits of value from the bones of the game. When every morsel helps, no corner is too remote to peer into. The advent of big and detailed data sets just made it easier to see into some of those corners. Efficiency has conquered the game.

In 2016, I worked with researcher Kate Morrison to turn the microscope around. We gathered information on MLB front office executives, the people who were making the decisions that drove the game. One of the things that we looked at were their educational backgrounds. It turned out to be easy since nearly all of them were college graduates (something less than half of United States adults can claim) and their university alumni magazines loved printing articles about the former students who helped to run real live baseball teams. More than half of the executives we looked up majored in business, finance, or economics.

We compliment teams when they sign a player to a bargain salary who then puts up MVP numbers. These are the teams that can win on a "shoestring budget." In a baseball world which had previously been dominated by the golden rule that whoever had the most gold ruled the standings, analytics represented a new way for teams to win, a way that was open to anyone who had a copy of Microsoft Excel. At first, efficiency was a great leveler.

Then something happened. There was a shift in the language that we used to talk about players. Teams were searching for "undervalued assets."

That meant players who had skills that the market was not properly valuing. We started hearing more about what players were "worth." I might not have been a great therapist, but I can still pick a few things up, not just in what people say, but in *how* they say them. In business and finance, you make money by finding assets to buy at a lower price than you will eventually sell them for. You look for ways that can bring down your costs or make things run more effectively. Somewhere along the line, players became assets.

THERE'S A DARK side to "efficiency" that we rarely talk about. In the labor negotiations that followed from the expiration of the Collective Bargaining Agreement between franchise owners and players after the 2021 season, one issue that the MLB Players Association consistently spoke about was baseball's forgotten players, the ones who make the minimum salary. There's a polite euphemism that has developed in baseball of the "cost-controlled" player. Before players obtained the right to free agency in 1976, salaries were effectively governed by the "reserve clause." Once a player signed with a team, the team could "reserve" the rights to the player. Contracts could be traded between franchises, but players could not move to other teams of their own will, even if they were not under contract. It meant that at the beginning of each season, teams could offer a player a salary and the player's choices were either to take it or sit out the season.

Since 1976, baseball's salary structure has been an odd mix of the reserve clause, the free market, and the strange space in between known as arbitration.

Table 23. How MLB salaries are set

Year in league	Salary is determined by...
1 to 3	League Minimum
4 to 6	Arbitration
7+	Free Agency

Part of the Collective Bargaining Agreement is a league minimum salary that also functions as the set salary for players in their first three years in MLB. Whether the player wins an MVP or pitches some garbage-time innings, their salary is the same. In years four through six of their careers, players are not eligible to leave their team, but are instead subject to the arbitration system. In their "arb years," players (and their agents) submit a suggestion for their salary for the upcoming year based on salaries for comparable players from years past. Teams do the same. A panel of arbiters picks one of them after literally hearing arguments from both sides. Alternately, teams and players can settle among themselves and skip the arbitration process, but arbitration provides a final backstop. It is widely known that arbitration salaries are well below what players could earn in the free market. It's not until their seventh season that players can negotiate with all 30 teams and sign where they will.

While players would most certainly like to get to free agency and its higher salaries earlier, franchise owners have resisted for the obvious reason that it keeps salaries lower, but also that it provides a way for teams with smaller budgets to compete. Identifying young players who are paid below their market value (i.e., are "cost-controlled") and who aren't allowed to leave represents a way for teams to be "efficient" with their payrolls.

There's a collision between this odd salary structure and one of the other forces we've already talked about. The most important ratio in baseball is the ratio of talent to MLB roster spots, and we've talked about how the talent pool has expanded considerably. While the superstars will still get paid, at the other end of the roster, there are now more humans who are talented enough to be bench players or "sponge arms" that soak up innings in a bullpen. Now consider a bench player who reaches his fourth year of service. He's not going to get millions of dollars, but he's going to get more than the minimum. If there's someone else who can do the same job and will only need to be paid the minimum, the efficient thing to do is for the team to wish the fourth-year player well and non-tender him.

There have always been players who wash out of MLB after a year or two, and no one is guaranteed a five-year career, but the number who even make it to arbitration has been falling. In Figure 32, we can see the percentage of players who debuted in each year (a debut means that they either batted at least 100 times or pitched at least 30 innings) that then went on to have at least three more years with similar playing time. Because of the shortened 2020 season, the graph ends with the 2016 debutant group.

Figure 32. Percentage of players reaching fourth year, by debut year

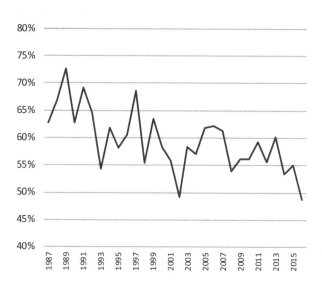

We can see that over time, the percentage of players who make it to a fourth year in MLB, much less four full years of service time, has fallen. As the talent pool expands, the pool of cheaper, less experienced workers becomes more plentiful, only for the cycle to continue. Certain types of players have become disposable.

In some cases, entire seasons have become disposable. While the ultimate asset is a World Series ring, there's a problem. To win the World Series, a team has to get to the playoffs, something that usually requires somewhere around 90 wins during the regular season. If a team looks at its roster and realizes that they don't have the talent to do that, then the next-most valuable resource available is the ability to find more and better cost-controlled players. Since MLB, like most professional sports leagues, awards the highest draft positions (and more importantly, allows the biggest pools of money to be given out in signing bonuses) to the teams with the worst records, the efficient thing to do is to chase the worst record in the league. There's no glory in finishing 81–81, but there might be a future superstar waiting for you if you go 60–102.

"Tank" has become a four-letter word in baseball. Teams have endured "rebuilding" periods for as long as the game has been around, but it was never as openly acknowledged or so brazenly done. General managers still use veiled phrases when they talk about "adjusting payroll to anticipated performance" and "focusing on player development" but everyone knows what they're doing. Even though the incentives for tanking have always been there, there used to be room for a little bit of irrational optimism. It's hard for the rationalist to look at a projection system that says you've got a 75-win team and do anything other than the next logical step. It might even be the right thing to do, but it feels like the breaking of a social contract. Sometimes what people want is to feel giddy about something, even if it isn't likely to happen. There's more to baseball and life than probabilities and logic. No matter what they might say, people don't always want everything to be so linear. They might be wrong, but they might also be human.

MAJOR LEAGUE BASEBALL teams hold a very strange place in the culture of the United States (and Toronto). Baseball teams feel like a part of a city. Wearing a Cubs shirt is one way to say "I'm from [the North Side of] Chicago!" While the franchises are privately run, for-profit companies that sell a product they want people to buy, they exist in a space that no other company does. If Consolidated Widgets has a *really* good sales year, that's wonderful for them, but there's no parade. There's no run on merchandise with the "CW" logo on it. Strangers don't high five each other randomly on the subway or strike up a conversation about widget manufacturing strategies as if either had any clue what they were talking about.

There are sections of the newspaper, websites, and radio shows for Ed from Lakewood to call in to that are devoted to discussing MLB teams. People feel genuinely entitled to express their opinion on whom *we* should start at third base. We?

MLB teams aren't beyond playing that dynamic when it suits their needs. When they want a new stadium, they threaten to move to another city unless the taxpayers kindly subsidize the new place for them. Research by economists has shown consistently that these stadiums bring very little financial benefit to an area, but it turns out that people are only too willing to hand over their tax dollars to keep "our team" around. It's not just about dollars and cents. It's about the identity of the city.

Franchise owners want to make money from their business. Fans want to be entertained. Players want to win and get paid and maybe even in that order. For a long time, everyone assumed that the nexus of those three was winning. After all, more people buy tickets and hats when the team is doing well. When analytics came along, it promised to find new ways to win, and so it sounded like a great idea. How did it all send the game crashing into dystopia? The new ballgame is what a hyper-focus on winning looks like. It turns out that people didn't like that.

The therapist in me always hears the word "we" loud and clear when people talk about their favorite baseball teams. Fans will swear that the thing that they most want from the fan experience is to witness their favorite team win a championship. In Chapter 1, we talked about the two languages of the game of baseball. In the newspaper the next day, there's a box score and a game story. The analytic mind reads the box score and looks for the patterns to be found there. Whether they wanted to admit it or not, what many fans were really hungry for was the other half, the ability of the game to tell a story, one interwoven with their own, *even more than winning.*

There are a few readers out there who just raised their eyebrows and are scoffing that of course they most want to see the Commissioner's Trophy come to their fair city. The therapist in me also knows that sometimes the head and the heart want very different things. When people talk about how analytics has "ruined the game," I think that split between story-telling and winning is what they usually mean, but it can be hard to verbalize that. There's a cultural taboo around winning. It isn't everything. It's the only thing. That makes it uncomfortable to say that you're more interested in the story than the results. When people are uncomfortable, they sometimes lash out at the thing that brings up that discomfort.

The old ballgame certainly had its power hitters, but it also had players who specialized in being fast and sneaky and able to steal away to places where they weren't supposed to. There were those who were skilled in refined hitting. There were some who weren't great, but were always hustling. There were delicious five-second bursts of dramatic tension as the players ran toward their goal, not knowing their fate. There were pitchers whose love language was to take as much of the game onto their shoulders as they could, and there were tactical specialist pitchers. There was genuine uncertainty about what each manager would do next and each had their own little quirks. It was an ensemble cast that had a character for everyone to identify with and see themselves in. For a long time, we thought that all of those characters were necessary to winning. They aren't all gone, but some of them have been deemed inefficient and politely asked to step to the sides of the stage.

As MLB tries to fix itself, it needs to first think about the game from this perspective. When I hear people tell stories about their favorite teams, I often hear two very important phrases: "I liked the way he played the game" and "That was the year when…" The latter is usually followed by an observation about what happened on the field that year, but also about what was going on in the person's life. Only one of the 30 teams in the game will win a World Series each year. Most fans will experience the thrill of a World Series victory a time or two in their lives. The majority of what they will take home from their baseball fandom are the stories that they experienced along the way. They saw themselves in those characters. Those years were important to them. Even in recounting the championships, they'll probably tell you who they celebrated with. Baseball isn't just about winning.

It's telling that most of the proposed solutions to make the game "less boring" have tried to fix the game with even more efficiency. We can dispense with the four wide throws in an intentional walk and just send the runner to first. We can discourage or outlaw mid-inning pitching changes so as to cut down on the time wasted there. We can add a clock. What if the problem isn't a lack of efficiency, but the game losing its ability to tell a rich and vibrant narrative? What if what fans really want is for someone to sit and listen to their stories? Must we always be so linear about everything?

WHEN BASEBALL'S BIG-DATA dystopia arrived, its herald was a garbage can. Unlike a breaking ball at Minute Maid Field, few saw it coming, but in the Spring of 2020, news broke that in 2017 and 2018, the Houston Astros had engaged in a sign-stealing scheme, the broad outlines of which have been publicly confessed to, if only minimally apologized for. Astros employees used a camera to observe the catcher's signs to the pitcher, and then used some light programming to break the code of what pitch was coming next. Once they knew, they would whack a waste receptacle in the clubhouse tunnel, sending out a coded message that could be heard at home plate. Worse than the thousands of trashy puns that it spawned is the realization that this could very easily happen again.

The game of baseball rests on the legs of the catcher. Long derided as the guy who wore the "tools of ignorance," if there is something we've learned about the game in the last 20 years, it's how sneakily important the catcher is and has always been. The pitcher might throw 98 mph, but it's the catcher who has think faster than that *and* to slow the pitch down to zero while calmly presenting it to the umpire for judgement of whether or not it's a strike.

The space between the catcher's shin guards might be the most valuable piece of real estate in the entire stadium because it makes the game of baseball possible. How strange it is that each pitch begins with a negotiation between the pitcher and catcher, and that there is an expectation that the *catcher* is the one who is "calling the game." It's important that the two of them are on the same page so that the umpire doesn't take a bunch of 98-mph shots to the chest protector, but it's the pitcher who has to make the pitch. And yet, there the catcher is behind home plate, moving his fingers around. That few inches of space between his legs is about the only bit of privacy that his team has on the field. The catcher has the advantage of being the one fielder whom the batter can't see, and his legs provide a natural shield from the signs being seen from either dugout. The only place that a member of the other team can really see those signs is if he is standing on second base. Codebreaking, when done from second base or anywhere else on the field, if someone can manage to sneak a peek, has been an accepted, if politely unspoken part of the game since the 19th century. If the runner can figure out the catcher's signs and relay them through subterfuge to his teammate at bat, that's considered fair game.

Signs are a form of cryptography and "What pitch should we throw?" presents a bit of a cryptographic problem. For a pitcher with a standard four-pitch (fastball, slider, curve, changeup) mix, it means there are four possible options (more if you consider the location of the pitch, but we'll leave that in the trash can for the moment). It's going to be a relatively easy code to break. The code has to be simple enough to be implemented by two people who may or may not speak the same language and who are in the middle of intense physical labor and who have nothing but their own hands with which to make the system work.

If they didn't have the space between the catcher's legs, keeping a secret in baseball would be nearly impossible. It isn't a foolproof system. "We've got your signs" is one of the oldest taunts in the book, but that space is enough that the game can function and we don't have to go back to the days when batters could just request the pitch that they wanted.

The Astros' scheme started when someone came up with a simple Excel sheet designed to break the pitch-selection code. It wouldn't have been that hard once someone made the decision to try it. Someone with a subscription to MLB.tv could do a low-budget version of this, watching games and logging catcher signs and pitch types. Sometimes just logging things into Excel, you might pick up on the pattern. After all, players can sometimes break the code on the field with no software assistance. The StatCast system even kindly provides the pitch type for you, so all you have to log is the sign sequence.

After some basic analysis, it would be easy to figure out a team's preferences. Do they like to use "second sign?" Is the motion of the hand or the fingers the key to look for? It's not a guarantee that they'll do the same thing tomorrow night, but all humans have their fallback positions, and if you assume no one is watching—and it was expressly illegal to use electronic surveillance to steal signs—you re-use the same strategies because they're familiar and easy to implement.

The Astros system required some work, but it's nothing beyond the capabilities of someone with a little bit of free time. The rest of the scheme apparently involved a camera, a video monitor, a bat, and a big ol' garbage can. From there, you just need to zoom in on that private space and then when you're ready, bang out the message. Before this scandal broke, "the Astros" were a cultural codeword for a team that was on the "leading edge" of the use of data analysis and technology in baseball. It's amazing how low-tech the whole thing really was.

IN MY REAL job as a mental health researcher, I do a lot of program evaluation work. I'm the person who gets to say things like "Six months after enrolling in this program, participants saw a 20 percent decrease in their levels of depression and anxiety." It's a lot different than my days seeing patients. In explaining the difference between the two professions to a researcher colleague who was considering pursuing a clinical degree, I told him that as a clinician, you can put a name and a face to your daily accomplishments. You helped Ed from Lakewood. When you work in policy, the victory that you get is a report showing that 5 percent fewer people were suffering from depression than a year ago. You will never know who those people are and perhaps never even be in the same room as one of them. You may literally have touched hundreds or thousands of lives in some way, but you don't get the same validation that you do in the clinic.

When I give a presentation to a professional audience, usually fellow policy researchers, and I get to the part about the gory mathematical details, I always stop somewhere and point to the screen and, after saying that rates of readmission to inpatient care fell by 17 percent, I pause to say "...and those are real people." I always find it to be an act of strange rebellion. When you stare at numbers all day, it's easy to think of them as dots on a screen. Just hearing "those are real people," even if I say it to myself, is grounding in a way that I never quite anticipate. This is real life. When everything is data, you sometimes lose track of that. Everything becomes just another potential market inefficiency.

I wonder if the Astros fell into the same trap. As a (former) therapist, I'm trained to look for the ways in which people rationalize their own behavior. It's rare that someone wakes up and decides to do something destructive. There is no diving board into the dark arts. You get there on an easily graded pathway that sometimes you don't even realize you're on. It's something that builds over time and a series of small decisions.

It's entirely reasonable for a major-league team to scout its opponents. It's entirely reasonable for a team to look for patterns in what the other pitcher likes to throw. It's entirely reasonable to use video to do that research. It's entirely reasonable to notice everything and put it in the scouting report. But there does come a moment where you cross the line—and that camera in center field that we're only supposed to use for internal research is already in place. All the pieces are literally right there, and you know that you're not supposed to, but...

Sign stealing has always been a sensitive topic in the game of baseball. It's part of the cat-and-mouse game within the game. Because everyone is on the same playing field (literally) and using only their eyes and brains, the ability to maintain a secret and the other team's desire to steal that secret is a fair fight. When technology gets involved, things change. Against a camera and a laptop, humans don't stand a chance. The commissioner's office disciplined the Astros because they broke a stated policy about the use of electronic surveillance. What I don't think the Astros fully appreciated is that they could have broken *the* game of baseball. The taboo is there for a reason.

What big data have done is to make it really easy to cross that line. You begin saying things like, "Well, in theory, what would the results be?" and calculating them out, all the while convincing yourself that it's all just a make-believe spreadsheet fantasy. Sometimes that gives way to rationalization, and big data can grease those skids. Take that technological capability and put it in the hands of someone whose job and career prospects might be enhanced (or perhaps, preserved) by coming up with a novel idea that might be a *little bit* over the line, and the temptation to "just see if it works" is going to be there.

For the first time in a century, there was legitimate doubt cast on a World Series. The 2017 World Series champion Houston Asterisks may go down in baseball lore in the same way that the 1919 Chicago Black Sox did. Baseball is a game where the point is to win, and in a real sense, all 30 teams are trying to get one over on the other 29. That's the nature of competition, but there need to be spaces in baseball and in life that are private, where data politely decline to go. These are real people after all. The bad news is that the data are only getting bigger. There will be more ways to peek where one shouldn't.

What MLB is really selling is the idea that two teams can enter a field and play a fair game. One of them will win, and the story of how that win came about will become legend or at least good copy for the paper the next day. There's no glory in winning an unfair game. "The integrity of the game" isn't just a marketing phrase. Without it, you don't have a game worth winning. The danger of analytics in baseball isn't in the decline of the sacrifice bunt. It's in everything becoming just another dry intellectual exercise in hacking the game.

THERE NEVER WAS a stats vs. scouts war. It was never that simple. It's not just the usual platitudes of "scouts are a valuable source of data." That's a true statement, but there was something deeper going on when we were all obsessing over which "side" was winning the WAR of baseball ideas. Most of the time, an argument isn't about what it's about. The therapist in me now recognizes that "stats vs. scouts" was a smokescreen. When people feel uncomfortable about a conflict in their lives, they sometimes frame it in a way that's more palatable to them.

Over the last quarter century, we have entered the era of "big data." It's worth going beyond the buzzword to appreciate how transformative large data sets are, not just for the fact that there are 10 million lines on the spreadsheet, but because of what kinds of questions those data sets allow us to ask. It's not that we didn't have data before *Moneyball* came out, but if you wanted to collect data in places where you didn't physically live, you had to send someone to that place and then get the data back to a hub somehow. It's a task that we now take for granted because of the internet. Before the internet, if the data were worth the effort, this sort of large-scale collection was possible, but there were the logistics problems. There's a limit to how much data you can pass back and forth by mailing pieces of loose-leaf paper or 3.5 inch "floppy" disks.

The luxury that the internet has bestowed on us is not just the ability to create a large data set, but a *complete* one. In a creepily obsessive way, I can know everything that happened at every MLB park on every day of the season. Not only do I have a few million observations to work from, but I have a full catalog of unbiased data and the benefit of having eyes everywhere. It's enough data to fill a book. Suddenly, we lived in a world where we could ask questions that had *an* answer. Hold on to that emphasis on "an."

The answers to those questions might be valuable. As baseball teams realized this, they quickly hired a lot of people who were skilled in working with data to find those answers. According to the popular narrative or at least that movie with Brad Pitt in it, that's when the war began, although the truth of it was much tamer. Reasonable people will listen to reasonable evidence.

Before "big data" could answer those questions, baseball decision-makers did the best they could with what tools they had. Humans are both blessed and cursed with the ability to construct a bigger picture from incomplete data. The world around us is far too complex for our eyes and ears to take all of it in and analyze it. Through experience, we learn which pieces to focus on and which to filter out, and we can sometimes accurately fill in the gaps in our attention. The problem is that humans aren't always sure about what pieces they are filling in with hard-won wisdom and what pieces they are filling in with guesses or magical thinking. Everyone does a little of both. The ones who are in the Hall of Fame probably had a great deal of wisdom *and* some guesses that they got right. There was also *a lot* of magical thinking that passed as wisdom—in baseball and in life—before big data came along. The first Sabermetricians took it upon themselves to knock down a lot of that guessing and replace it with good, solid science.

I think baseball is better off with the findings of Sabermetrics. I don't know of any serious person in the game who doesn't. It makes for measurably better decisions and none of it should be tossed to the side. I'm sure some of the readers out there picked up on the odd phrasing "the findings of Sabermetrics." This is why a moment ago, I asked you to hold on to the idea of questions that had *an* answer.

If the "old school" was overrun with magical thinking, then the "new school" needs to recognize that it's overrun with linear thinking. Perhaps the Sabermetric movement has become the villain it once sought to conquer. The decision-makers in the game buzz with words like "solutions-focused" and "data-driven" and of course "efficiency." It hides the fact that we are too often seeking out the questions that fit our tools. Specifically, we look for the questions that have *an* answer, because analytic methods are really good at that. You find a data set. You hit the correct buttons. You get to the endpoint. Everyone's out to find the #NewMoneyball, and we're mighty proud of ourselves when we find it. What happens when the question that really needs answered is, "Can baseball tell better stories?" or "Is this idea ethical?"

You can't find those answers on a spreadsheet, and so we've mostly ignored them—and it shows. That's how analytics ruined baseball. Baseball analytics was hailed as a revolution, but I wonder if baseball *needs* another one, some group of outsiders to come in and put all of this overly rigid thinking in its place. I wonder whether there are questions that we've just not even considered asking because they don't have *an* answer. There could be wisdom in those questions too, but how does one begin to answer a question that you don't even know how to ask?

Chapter 9

Can Analytics Fix Baseball?

When my phone beeped, I figured it was my wife. It was December of 2018, and I was driving around my native Cleveland (fact one) with two sleeping toddlers (40 percent of my fourth fact) in the backseat of our family minivan. We were back visiting my parents for Christmas, and the twins needed a nap. Badly. Since I was going to be driving for a little while, I decided to see some of my favorite sights in Cleveland, and I knew which one I wanted to see first. I hopped on I-90 and headed eastward toward downtown. At the East 9th exit, there's a cloverleaf that spins you around, first away from Carnegie Avenue as if to tease the glory that is about to unfold. But soon enough, you are on 9th, and as you come back under the highway and into the downtown streetscape, it waits for you. I still call it Jacobs Field even if Progressive Insurance bought the naming rights. I knew it was just going to be a drive-by. It was December, and there wasn't any baseball going on in there, but it was nice to see my old friend.

It's weird that my phone beeped right then, considering what happened next. I was driving, so I couldn't stop to look at it until a little while later as I pulled up to a stoplight. Plus, I figured it was Tanya just checking in to see whether the twins were asleep. They were, but the beep wasn't from her.

It was the newly hired assistant general manager of the New York Mets, Adam Guttridge. He sent along a pleasant message and asked me if I'd like to chat about some ideas they had for the team. It was a good thing I was at a stoplight. The suddenness of the message induced a haze that was kindly broken for me by an F-sharp note played by the car behind me.

Growing up, I had no emotional connection to the Mets, but two months later, I was standing in Port St. Lucie, Florida, watching Noah Syndergaard throw a Spring Training bullpen. I wasn't going to be a full-time Met. This was going to be fact 3a in my life. I was mental health researcher, but I was now also a consultant to a real live baseball team. I had a seat at the table, or more accurately, an account on the Mets R&D Slack.

My trip to Port St. Lucie to meet my new coworkers coincided with the first game of spring training, and the Mets happened to be taking on Atlanta. Before I left for the trip, my daughters asked me whether they were still allowed to cheer for their hometown team. I told them that they could cheer for whomever they wanted to, but Daddy might have to be a little quieter when the subject came up. After the game, a 4–3 Mets win that didn't really count for anything, I was happy. *We* won and I could actually say that. I eventually committed the ultimate act of baseball betrayal and bought a Mets hat.

If analytics is ruining the game of baseball, then I was on the front line of ruining it in the Mets Research and Development department. Or at least, I was consulting to the people who were ruining it. The dirty secret of working for a baseball team is that it's a mountain of minutiae, but every once in a while, there was a decision point and senior management would ask for our input.

In August of that year, second baseman Joe Panik had been designated for assignment and then released by the Giants. Every line in the transaction column hides a broken heart, but Panik wasn't having a great year in San Francisco. At the time though, the Mets were in a bit of a crunch

August 9, 2019—Washington at New York (Regular Season)

Washington	AB	R	H	RBI	New York (N)	AB	R	H	RBI
Turner, ss	3	2	2	0	McNeil, rf	4	1	0	0
Eaton, rf	5	1	3	0	Rosario, ss	5	0	3	0
Rendon, 3b	5	2	2	3	Conforto, cf	5	0	2	1
Soto, lf	5	1	3	2	Alonso, 1b	4	1	1	2
Adams, 1b	5	0	2	0	Davis, lf	4	2	2	1
Suzuki, c	4	0	0	0	Ramos, c	3	1	1	0
Dozier, 2b	4	0	0	0	Frazier, 3b	4	1	1	3
Robles, cf	3	0	1	0	Panik, 2b	4	0	1	0
Strasburg, p	3	0	0	0	Stroman, p	2	0	0	0
Stevenson, ph	1	0	0	0	Wilson, p	0	0	0	0
Hudson, p	0	0	0	0	Guillorme, ph	1	0	0	0
Doolittle, p	0	0	0	0	Gsellman, p	0	0	0	0
					Avilán, p	0	0	0	0
					Lagares, ph	1	1	0	0

Washington —	000 300 201	6 13 0	
New York (N) —	000 300 004	7 11 0	

2B—Soto (8), Rosario (22), Davis (16); 3B—Rendon (3); HR—Soto (22, 4th inning, 1 on, off Stroman), Alonso (38, 4th inning, 1 on, off Strasburg), Davis (13, 4th inning, 0 on, off Strasburg), Frazier (15, 9th inning, 2 on, off Doolittle); SB—Turner (24), Soto (10), Eaton (11), Conforto (6); CS—Robles (7); DP—New York (Frazier-Panik-Alonso); WP —Wilson (3), Avilán (2) LOB—Washington 8, New York 6; T—3:20; A—39,602

Washington	IP	H	R	ER	BB	SO
Strasburg	7	4	3	3	2	6
Hudson	1	1	0	0	0	1
Doolittle BS (5), L (6–4)	0.2	6	4	4	0	0

New York (N)	IP	H	R	ER	BB	SO
Stroman	6	9	4	4	3	9
Wilson	1	2	1	1	0	2
Gsellman	1.1	2	1	1	0	1
Avilán W (3–0)	0.2	0	0	0	0	2

Stroman faced one batter in the seventh; Two outs when the winning run scored.

at second base. Regular second baseman Robinson Canó was hurt, and the plan to have Jeff McNeil play all nine positions at once was running into some serious limitations. Perhaps Panik was worth a short-term flyer as cover at second? Suddenly, I was being asked for my opinion on a real-life MLB roster decision. While I have no illusions that my voice alone carried the day, I can honestly say that someone asked.

There's a story in every box score, but sometimes you never get to hear them.

IF YOU'RE SOMEONE who has the dream of working for a major league team, I suggest doing a little reading first—after, of course, you're done with this book. It's amazing how much can be gleaned by reading through the "help wanted" ads in baseball. Not all jobs in baseball are listed on LinkedIn, but MLB teams are business organizations that employ accountants and security guards and plumbers and I hate to break the illusion, but there's a real person in that mascot costume. My guess though is that you, reader of a book about baseball written by an "analytics guy," want to work in Baseball Operations. Those are the people who make the decisions about players and strategies. And since you're now nine chapters deep into a book that's filled with charts and graphs, you probably want to work in the Stat Cave.

Even if you're not looking for a new job, it's worth reading a few of those job postings, because they tell us something about what's become of analytics in MLB and of the front office more generally. To start, when the league's unofficial hiring season begins in October, most teams post openings for data-centric positions. They aren't always newly created positions. Some are the result of natural turnover, but it tells us that all 30 teams are looking at the data.

What can the classifieds teach us about what happens on the inside? For one, what we call "analytics" is mostly data management. Many readers of this book will be familiar with "Moore's Law," the idea that the number of transistors that can be placed on a semi-conductor chip doubles every two years. The law is named for Gordon Moore, co-founder of Intel, and describes the evolution of microchips fairly well over the last few decades. There's debate on whether or not this "law" can be sustained and whether there's a physical limit to how many transistors can dance on the head of a pin, or more importantly, whether the model can be financially sustained.

For those of us who enjoy the fruits of that law, with ever faster and more powerful chips for our gadgets, it can seem like this growth happens on its own. The reality is that the cost of doubling the number of transistors increases every time, both in the R&D costs to find new ways to make smaller transistors and the manufacturing techniques needed to make them.

If there's something that immediately sticks out when reading the MLB classifieds, it's how many of the positions are for data engineers, with job descriptions that are heavy on skills like data acquisition and warehousing. It makes sense. MLB has invested heavily in data infrastructure, beginning with StatCast, which tracks the ball and the players all over the field and has powered some neat in-game graphics, and more recently, FieldVision, which can track individual arms and legs and elbows and all their movements. That's a lot of 1s and 0s to slice and dice.

I think there's a romantic idea left over from the days of *Moneyball* that baseball analytics is mostly people sitting around bouncing ideas off each other. Maybe you run a few regressions afterward to see if they work. Some of the earliest advances in baseball analytics, like appreciating the importance of OBP rather than batting average, required little more than some rudimentary Excel skills. It's not that simple anymore. The full StatCast data feed for even one game would overwhelm most casual analysts. Goodness only knows what the FieldVision data sets look like.

Every once in a while, someone writes a column that proclaims, "There is nothing further to be discovered about baseball." There's plenty more to be discovered about baseball, it just takes a lot more effort than it did even 10 years ago. Thinking that you have baseball all figured out is *the* fundamental mistake of the game, but I think that baseball analytics is running up against its own version of Moore's Law. Knowledge continues to expand, but the R&D costs to get there are much higher now, to the point that only teams can really justify them, and they need a small task force of people just to manage those huge data feeds.

There's a cultural shift that goes along with that. Baseball analytics used to—and maybe still does—pride itself on being an open field full of "outsiders." I started researching baseball in 2006. At the time, there were people who had no formal baseball experience who were providing MLB teams with insights that they didn't previously have. The data sets being used were mostly *public*. Now, most of the data aren't public, and to gain access to them, you need to be an insider. We've witnessed the slow de-democratization of baseball research. Sabermetric writers at places like *Baseball Prospectus* used to celebrate every time that one of their own made it to "the inside" and longed for the day when we would be fully welcomed in front offices. Well, we made it. And now I wonder how much of it will ever make its way back out. In the new ballgame, it's hard to be a baseball researcher on "the outside."

EVEN AMONG THE jobs that aren't obviously data *management* gigs, a lot of teams are looking for candidates who have experience with web development. Sure, teams will expect their candidates have some chops in data analysis, but data analysis will only get you so far. You have to know how to *present* information too.

Consider pitch framing, which is the idea that catchers can "steal" strikes on borderline pitches if they catch the ball in ways the fool the umpire. For a few years, the best work on pitch framing was publicly available, but once the value of pitch framing was widely known, teams reacted quickly and began incorporating that skill into how they rated and even trained catchers. It turned out to be such an important skill that statistically savvy fans learned to say "Smith is a horrible framer! We should get someone better!"

Your favorite team knows that Smith is a bad framer. They can read a leaderboard, but so can the other 29 teams. There's no pawning off Smith on some unsuspecting chump who isn't with the times anymore. Even if a team wanted to trade up at catcher, it's not often that you really have the chance to make that sort of swap. You're sitting still if you're just waiting around for that deal to materialize. The better use of those framing data and an analyst's time, the one that will provide the most benefit to the team, is to help Smith get better at framing, even if it's just going from terrible to below average. Fixing the players that you have has real value and is often a better strategy than finding new ones. Sometimes you don't have any other choices.

That requires us to go beyond "framing is important" and "Smith is bad at framing" and get into "Smith needs help with framing pitches on the outside edge against right-handed hitters." You have to be able to show Smith and the catching instructor where he's missing chances to frame, work on a plan to fix it, and then monitor Smith's progress. Your challenge isn't to find some deeply meaningful thing about baseball in the data. Your job is to make the data deeply meaningful to Smith. The best analytics department might not be the one who figures out the next big inefficiency. It's the one that can communicate a hundred little ones to the people who need to see them and in ways that help them to change.

THE NEW DATA frontier in baseball is an old friend: video. There's a field of study in data science known as "computer vision" which is the extraction of data from visual sources. Normally, teams need trained people to watch video to look for actionable intelligence and some of them will always be necessary. Computer vision speeds that process up. An algorithm can "watch" much more baseball than any human, and it doesn't need snack breaks.

Teams might pick up on "tells" that a pitcher is tiring or at risk for injury that might not be entirely obvious. Maybe it's something about how far the right shoulder drops that they then know to look for live during the game. Maybe they can pick up on bad habits that the pitcher has fallen into and relay that information to the pitching coach. Maybe, a little more cynically, they could pick up a "tell" from what the opposing pitcher does *between pitches* that means a slider is coming.

A computer vision engineer doesn't come cheap. The median salary for such a person in the private sector has six digits in it. MLB teams have long had the advantage that they could pay professionals less than the market rate in their fields, because *you get to work for a baseball team*, but there's only so much of a discount that people will take. Eventually, front offices are going to run into a problem. Not only do the nerds have an outpost on the third floor, but some of them will be making salaries that rival what major movers in the organization make. What began as a small independent movement of outsiders is now a well-compensated battalion of professionals.

IN THE LAST chapter, I asked the question of whether analytics had ruined baseball and answered it with a "Yes." Sorry about that. I suppose that I ought to do something about the mess. That's a tough order to fill. Most of the "problems" in the new ballgame are caused by people behaving rationally within the rules that baseball has set up. In order to change their behavior, we might need to change the rules of the game.

In 2017, during the World Baseball Classic, fans saw something that they likely never had before, assuming they were up watching baseball at 9 AM. With a game between the Netherlands and Japan tied 6–6 after the 10th inning, Japan's Seiya Suzuki was scheduled to leadoff the top of the 11th. He came to bat with teammates Nori Aoki and Ryosuke Kikuchi having magically appeared on first and second base, respectively. While technically just an exhibition, the WBC was sponsored by MLB, and so this was the first test of whether civilization would collapse if baseball had this slightly different rule. Suzuki bunted his teammates over and first baseman Sho Nakata singled them in, giving Japan an 8–6 lead that proved to be the final score. Civilization did not, in fact, collapse.

In 2020, MLB adopted a form of this rule for regular season games, with a runner placed on second base during any extra innings. Angels' pitcher/designated hitter Shohei Ohtani had the honor of being the first "automatic runner" in MLB history. The rule was meant to cut down on marathon extra-inning games that would last beyond the second singing of "Take Me Out to the Ballgame" during the 14th-inning stretch. Or the third one. Given that both teams got the same runner, it seems odd that the rule would shorten games, but a little bit of math shows us why the rule worked.

Table 24. Number of runs scored, by base/out state, 2018–2022

Runs Scored	No outs, no runners	No outs, runner on 2nd
0	72.4%	39.5%
1	14.7%	32.6%
2	7.0%	14.5%
3	3.3%	7.3%
4	1.5%	3.4%
5+	1.1%	2.7%

By definition, an extra-inning game continues if both teams score the same number of runs in their respective half-innings at bat. In regulation play, the most common thing to happen is that both teams fail to score and the game continues. With no runners and no outs to start an inning, teams go scoreless 72.4 percent of the time. The chances of both teams getting goose egged are 52.4 percent ($.724^2$). There's also a chance that both teams will score one run, and so on.

Gifted the runner on second, teams score zero runs only 39.5 percent of the time, which means that there's only a 15.6 percent chance of both sides remaining scoreless. With the ghost runner, the chances of both teams each scoring one run go up to 32.6 percent, but here, the power of squares is our friend. The chances that both teams score one run is 10.6 percent (.326^2). With no runners on, there's a 55 percent chance that both sides will match scores at the end of the inning. With the runner on second, that drops to 29 percent. Anything can happen, but the chances of the game dragging on into the 15th inning are much lower. That was the entire point of the rule.

The rules of the game aren't set in stone. Some of them are enforced by a literal chalk line that they have to reapply every night because it's so easily brushed away. While the "ghost runner" rule shortens games, it has a problem. It feels a bit like mutant baseball. It's not completely unrecognizable. Other than the runner at second, they're still playing *baseball*. This isn't deciding a game after nine innings with a home run derby. It's weird though that the rules change midway through the game. This is the problem that MLB finds itself with. Baseball has some things that need fixing, but the medicine might be worse than the disease.

We're going to focus on four of baseball's problems that we met in the previous chapter. The games are too long. There are too many strikeouts. There's not enough action. Teams are tanking. What if we made things a little different? If there's something that analytics is good at it, it's gaining insight into what things could be like with a few changes. Could we use it to improve the game *without* turning it into mutant baseball?

The games are too long.

Let's diagnose the patient first. We can make a short list of the items that consume time within a baseball game. There are the pitches (and the spaces in between them), throws to first, actual plays once the ball has been hit, between-inning breaks, mid-inning pitching changes, instant replay, and visits to the mound by either the pitching coach or the catcher.

There's no way to shorten up plays in the field, aside from silly things like making the bases 60 feet apart. That might shave a second or so off a single, but that would completely rewrite everything else about the game. That's out. The length of between-inning breaks is regulated by MLB and is set to two minutes and five seconds (longer for nationally televised and playoff games). In theory, MLB could cut the breaks down by a minute and shave 17 minutes off a game, but during those 17 minutes, they sell advertising. Those breaks aren't going anywhere either.

Mid-inning pitching changes, where they also pause for a few words from our sponsors, are on the same schedule as the between-inning breaks. Many fans often wonder why a pitcher who just spent 10 minutes warming up in the bullpen needs an extra two minutes on the real mound to throw even more pitches. The reason is that pitching is more than just arm action. The bullpen is basically a shoebox, while the real mound is a larger open-air area. You need a moment to pick up on the visual cues that go with pitching from the real mound, so the warmup tosses after coming in from the bullpen *are for your brain.* You also need to make sure that your landing spot for your delivery doesn't have a divot in it from the others who have used that mound before you.

In 2020, MLB instituted a rule stating that relievers must remain in the game to face three batters (or pitch to the end of the inning) in an attempt to cut down on mid-inning pitching changes. The new rule did bring down the number of those changes, by a little bit, and other than outlawing them altogether, there's not a lot of options left to cut further down on them.

Figure 33. Average number of mid-inning pitching changes, 1993–2022

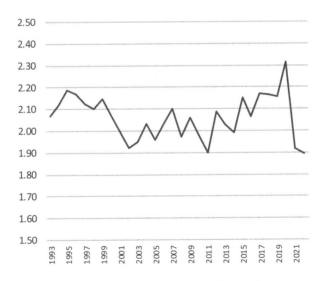

The impact of instant replay is also fairly minimal. In 2022, there were 1,434 plays reviewed, roughly one every other game, and the reviews averaged a little more than a minute in length. That time could be reclaimed, but spending it "buys" the ability to right obvious wrongs in the game. The impact of limiting visits to the pitcher's mound by the pitching coach or the catcher would be similarly minor. MLB limited the length of mound visits to 30 seconds in 2016, and then limited the total number of visits allowed in the first nine innings to six in 2018 and five in 2019. It didn't change the game significantly, so it went largely unnoticed, save for the fact that many teams started listing the number of remaining mound visits on the scoreboard.

Throws to first do add time to the ledger, although in 2022, there were six per game. Near the end of the 2022 season though, as part of the new pitch clock, MLB created a rule that limited the number of pickoff throws a pitcher is allowed to make to two per at-bat. On the third attempt, the runner is awarded the next base if not picked off. While that might initially seem like a way to cut down game time, we have to think this one all the way through. Once the pitcher has made two unsuccessful throws over (and only about 2 percent of pickoff throws result in an out), the runner now knows that the pitcher can't throw over again without risking giving up a base. That might shorten up the game a bit, but the rules of the running game have been rewritten.

That leaves us with the major contributor to game time and the lever which MLB has decided to press on to address the problem, which is the time between pitches. For the 2023 season, MLB introduced a pitch clock, with a 15-second limit (20 with runners on base) between when the pitcher receives the ball and the wind up for the next pitch. In 2022, there were 291 pitches thrown per game by both teams, although 75 of them ended plate appearances. That leaves 216 pitches that were thrown that would be subject to a pitch clock. The average time between those pitches in 2022 was 23.1 seconds. Dropping the average time between pitches to even 20 seconds would save 11 minutes per game. During the 2022 *minor* league season, a modified version of the rule saw a drop in game times of about 20 minutes.

The pitch clock comes with a price. Baseball has famously been "the game without a clock." That's been part of its charm, and adding one feels like creeping into the land of mutant baseball. Eventually, someone will win a game in part because of a shot clock violation. The pitch clock is now the best illustration of the fundamental question of the new ballgame: *How far will baseball go to reshape itself?* MLB has started to answer this one, moving to solve the problem of long games by violating one of its most treasured non-rules. This truly is a new ballgame.

There are too many strikeouts.

If the length of a game is mostly a function of the number of pitches thrown and the time between those pitches, then one way to shorten games is to encourage fewer pitches. In Chapter 7, we saw that as strikeouts have increased, so have pitches per plate appearance. Those extra pitches add up. As the game tilts more in the direction of strikeouts (and walks), the number of pitches in a game will go up too.

Table 25. Average number of pitches, by outcome, 2022

Event	Average number of pitches
Strikeout	4.73
Walk	5.75
Everything Else	3.32

For every strikeout (and walk) that MLB can turn into something else, they will save a pitch or two from being made, but it's not the walks that are out of control. Getting rid of a few strikeouts could knock a few more minutes off the game time.

In the rulebook, the strike zone is defined by "the area over home plate from the midpoint between a batter's shoulders and the top of the uniform pants—when the batter is in his stance and prepared to swing at a pitched ball—and a point just below the kneecap." In theory, it's a rectangle. In reality, it's a blob. Because human umpires call balls and strikes, the actual strike zone extends a bit off the plate on the outer part of the zone, and isn't quite as tall as the rulebook suggests. It looks more like an oval.

The immediate reflex that most people have around solving the issue of strikeouts is to tinker with the size of the strike zone. The size of the zone that gets called varies a bit from umpire to umpire, and we can use that variation to our advantage. What's fascinating is that there are theories on why both decreasing the size of the strike zone and increasing it would cut down on Ks. The case for shrinking is fairly obvious, but the one for increasing its size suggests that with more area to "protect," batters would be incentivized to swing and put the ball in play more often.

It turns out that the "shrink the zone" theories have more evidence to back them. Umpires who have smaller strike zones yell "strike three!" less often, even after controlling for how often the batter and pitcher usually record strike outs on their lines in the box score. The effect of the smaller zone wasn't big, and it had the obvious side effect of increasing walks. MLB could easily redefine the strike zone, perhaps bringing the bottom of the zone above the knee and cut down some on the K's, though it wouldn't move the needle very much on game time.

Let's set a goal that we're trying to reach. There's no fundamentally correct strikeout rate in baseball, but in 2000, 16.6 percent of batters struck out, and in 2010, it was 18.5 percent. Maybe we can get back there from the (gulp!) 23.2 percent peak rate that MLB had in 2021. In 2022, MLB implemented one of its most obvious anti-strikeout ideas, which was to stop letting pitchers strike out so much, but even that only brought the number down by a few tenths of a percent league-wide (to 22.4 percent) compared to 2021 when (some) pitchers did still bat.

In Chapter 7, we briefly discussed killing the octopus. Because teams routinely roster 13 pitchers, it allows for an eight-armed bullpen. MLB could enact a rule that artificially limited rosters to 10 pitchers. Teams would cut their three worst, but the remaining pitchers would have to cover more innings. Pitchers become less likely to strike out batters the deeper into games that they go. In 2022, starting pitchers, in the first inning of games where they eventually completed six innings or more, struck out 24.6 percent of batters they faced. By the sixth inning, it was down to 20.9 percent. When relievers came into the sixth inning in 2022, they struck out 23.4 percent of the batters they faced. In the new ballgame, with shortened starting assignments and four relievers finishing the final four innings, teams can effectively sustain a high strikeout rate all game. With only 10 pitchers on the roster, they'd have to think twice about doing that.

Making pitchers work longer hours would bring down the strikeout rate a little bit, but even if all pitchers reverted to pitching like tired starters at the end of their day, a 20.9 percent rate only gets us back to the rate of 2016. It's a tribute to how overrun the game has become with strikeouts. The other option would be to expand the league. Two new teams would require 26 pitchers who weren't good enough to be on rosters last year. But even the players who had a negative WAR in 2022 (meaning they performed worse overall than an end-of-the-bench or AAA call-up pitcher) had a combined strikeout rate of 18.8 percent. The really bad pitchers are getting whiffs too.

If we're going to fix the strikeout problem, we may have to look instead to the batters and see if we can incentivize them to be a little more disciplined at the plate. Maybe we can even address another issue plaguing the game and feed two birds with one scone.

There's not enough action in the game.

In the last chapter, we saw that the average number of minutes between balls that are hit into play had risen sharply. Baseball might not suffer so much from a *time*-of-game problem as a *pace*-of-game problem. Because strikeouts and walks don't register with most fans as "action," perhaps MLB needs to gently guide the game away from those outcomes. It's easier said than done. We also saw evidence in Chapter 7 that hitters are favoring a "swing real hard in case you hit it" approach. It has led to more swinging and missing, but also louder contact when they do hit the ball. How can we convince batters to take a more level swing?

In Chapter 5, we talked about banning the infield shift as a way to get more contact into the game. The data didn't provide much optimism. The biggest problem with the infield shift wasn't what it did to the balls that went into play, but the way hitters reacted to it. Knowing that the shift was a trap just waiting for a ground ball to be hit into it led to more swinging for the fences. That led to more strikeouts. Under MLB's new shift rule, what has been called a "partial shift," where the shortstop plays as close to the second base bag as possible without stepping over to the dark side, remains legal. As we might expect, teams didn't get *quite* the same fielding benefit from the partial shift as they did from the full shift, but the increased strikeouts were still there in both formations.

If MLB were to not only ban three fielders on one side of the infield but to restrict them from being a certain distance from second base (a rule that MLB has already begun testing in the minors), forcing them to line up in a "traditional" 2–2 defense, we might get somewhere. When you combine both the now-illegal full shifts and the still-legal partial shifts, almost two thirds of left-handed batters in 2022 saw some form of mutant infield configuration. We saw that the infield shift and the partial shift raised strikeout rates by 3.5 and 3.2 percent, respectively, compared to the

2–2 defense. When we multiply all of that together, enforcing a strict ban on shifting could drop the strikeout rate overall by about nine-tenths of a percentage point, just from left-handed batters being able to feel a little less closed in by the defense. To put that in perspective, from 2021 to 2022, the MLB overall strikeout rate dropped by about the same amount. Some of that can be attributed to the fact that non-pitchers struck out a bit less, but most of it was implementation of the universal designated hitter. A full and strict ban on the infield shift would have an effect on strikeouts that was stronger than getting rid of pitchers hitting.

The ban on the infield shift should also take some walks off the board as pitchers don't feel the need to nibble as much and avoid certain parts of the strike zone. Instead, there should be more balls in play, and more of them should go through the infield as hits. In theory, this is exactly the outcome that MLB wants, but we now reach a very sticky question. The infield shift developed because MLB had no rules about where the seven fielders who aren't the pitcher or catcher could stand. It took a century before teams realized the power of the infield shift. When it appeared, it looked weird, and it started pulling the game in a very dark direction, away from contact and "action." On the other hand, baseball has always been a game of move and counter-move. The shift was crafty, but legal, and it had traditionally been the responsibility of the other party to figure out some antidote. You will recognize them by their battle cry: "Learn to hit the ball the other way!" We want to nudge baseball in an aesthetically pleasing direction, but we don't want mutant baseball. Problem is, who's the mutant?

In the therapy room, it was often my job to work with a patient on making a tough decision. Some decisions were important ("Should I change careers?") and some were more mundane, but they usually didn't have a clear answer. If the answer were clear, the patient would have already done it. The hardest decisions to make are the ones that have positives and negatives on both sides and arrows pointing in both directions. As a therapist, it was never my place to decide for the patient, but afterward, it was often my job to work with them around one of the hardest parts of life: It's possible to both feel good about picking the side that had the most positives *and* to feel sad about the positive things that you had to leave behind *and* to be mad at the fact that you had pick between the two.

Forcing teams into a traditional 2–2 defense would probably inject more action into the game. It would preserve the "traditional optics" of the game. It would also involve MLB outlawing something that was the product of a good amount of honest research and creative thinking. There isn't a right answer. As my wife, who holds a Ph.D. in cell biology, is fond of saying, "We are all mutants."

THE OTHER OPTION that MLB might consider to put more action back into the game is to purposefully deaden the baseball. It's a topic about which MLB has been notoriously tight-lipped. After the game experienced a home run surge in 2015 and into 2016 and 2017, with home run rates not just jumping up, but leaping from previous norms, MLB commissioned a report by a group of well-known researchers whose third facts were that they were physicists and engineers and whose fifth facts were that they loved baseball.

The group concluded that the baseball had indeed changed from 2015 to 2017 and had become a little "bouncier" and thus, more likely to leave the park. They explicitly stated that the changes did not appear to be the result of any intentional actions by MLB or Rawlings, which manufactures the balls (and of which MLB is now part-owner). This wasn't a juicing conspiracy. However, in 2018 and 2019, home run rates continued to increase, something that the committee, issuing its report after the 2019 season, chalked up to changes in player behavior. Seems that players got used to the bouncier ball and started swinging for the fences.

One of the recommendations that the committee made in their report was that MLB install humidors in all 30 parks, specifically to regulate the storage conditions for all game balls. In 2022, MLB did exactly that. A dry baseball is a bouncier baseball—the well-known "Coors Field Effect" owes to the low humidity in the mountain air of Denver—and in 2022, home run rates fell. It's hard to draw direct links between the events (the old saw about correlation not equaling causation is appropriate here), but it's also hard to ignore.

A simple measure of how juicy the ball is in a given year is the percentage of fly balls that become home runs (HR/FB). Once the batter has hit the ball in the air, how likely is it to fly over the fence? For much of this century, the rate held within a range of between 9 and 11 percent. In 2019, it reached 15.3 percent. As the rate of home runs on fly balls increased, so did swings-

and-misses and the strikeout rate. There was plenty of incentive to swing real hard in case you hit it. The ball was doing a lot of the work.

We have data on HR/FB league-wide back to 2002, and not surprisingly, there's a strong correlation (there's that word again) between HR/FB and metrics like league-wide strikeout rate and league-wide swing-and-miss rate. Even more interesting, the correlations get stronger if you use last year's HR/FB rate. It suggests that if the ball changes, it takes batters a little time to adjust their collective approach, but that they do respond to the incentives in the environment. A little extra math tells us that a one-point reduction in HR/FB is worth about a one-point decrease in strikeout rate. Players won't swing from their heels as much if it just means flying out to the wall, but there's only so far you can go in that direction before fans start missing the dingers.

There are plenty of not-so-hidden forces that are trying to shape baseball, but *you can change the game by tinkering with the rules, but only by so much.* Some of the changes that have influenced the development of the new ballgame are bigger than the game itself and MLB is mostly powerless to do anything about them. On the flip side, there are steps that MLB could take and there's a decent case that they would at least address some of its biggest issues. Whether or not those steps would be enough to "fix" things is a matter of taste. What's clear though is that the strikeout problem, the length-of-game problem, and the lack-of-action problem are all interrelated, and perhaps even the *same problem.* MLB has now taken some of those steps and *could* take more to further put their thumb on the scale, if they wanted to. Would the result be mutant baseball?

MAYBE THERE IS a way that analytics can save the day after all. Or at least help. Does "swing real hard in case you hit it" actually work? That's a question we can answer with a little math. In this book, we've already seen the idea of the run expectancy of a situation, the average number of runs that score from a given combination of runners and outs. Other than a home run, a batter can't produce a run all by himself, but we can track how much he helped his team toward a run. For example, in 2022, with no runners and no outs, the average team scored an average of .47 runs before the inning was over. If the leadoff batter singles, he creates a situation (runner at first, no outs) where the run expectancy is .87 runs. He has increased his team's run expectancy by .40 runs. If he makes an out (now, no runners, one out), the team's run expectancy falls to .25, a drop of .22 runs.

We can look at these changes in all plate appearances that go to two strikes. With a two-strike count, we expect that outcomes will tilt toward the negative, because there's now a pretty good chance that the batter will strike out. When we look at how hitters have done across the years in these situations, we see something interesting.

Figure 34. Run expectancy added on two-strike counts, 1993–2022 (pitchers batting excluded)

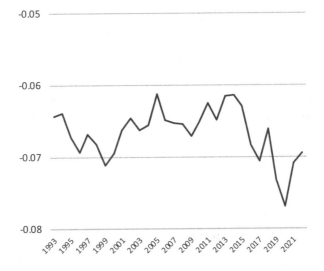

Around 2014, when the "swing real hard in case you hit it" style began to emerge, production on two-strike counts began falling. The losses from the strikeouts outweighed the gains from the extra power generated. We've talked about why the strategy made sense to try, but it's important to go deeper than that. As the infield shift gained prominence in the game, press interviews with hitters found an emerging sense of frustration. It seemed that all of the recent major improvements in strategy and technology had benefitted pitching and defense, leaving batters to fend for themselves. It was tough to line a ball through the infield only to see it caught by someone standing in a position that didn't exist when the batter was growing up.

Analytics has prided itself on being the antidote to overly emotional—but very human—reactions on the part of baseball players. It might seem like a trifle that run expectancy on two-strike counts has gone down by a mere hundredth of a run per plate appearance, until you realize that in 2022, the average team had 3,241 plate appearances that got to that point. If each is bleeding away a hundredth of a run that it doesn't need to, that's more than 30 runs of value, which is a run every five or six games. If a team could recover even some of that by convincing their hitters to shorten up with two strikes and not swing from their heels, it would make their offenses much better and, more importantly, cut down on the Ks in the game. In a perfect world, just showing everyone Figure 34 would be enough.

If only it were all that easy. It's not enough to tell people that they need to do something different. You have to engage with the reasons they are doing it in the first place. There is a branch of research in public health known as "translational science." It includes the study of how you can get a rational message out to people who aren't always going to behave rationally. Consider for a moment how many people do things that we know are horrible for them to do. They overeat, put off preventative medical care, drive too fast, and sleep too little. And that's just me. All of these are demonstrably bad ideas. If it were as easy as showing someone 10 different studies by ten respected experts at ten different medical schools, we'd have a society of health nuts. We don't.

Suppose that someone asked you to increase your intake of fruits and vegetables to five servings per day, because the scientists all say that "five will keep you alive." Right now, you maybe get two or three per day, but there aren't that many fruits and vegetables that you like and you don't know a lot of recipes that contain vegetables. Our well-meaning public health worker hands you a cookbook. You politely inform the veggie pusher that your local grocery store doesn't have a wide selection of produce and that you prefer to eat the foods that you grew up with. It's not that our vegetable-loving friend is incorrect. Broccoli really is good for your health. The message of "just eat more vegetables" sounds easy until you notice all of the unspoken requests that are buried in there. You're going to have to change your grocery store, buy a bunch of expensive produce and throw some of it away when you inevitably don't like it, read a big cookbook and learn a lot of new recipes, eat foods that are unfamiliar, and potentially give up some comfort foods. Where's the line of people to sign up?

If analytics wants to be seen as more than just a fringe element in baseball, then it needs to solve the Broccoli Problem. It's not enough to simply point out the places where people are being inefficient. You also need to look at the underlying causes of why people act that way to begin with. If some of the "swing real hard in case you hit it" trend is being driven by frustration, then that frustration needs to be directly addressed. That's not easy, but the team that understands *both* the rational explanation of a behavior *and* the irrational people whose behavior that they are trying to change will have the edge.

Teams are tanking.

When I was growing up, it was hard being a fan of Cleveland baseball. I'd lived through three seasons of 100 losses by my 12th birthday. In 1991, the team hit rock bottom and lost 105 games. They hadn't even finished in *third* place since 1968. Cleveland's fan base grew weary of what seemed like an endless cycle of losing, and Municipal Stadium became a dreary, empty place most nights. Free agents would avoid the city and the few young stars that the team did find seemed to always end up having their best days somewhere else. In the late 1980s, the team took matters into their own hands. Veterans like Julio Franco, Greg Swindell, and Joe Carter were traded for what young talent they would bring back, and by 1991, the major league roster and my 11-year-old heart felt the pain.

Cleveland eventually pioneered a strategy that became common in MLB, signing their talented young players to long-term contracts, before they had fully developed, but also before they reached free agency. It was a gamble. In the mid-1990s, it paid off. It helped that Manny Ramírez and Jim Thome, both of whom would go on to hit 500 home runs in their careers, stepped out of the team's farm system at roughly the same time. For every hit on their new strategy, there were some misses too. No one in Cleveland talks about the legendary exploits of Scott Scudder or Dave Otto, but in 1995, on the backs of that new generation of players, Cleveland made the World Series for the first time in four decades, even if Jim Poole did give up *that* home run.

When I was growing up, this process was called "rebuilding." Most teams went through the cycle every few years. Father Time is undefeated, after all. Teams assembled a group of talented young players and added to them a few veteran leaders. The veterans eventually retire and the young players become old (and expensive). At some point, it makes sense to start over. It's hard to know where "rebuilding" stops and "tanking" starts. Rebuilding is a painful, but necessary process. Tanking is a tactical one. Perhaps the dividing line is shame.

What if we could incentivize teams not to be so quick in giving up on an entire summer of someone's life? There will still be bad teams, but maybe we could take the phrase "This team *only* has 83-win potential" and remove the word "only." We may have seen part of the answer in 2020, not that there's a whole lot of that year that anyone would want to repeat. After a delayed start, MLB held a 60-game regular season, followed by a 16-team playoff. Like the universal DH, the expanded playoffs were supposed to be a temporary measure, but I'm sure someone at MLB noticed that it gave them some new playoff games to market. Since 2012, MLB had included five teams per league in its postseason, but in 2022, MLB added a sixth team to its playoff schedule and a new "Wild Card round."

Expanding the playoffs comes with a cost. The short version is that it "cheapens the regular season" but it's important to understand exactly what makes it so cheap. The American and National Leagues used to select their World Series representatives by simply sending the team with the most wins. It wasn't until the introduction of divisions in 1969 that the modern *intra*-league playoff series was born.

Divisional play had a specific reason for coming into being. Prior to 1957, the only cities with an AL or NL team west of the Mississippi River were Kansas City and St. Louis (by a couple of blocks). In 1958, the Brooklyn Dodgers and New York Giants famously decamped for California, and the Kansas City Athletics followed them 10 years later. Expansion teams in San Diego, Seattle, and Anaheim meant that baseball was no longer just an East Coast game. It also meant that East Coast teams were hauling out to see the Pacific Ocean several times a year and vice versa. With the advent of two divisions, teams began playing 18 games against teams inside their divisions and 12 games against those outside. It was supposed to mean less travel, although implementation was lacking. I grew up in the two-division era with the absurdity of the Chicago White Sox, members of the AL West, playing more often against Seattle and Oakland than they did against the then–AL East residing Milwaukee Brewers, who were a mere 90-minute bus ride away.

Divisions were effectively interleague play before interleague. It just didn't seem as much of an outrage. The AL and NL each effectively split themselves into two sub-leagues, and while there were games played between the divisions, teams in the Western Division ultimately had no concern about how teams in the Eastern Division were doing. It didn't matter other than to figure out whom they might play in the League Championship Series.

Divisional play did something else. In the 1950s and 1960s, baseball in the western half of the United States was still an economic experiment. We know now that the experiment worked out just fine, but at the time, there was a legitimate fear that the teams back east would dominate the World Series and leave fans on the West Coast with nothing to look forward to. If you're trying to sell an entire region on a game, you might want to give them a reason not to give up.

The price of that was to cheapen the benefit of having the best record in the league. It used to guarantee a trip to the World Series. Now it meant playing a short series another team that had a decent shot of de-throning you. In 1973, the New York Mets finished 82–79, barely over .500, but somehow, the best in the NL Eastern Division. They advanced to the World Series over West Coast representatives, the 99-game winning Cincinnati Reds, on the strength of a 3–2 National League Championship Series win. As the presence of a "League Championship Series" went from sacrilege to sacred tradition as so many things in baseball do after two or three years, another problem appeared.

In 1993, the most famous case happened, when the San Francisco Giants won 103 games—a mark that would have dominated both divisions in the 1993 AL, as well as the NL East and just about every other division in the modern era—only to be playing for their playoff lives on the last day of the season. Earlier in the day, their West Coast neighbors in Atlanta had won their 104th game. The Giants lost game 162 and in the last season before the Wild Card, went home.

Cutting leagues into three divisions in 1994—including one for the "Central" part of the country and all those Midwestern "small markets"—along with the new Wild Card, was supposed to get rid of those sorts of omissions. They quickly ended up bringing about their own problems. Now, there was a backdoor way to get into the playoffs and maybe the World Series without even winning a division. In 1997, the Florida Marlins did just that, but they at least had the second-best record in the National League that year. The 2002 Angels-Giants World Series featured the first matchup of two Wild Card teams, and more importantly, between the holders of the third-best record in the AL and the fourth-best in the NL. If a team can get to the World Series with the league's fourth-best record, what was the point of that 162-game marathon?

Table 26. Average number of wins by position in overall league standings, 2000–2022 (2020 excluded)

Overall Place	Average Wins
1	100.0
2	96.2
3	93.4
4	91.1
5	88.8
6	86.5
7	83.8
8	81.4

There aren't many teams who can honestly say that they have a chance to win 100 games before a season starts, but at eight teams per league, the playoffs would basically be for anyone who can break .500. Once you get into the playoffs, especially in a short series, anything can happen. Just about every weekend during the regular season, there's a series where a so-so team travels to the home of a division leader and they win two of the three games that they play. It doesn't happen all the time, but it happens enough that we know not to be surprised by it. That's baseball.

With a little math, we can even put a number to that. In an eight-teams-per-league format, an 82-win team (eighth seed) playing a three-game series in the home park of a 100-win team (the top seed) will come away with two wins about 30 percent of the time. You can call it the romance of the upset. You can call it ruining the regular season. You can call it a shameless way to sell more tickets. That 30 percent chance is *the point*. If teams can get to 82 wins, they could have a 30 percent chance at making it to the Division Series round, something they used to have no shot at whatsoever. That wouldn't end all tanking, but it would make a lot of teams think twice about doing it and it would speed up some of their plans to "spend when the time is right." The cost is that 30 percent of the time, the team with 100 wins would quietly bow out after a three-game series with a team that "shouldn't have even been here." All decisions involve trade-offs. Is a sixth-place team winning the World Series one mutation too far?

There's something about all that which doesn't sit right. Having the best record in the league still feels like it should count for *something*. We have an easy way to make it count. By using a six-team field in each league, MLB has given the best two teams a pass into the Division Series round. We still have the problem that a team that won 86 games can knock out a team that won 93 games, but there was a way that the third-place team could have avoided the series altogether. The nice thing from a marketing standpoint is that coming down the stretch in September, there's now a race both for the last playoff spots and for the top spots in the standings. MLB has to walk the line between allowing as many teams and fans as possible to think they have a chance, but also to not cheapen the regular season so much that no one bothers watching until October.

We can see an argument both for and against expanding the playoffs. If more teams have a chance at the playoffs, fewer should tank, but once they get in, the system is going to feel a little unfair. To this point in the book, we've solved those conflicts by asking "Which arrow is bigger?" When the outcome that you want is more runs or more wins, that's easy to figure out.

Since the turn of the 21st century, the fundamental question of baseball has been, "How can we play the game more efficiently?" Efficiency is measurable. It can be analyzed. That question is beginning to change, because what began as a quest for brutal efficiency has become brutal to watch. MLB has long been willing to let the game alone to develop on its own, but we got here because we've done a lot of avoiding the questions of what baseball *should* look like. Now MLB is having to make some tough choices. It's embracing what previously would have been considered mutant baseball.

What happens when the outcome that you want is to build the system that is the fairest or the most entertaining? What happens when no one can agree on definitions of "fair" or "entertaining?" Maybe we shouldn't be surprised when MLB defaults to judging things by something that they can quantify: how many dollars each decision might yield. Baseball is a game, but MLB is a business.

Analytics isn't going to save baseball. It can't, and we need to stop pretending that it can. About the best that analytics can hope for is to encourage creative thinking about how things might be a little different. That's an important role to play and one that analytically-minded fans should take seriously. But the biggest challenges that MLB now faces involve figuring out what the game *should* look like. Those are questions without *an* answer, and you can't just efficiency your way out of a philosophical question.

Chapter 10

The Beauty Unseen

Somewhere at my parents' house, there's a Starting Lineup figurine of José Canseco that I got for Christmas one year. It shows him during his "Bash Brothers" days with the late 1980s Oakland A's. They say baseball is never more perfect than it is when you are 10 years old, and when I was 10, he was the best player in the game. Canseco had won the 1986 Rookie of the Year award at 21 and the 1988 MVP at 23, hitting 42 home runs and stealing 40 bases in the same year. He was the first to make it to the 40/40 club. At the time, he seemed like the guy we would all look back on and tell our kids that we saw *him* play. I have yet to mention José Canseco to my kids.

For those who don't remember Starting Lineup, they were small action figure-like toys in the form of pro athletes. They didn't really *do* much other than stand there and look like José Canseco or Kevin Mitchell or Pat Tabler—if Canseco and Mitchell and Tabler were plastic men who stood about four inches tall. I had a few of them, but Canseco was the pride of my collection, because he was the best player in baseball *and* he was hard to get. The figurines were mostly sold regionally, so there were plenty of Tablers in Cleveland's toy stores, but few who played in other markets. Fortunately, my father happened to "know a guy."

I wish I still had that Canseco figurine. The Tabler one too. Not because they'd make me rich, but because they'd help me to be a better researcher. I no longer see patients but I might still remember a thing or two though from those days that can help me. "Therapy" can take many forms, especially when working with kids. Most people think of therapy as talking to a counselor about whatever's going on, and that certainly is one form. The thing about kids is that they don't always have the vocabulary to speak in the same way that adults do. Kids are more likely to express themselves through *play*.

If you go into the office of a child therapist, there's a good chance you'll see a dollhouse or a sandbox, strategically stocked with toys that allow a patient to play out a range of scenes. There are always human dolls, but sometimes kids will prefer to play with toy animals or superheroes or historical figures instead. Superheroes and animals can give them a little more emotional distance from what they're "talking" about, but they might also serve as a metaphor for a specific character trait in a person. A tiger might be a stand-in for someone who's ferocious. A dog might be a playful and loyal person. Pat Tabler might be a stand-in for a guy who sticks around for 11 years mostly because he hit nearly .500 with the bases loaded.

In fact, half the time, the therapist puts specific items into the dollhouse before a session to encourage a child to engage a specific issue. A child might not be able to talk about what's going on at home, but if you see them using a doll family to play out scenes where a parent is always yelling, that's a clue. Sometimes, it's just a more comfortable way to bring up the topic, because the child can say that they were "just playing around." Adults do this too; they call it humor. The first rule of child psychology is that it applies throughout all of life.

There's something about play that we often overlook. It's a wonderful way to explore new ideas. Kids don't have a wealth of experience to draw from. Even simple social situations are new to them, so they need to rehearse what they're going to do out in the real world. In the dollhouse or the sandbox, you can set up whatever situation you like and play it out a bunch of different ways. You can get feedback on which responses work best. When you play in a dollhouse or a sandbox, you have to think things through for all of the characters involved. What would the dinosaur think about this situation? What would Abe Lincoln's response be to the dinosaur? It's an exercise in perspective-taking, which is a skill that everyone can use more of in their lives.

WE LIVE IN an era of screens. What we don't always recognize is that computers change that way in which we engage information. In 2013, two researchers at Dartmouth College, Geoff Kaufman and Mary Flanagan, had participants play a game in which the objective was to contain an outbreak of a deadly virus. (At the time, this was just a hypothetical.) The game could be played either on a computer screen or as a board game. What the researchers found was that the screen players tended to focus their efforts on responding to the immediately present "cases" of the virus, a strategy that didn't actually limit its spread. The better alternative was to put resources into vaccination and prevention and the people who played the game on the board were more likely to hit on the right answer. The researchers chalked up the discrepancy to the idea that screens prime people to look for quick answers, rather than to deeply engage the problem.

One of the nice things about computers is that you can do a lot of complicated math quickly. In baseball, it's led to people asking questions that prior to the computer age, couldn't have been solved with just pen and paper. That speed comes at a cost. I can come up with an interesting question, represent it mathematically, and have the answer to that question within a few minutes. The cost is that it's easy to focus on, "Hey, I got an answer!" Unlike the sandbox, computers don't leave a lot of time to take the dinosaur's perspective.

Most baseball research is mediated through a computer screen. It's an old critique that maybe baseball analysts ought to pull away from the spreadsheet once in a while, but there's something to be said for that. Yes, you can figure out the mathematically optimal bullpen usage quickly, but why not slow down and think about how the dinosaur feels about pitching in the seventh inning. You could just tell him to shut up and pitch when he's told. He might bite your head off.

Play is a slow process. It's the opposite of the computer. It draws a person into a different way of thinking. If working on a screen—or perhaps more importantly, the processor capable of billions of operations per second connected to it—encourages quick and immediate thinking, play requires that a person think about a situation more deeply. Consider a team thinking about some different positioning ideas for their fielders. On a computer, it's easy to generate a batted-ball profile and spray chart that shows why a particular hitter might be a good candidate to be played that way. Now imagine studying the same problem in the sandbox with those Starting Lineup figurines. José Canseco could be the batter, while Abe Lincoln and the dinosaur played in the outfield. You'd have to envision where they would stand. Would they overlap? Do we need to think differently about who should "call" a ball that two fielders might both get to? If the ball were hit to one of them, would the visual cues that they usually use to track down the ball be all messed up? What about the batter? Looking out, what would he see, and what would be the logical thing for him to try to do?

To play it out in the sandbox might take 30 minutes and would involve moving physical objects through space, and maybe moving yourself around to consider the view from various points on the diamond. It's quite different than using a machine that can simulate an entire season of games in 30 seconds. Play engages multiple senses and forces a person to slow down as a result. All ideas have their downsides and some are still worth it, but if you slow down a bit, you have a better chance of thinking of some of those possible pitfalls in the first place. Sometimes when you move too fast, you don't think enough about the consequences.

I think all baseball researchers should spend some time in the sandbox. Find some old action figures from back in the day. Bring a Superman figure because at some point, you'll construct some weird hypothetical involving Mike Trout. Create a small baseball field for them to stand on and once in a while, test out your ideas in the land of make believe. Maybe MLB teams ought to have little sandbox annexes next to their Stat Caves too. It's better than thinking up revolutionary ideas and then jumping into trying them on real people. Let the plastic people try first. You aren't going to prove whether your idea is brilliant in the sandbox, but by engaging with it in a different way, you might have a chance to see nuances that you hadn't considered. It's decidedly low-tech, but technology will only get you so far in baseball. And life.

IF YOU'VE PAID attention to baseball since the turn of the 21st century, you've heard about WAR. Wins Above Replacement has become *the* face of the baseball analytics movement, that is if numbers had faces. WAR attempts to put one number on how much a player was worth during a season. It begins with the question "What would have happened if Smith had decided not to play?" The team would have found another warm body to take the playing time that Smith got, but it would have been someone from the bench or AAA who wouldn't have been as good.

WAR is a measure of marginal, rather than absolute value. Consider two players who are both league-average hitters and baserunners. Both play average defense at their positions. One is a shortstop, the other a first baseman. Both contributed the same amount to their teams, but WAR says that the shortstop is worth more, because of who he *isn't*. The backup first baseman is probably a better hitter than the backup shortstop, and the space between the two backups is where the difference in value comes from. That trips a lot of people up. Part of what made WAR so different was the ability to see those negative spaces, not only what happened, but what *didn't* happen. People have a hard time with negative space.

If there's something else that stands out about WAR, it's that it cuts to the chase. How much was the player *worth*? This might be a player who plays Gold Glove defense with a decent bat or a power hitter who is hiding in left field in the hope that no one will hit anything to him. WAR is *very* good at putting all of the pieces of the game onto the same scale, but it's a measure built for efficiency. It's also given in the language of *value* rather than performance. The question that most fans are used to asking is, "What did the player do?" WAR asks how much it was worth.

At first, WAR was scorned by the Domestic Horticultural Anti-Trespassing Brigade as good for absolutely nothin'. (Say it again!) As more people have understood the logic behind it, WAR has gained broader acceptance, even among those who aren't entirely sure how it's calculated. Getting to even that level of acceptance has been hard-won. Many people held on to the "old-school" stats because they were familiar (and more easily calculated), even though many of them contain assumptions about baseball that weren't true. Batting average famously pretends that walks never happened.

WAR is the single best one-number summary of a player's season or career that's out there, but it is starting to run into a problem. The "bones" of WAR were laid down in the mid-1990s, and some people who grew up with WAR now own lawns that they don't want the kids to step on. The game has evolved since then, and I worry that WAR is in danger of becoming ossified. There are not-so-hidden forces that act on baseball's numerical language too. *As the game changes, the numbers that describe it take on different meanings.* Sometimes we need to find better numbers. WAR is no exception.

In 2018, when the first "openers" appeared, WAR was caught flat-footed. Starting pitchers and relievers are treated differently by the measure, but the opener, while technically the "starting pitcher," was clearly a reliever being used out of order. No one quite knew how to handle that. Analytically-inclined fans need to be careful. Like the people who clung to batting average without stopping to think about whether batting average made sense, I worry that the question has become, "What is Smith's WAR?" rather than the question that produced WAR in the first place: "Is this stat really measuring value?" If you want to understand the new ballgame, you have to be willing to engage that question.

I WANT TO study this particular box score from May of 2022. The game that it represents wasn't especially important. The two teams played a much more interesting game the day before, when Angels starter Reid Detmers threw a no-hitter. This one was a closely-played 10-inning affair, with the visiting Rays bouncing back from being no-hit and coming away with the win.

Taylor Ward of the Angels hit a pinch-hit two-run home run in the bottom of the eighth to tie the game. In the top of the 10th, Vidal Bruján's double scored "ghost runner" Kevin Kiermaier to put the Rays ahead and then Bruján scored on Harold Ramírez's single to add an insurance run. That's the game story, and the box score tells it nicely. There's something more important about this box score that I want to focus on: what it's hiding. It's a case study in how even advanced statistics, and espcially WAR, sometimes struggle to accurately capture pieces of the new ballgame.

May 11, 2022—Tampa Bay at Los Angeles (Regular Season)

Tampa Bay	AB	R	H	RBI	Los Angeles (A)	AB	R	H	RBI
Díaz, 3b	4	0	0	1	Marsh, lf	5	0	1	0
Franco, dh	5	0	0	0	Rengifo, 2b	4	0	1	0
Choi, 1b	4	0	0	0	Wallach, c	0	0	0	0
Arozarena, lf	3	0	0	0	Ohtani, dh	4	0	1	0
Mejía, c	4	0	0	0	Rendon, 3b	4	0	0	0
Kiermaier, cf	4	2	1	1	Walsh, 1b	4	0	0	0
Bruján, 2b	4	1	1	1	Whitefield, cf	4	0	0	0
Walls, ss	4	1	1	0	Mayfield, rf–2b	3	0	1	0
Phillips, rf	1	0	1	0	Romine, c	2	0	1	0
Ramírez, ph-rf	1	0	1	1	Wade, ph-ss	1	1	0	0
					Trout, ph	0	0	0	0
					Velazquez, ss	2	0	0	0
					Ward, ph-rf	2	1	1	2

Tampa Bay — 010 000 010 2   4 5 0
Los Angeles (A) — 000 000 020 0   2 6 0

2B—Bruján (1); HR—Kiermaier (3, 2nd inning, none on, off Ohtani), Ward (7, 8th inning, 1 on, off Kitteredge); SH—Phillips (1); SB—Walls (5), Arozarena (5), Bruján (1), Mayfield (1), Ohtani (5); PO—Marsh (by McLanahan, 1); LOB—Tampa Bay 5, Los Angeles 6; WP—Ohtani 2 (4); T—3:17; A—21,045

Tampa Bay	IP	H	R	ER	BB	SO
McClanahan	7	3	0	0	1	11
Kittredge, BS (2)	0.2	3	2	2	0	0
Poche	0.1	0	0	0	0	1
Feyereisen, W (3–0)	1	0	0	0	0	1
Raley, S (3)	1	0	0	0	1	1

Los Angeles (A)	IP	H	R	ER	BB	SO
Ohtani	6	2	1	1	2	5
Herget	1	0	0	0	0	2
Tepera	1	1	1	1	0	0
Iglesias	1	0	0	0	1	1
Loup, L (0–2)	1	2	2	1	0	2

Rays starter Shane McClanahan pitched seven shutout innings, facing 24 batters, while his counterpart, Shohei Ohtani, notched six innings, giving up only a run on two hits to the 22 batters whom he faced. Both starters had good outings, but how good? Let's compare them to what other starters did on that same day.

Table 27 shows all of the pitchers who got credit for a "start" on May 11th, although we can see a few obvious openers in the mix (Speier, Bush). We also see a few starters who were lifted either at the 18-batter mark (Thompson) or just after it (Falter, Cobb), despite giving up a combined total of four runs among the three of them. Ryan Pepiot and Dillon Peters faced off against each other. Each pitched three scoreless innings and then departed. I'm not even sure what to call that sort of an outing. How can we compare Shane McClanahan to other pitchers who clearly weren't doing the same job that he was? The new ballgame has muddied the waters on what exactly a "start" is.

Table 27. Starting pitcher outcomes, May 11, 2022

Pitcher	IP	R	BF	Pitcher	IP	R	BF
Zach Logue, OAK	7.0	0	26	Chad Kuhl, COL	4.2	5	25
Sandy Alcantara, MIA	7.0	1	26	Keegan Thompson, CHC	4.0	2	18
Miles Mikolas, STL	7.0	1	25	Nick Martinez, SDP	4.0	5	18
Nathan Eovaldi, BOS	6.1	3	26	Adrian Houser, MIL	4.0	7	23
Alex Cobb, SFG	5.1	1	20	Spenser Watkins, BAL	3.2	7	21
Ian Anderson, ATL	5.1	3	23	Ryan Pepiot, LAD	3.0	0	16
Aaron Sanchez, WAS	5.1	3	22	Dillon Peters, PIT	3.0	0	11
José Berríos, TOR	5.1	5	22	José Urquidy, HOU	3.0	1	12
Jameson Taillon, NYY	5.1	2	24	Chris Archer, MIN	3.0	5	17
Merrill Kelly, ARI	5.0	3	22	Joey Wentz, DET	2.2	6	16
Logan Gilbert, SEA	5.0	4	20	Gabe Speier, KCR	2.0	0	6
Bailey Falter, PHI	4.2	1	19	Tyler Megill, NYM	1.1	8	14
Vladimir Gutiérrez, CIN	4.2	4	21	Matt Bush, TEX	1.0	0	3

If Shane McClanahan had decided to go to Disneyland rather than pitch in Anaheim that night, someone would have taken his place. WAR assumes that "someone" would have replicated McClanahan's seven innings, albeit pitching much worse than McClanahan did. Would they? We can see that there weren't that many pitchers who even made it to five innings around the league. If our replacement didn't make it to the seventh, it would have meant a heavier workload on the Tampa Bay bullpen.

Table 28 shows us the valley between pitchers like McClanahan and the replacements. We can rank all of the starting pitchers in a given year by how many total outs they recorded during the season. We can rank numbers 1–30 as our aces, 31–60 as our "second starters" and so on. The type of pitcher who would have replaced McClanahan is going to come from the last group.

Table 28. Outs recorded, by starter tier, 2018–2022

Group	Avg. Outs Recorded	Finished 5th Inning	Team Win Pct.
Aces	18.0	89%	57%
2nd	16.6	79%	53%
3rd	15.9	74%	50%
4th	15.3	67%	49%
5th	14.9	64%	46%
Replacements	12.2	42%	44%

Ace starters tend to go almost two more innings on average than do replacement pitchers, and are twice as likely to make it through the fifth inning. The fact that Shane McClanahan pitched seven innings meant that Rays manager Kevin Cash didn't have to find two or three extra innings of bullpen coverage. His bullpen was better rested the next day and I've done research that shows that the extra workload saved has a positive effect on the bullpen later in the season. Cash also had the luxury of skipping to the good relievers in what was a close game. McClanahan gave his team a better chance to win both that day *and* down the road. WAR doesn't have a way to capture the value that McClanahan provided the Rays by virtue of who *didn't* have to pitch.

NEXT, WE LOOK at what happened after McClanahan and Ohtani finished pitching for the night. Let's consider the case of Angels reliever Jimmy Herget, who took over on the mound from Ohtani with the Angels down a run in the seventh inning. It's not the most pressure-packed assignment that Herget got, but it's still a tough one. You don't want a close game to get away from you. He did well to get three outs without incident (including two strikeouts). Had Herget been replaced by a AAA call-up who had given up a couple of runs, that would have been a disaster for the Angels. The fact that Angels manager Joe Maddon put Herget into a close game says something about his belief in Herget's abilities. These are the situations that relievers get paid for.

Herget had pitched two days earlier, again facing the Rays. That day, he pitched the eighth inning of a game where the Angels were already winning 11–3. In those situations, managers will often look to see which pitchers might need an inning of work to keep them "sharp." Sometimes, even the really good relievers get called because they haven't worked in a few days. It doesn't matter who throws those pitches. You're just trying to get to the end of the game. Herget threw a one-two-three inning with two strikeouts in the blowout as well, but had he been replaced by a AAA call-up who had given up two runs, the Angels were still going to win. Herget was just "an arm" that day and everyone in the stadium knew that.

In Sabermetrics, there's a concept known as win expectancy. It's similar to run expectancy. Given the score, inning, runners, and outs, we can look back in history and find other games where the same situation happened and see what percentage of the time the home or visiting team won. As each event happens, we can look to see how much that win probability changes. Late in a close game, those chances of winning can change in a hurry. Those situations are known as "high leverage."

In the 11–3 blowout, the leverage of the situation was nearly zero, but in the seventh inning down a run, Herget was pitching in a situation that was right about average for leverage. He entered with the Angels having a 31 percent chance of winning. By holding the Rays from scoring, he increased the Angels chances to 37 percent. His win probability added (WPA) for the game was 6 percent of a win. As a point of comparison, Brooks Raley pitched the bottom of the 10th for the Rays and closed out the game. He entered with the Rays having a win probability of 79 percent. By getting three outs without allowing a run, he raised the Rays by 21 percent of a win. That's the power of pitching in the late innings. You'd better be good or else your team will see some wins slip away that they thought they had in their hands.

In Chapter 4, we talked about how baseball is most commonly viewed from the perspective of the batter. One of the strengths of WAR—at least for hitters—is that it rewards them for the things that they control and not the situations that they find themselves in. Batters can only come to the plate when it's their turn. If the bases are loaded in the bottom of the ninth and the batting team is down by a run, that's a wonderful opportunity to win an actual game, but which batter is standing there is mostly a matter of chance. It's why stats like RBI are so suspect. How many runners are on base when you come up is not at all a reflection of your talent.

WAR uses some of those same assumptions for pitchers, even though they don't fit as well. Relievers aren't on a rotating system. The manager has full control over who pitches and in that ninth inning, bases loaded situation, the best available reliever is going to be out there. As you become a better reliever, you get to pitch in situations where you affect the game more. The context that you play in tells us a lot about your talent level (or at least what your manager thinks of your talent level compared to the other pitchers in the bullpen). When we study relievers, is a context-free measure like WAR the correct tool to use?

Going back to Herget, WAR sees his two performances as equals, as do most of his other "traditional" stats. His ERA doesn't care about the situation either. The major WAR indices do try to give a bit of a bonus to high-leverage relievers by looking at the average leverage that a pitcher faced over the course of a season. The problem is that each of those "just an arm" outings in blowouts artificially brings down that average, and it tends to undersell the differences among relievers and the effect that high-leverage pitchers have on games. When we strip out the context, the top relievers tend to have WAR values below three wins, but when we include the context and ask how much they added to their team's chances of actual wins in actual games, we get a very different answer. In Table 29, we can see the top 10 pitchers by WAR in 2022, along with the top pitchers by Win Probability Added (WPA).

The first list is completely dominated by starters. The second is a mix of elite starters and relievers. Why the difference? Starters pitch a lot more innings than do relievers, and if a starter were to be injured, their replacement would be a "sixth starter" (or worse) from the team's minor league system, and we've already seen that's a very large gap in quality. The closer would likely be replaced by the eighth-inning specialist (though someone would likely have to fill in for the eighth-inning guy, and on down the line). While the difference between the two of them isn't going to be that much on a per-batter basis, closers pitch at a time in the game where the effects of additional mistakes are magnified. While a starter giving up an extra run isn't great, a

Table 29. Top 10 pitchers by WAR and Win Probability Added, 2022

Pitcher	WAR	Pitcher	WPA
Aaron Nola	6.3	Sandy Alcantara	5.08
Carlos Rodón	6.2	Daniel Bard	4.81
Justin Verlander	6.1	Jhoan Durán	4.59
Sandy Alcantara	5.7	Max Fried	4.38
Kevin Gausman	5.7	Zac Gallen	4.18
Shohei Ohtani	5.6	Justin Verlander	3.97
Max Fried	5.0	Alek Manoah	3.78
Spencer Strider	4.9	Emmanuel Clase	3.75
Shane Bieber	4.9	Yu Darvish	3.69
Corbin Burnes	4.6	Edwin Díaz	3.65

closer doing the same thing could be the difference between winning and losing the game.

The strength of a measure like WAR—its ability to strip away the things that a player can't control around him—can become a weakness. If we're so caught up in neutralizing the context of everything, sometimes we forget that the context can be the entire point.

NEXT WE CAN look at the Angels decision to pinch-hit for their catcher, Austin Romine. Tyler Wade entered the game and reached on a fielder's choice, and then scored when Taylor Ward homered. When the Angels were put out, they had to do some defensive shuffling. Wade went to shortstop to replace starter Andrew Velazquez, for whom Ward pinch-hit. Then, into a game where one hit could be the difference between winning and losing, the Angels brought in backup catcher Chad Wallach. What was Wallach, owner of a sub-.200 career batting average, doing in the game? Why not leave Ward behind the plate? He was clearly athletic enough, considering he entered the game at shortstop. Or what about Mike Trout, who was still on the bench (and would eventually pinch-hit in the 10th inning)? Why not have him catch?

Some of the readers out there just scratched their heads. Neither Wade nor Trout had ever caught in their professional careers, and you can't just put someone behind the plate who's never done it unless it's a dire emergency. If a catcher gets hurt, the team doesn't call up their big bat third-base prospect and shift their regular third baseman behind the plate. Even if the "depth" catcher you have stashed away at AAA is Chad Wallach, you pretty much have to call him up. Teams might slide infielders around the diamond or put utility infielder Jack Mayfield in right, but catcher is a species unto itself.

We ask a lot of catchers. In addition to the physical beating that they take from all the squatting and foul balls, they also function as on-field social workers. If the pitcher is the most important player on the diamond, the catcher often plays the role of his emotional support giraffe. It's the catcher, not the second baseman, who goes out to the mound to calm the pitcher down after giving up an RBI double. The catcher also has to call the game, which means he has to be in tune with the pitcher's abilities and how best to use them. Then there's framing pitches to fool the umpire into calling an extra strike and blocking the pitches in the dirt and putting on the knight's armor every 20 minutes. The catcher has to be an athlete, a scholar, and a therapist. If you can handle all that and hit .240, you have a 10-year MLB career and a manager's job waiting for you.

Sabermetrics has begun to understand the previously unrecognized things a catcher does (and probably has always done) for which we never gave him credit. When I was growing up, a catcher was mostly evaluated on defense for his proficiency in throwing out would-be base-stealers, even though we now know that the best predictor of stolen bases is how well the *pitcher* holds on runners. There were always stories about the guys behind the plate whom pitchers "loved to throw to" and who "handled a staff well" and who "called a good game." Presumably there are some catchers who are better at those skills than others, but we lack any way of knowing who's who, and we lack a sense of how important each ability is. We understand so little of what's going on behind the plate. If there's a very hidden force that shapes the game, it's that while the person who pitches the ball is the most important player on the field, *the second most important is the one who catches it.*

WAR doesn't do a good job with any of this. One of the conceits of WAR is that we can compare players across different positions through a series of positional value adjustments. For example, shortstop and second base are generally considered to be five runs apart. The way that number comes about is through studying utility infielders. They spend time at both positions during the same season, and that makes for a nicely controlled comparison. The idea is that if you had a second baseman who was three runs above average and moved him to short, he'd probably perform two runs below the average shortstop. In Chapter 6, we talked about how that doesn't completely fit with reality. When a player moves to a new position, even a move that seems fairly straightforward (short to second), his performance is likely to be among the worst in the league, at least for a while.

Nowhere would this be more obvious than someone trying to "fake it" as a catcher. It doesn't matter how amazing your center fielder is with the glove. He's never going to catch. You can really only compare catchers to other catchers.

WE HAVE TO pause for a moment to marvel at the Angels' starting pitcher and designated hitter, Shohei Ohtani. I suppose there once was a time in MLB history where pitchers would regularly bat, but Ohtani has been one of the best power hitters in the game while at the same time acquitting himself just fine as a major league starter. There have been players who have played two ways, but for the most part, they have been good at one half of the game and barely adequate at the other. Sometimes they were just barely adequate at both. Ohtani is a marvel and has quickly become the go-to answer for just about any baseball hypothetical that could double as the plot for a sci-fi movie. It's now a race for second place to see which player I would clone 26 times. MLB even wrote a rule that basically applies only to him, allowing a pitcher to bat for himself as the designated hitter during a game that he starts and to remain in the game as a hitter even after he is removed as a pitcher.

In Chapter 6, we noted that the new ballgame is multi-positional. That's a bit of a problem for WAR, which was developed during the days of the starter/backup model of position players. There were multi-positionalists, but they were mostly "utility" players. Ohtani is the case that lays this in its most clear light. We see him filling two roles at once in our box score, as though he were two separate people. We know how to value what Ohtani did, both on the mound and with the bat. How do we calculate the fact that Ohtani gave the Angels an extra roster spot to play with?

WAR assumes that if the Angels had lost Ohtani the pitcher to injury, they would call up someone from the minors and have them take over those innings. Similarly, if the Angels lost Ohtani the hitter, they would probably promote the best of their bench hitters into Ohtani's customary DH role and call up someone from AAA to sit on the end of the bench. They couldn't actually do both. On the flip side, with a healthy Ohtani, the Angels can roster an extra "clubhouse influencer" or a defensive specialist or yet another reliever. That additional reliever might be a replacement-level pitcher, but can he soak up some garbage innings allowing the Angels to keep their good relievers a little fresher?

There are softer examples of this. Suppose that a team had a regular starting third baseman who was fully capable of handling shortstop and doing fine there. It's just that the team already happened to have a good shortstop. Now they have an interesting bit of flexibility. Knowing they already had built-in cover at shortstop, they could realistically look at a bench player who had a better bat and could play at third a time or two per week, but wasn't a good idea as a shortstop. Maybe that player isn't out there and available, and they end up signing a more traditional former shortstop who will hit .240 as their backup infielder. The third baseman might never step foot into the short spot, but the team had a broader range of options to pick from. There's value in not having your choices foreclosed before you have a chance to make them.

As baseball becomes more multi-positional and the position that you end up playing on a given day becomes less important than the spectrum of positions that you *can* play, we're going to need a new language to describe what players are capable of, rather than what position they end up playing. Those aren't always the same thing. How do you value something that a player could have done, but didn't need to?

FINALLY, WE COME to the story of why Austin Romine was starting the game for the Angels behind the plate. Regular Angels catchers Max Stassi and Kurt Suzuki had both contracted COVID-19 and were unable to play, and so Romine (and as we saw earlier, Chad Wallach) were called up to catch. The Angels also had Aaron Whitefield playing in center field and making his first ever MLB start so that Mike Trout could have (most of) the day off. Romine went 1-for-2 before being lifted for a pinch-hitter and Whitefield went 0-for-4.

The way that WAR defines "replacement level" comes from appearances like this. Romine and Whitefield weren't even in the majors a few weeks later, but they both got playing time in a major league uniform. MLB teams run through a lot of these types of players. Some of them stick around for longer than others, but they're the ones at the fringes of the roster. If someone can't play, these replacements are the ones who step in.

The term "replacement level" has developed an unfortunate shorthand meaning. Most people quickly assume that if a player is called up from AAA or signed off the waiver wire, they will perform at "replacement level." That's not how it works. Replacement level is supposed to approximate the *average* performance of all of those bench and part-time players. Like any average, there are some players who are above it and some who are below it. The ones who are a little better than average are usually the ones who stick around on the bench.

In 2022, for each of the three major WAR indices (Baseball Prospectus, Fangraphs, Baseball Reference), I looked to see, given a minimum of either 100 plate appearances or 30 innings pitched, how many total players functioned at or above replacement level.

Table 30. Number of players above replacement level, per team, 2022

WAR Index	Batters	Pitchers
Baseball Prospectus	13.4	13.2
FanGraphs	11.9	12.7
Baseball Reference	11.9	11.8

Baseball Prospectus is a little more lenient about where they set their replacement level, but we can see that among the players who got even semi-regular playing time, there's not really enough to even fill out the 26-member active rosters of all 30 teams, and teams go through so many more players than even that. In 2022, MLB teams sent an average of 28 batters to the plate and 29 pitchers to the mound over the course of the season.

Resetting our filters, Table 31 shows, for each of the major WAR indices, how many plate appearances and innings pitched were taken by players functioning *below* replacement level and how many WAR those players "contributed." Since they were all below replacement level, the number will be notably negative.

Table 31. Playing time and WAR for sub-replacement players, per team, 2022

WAR Index	Batter PA	Batter WAR	Pitcher IP	Pitcher WAR	Total WAR
Baseball Prospectus	595	−0.9	220	−1.5	−2.4
FanGraphs	1,147	−3.2	227	−2.3	−5.5
Baseball Reference	1,125	−3.6	317	−4.3	−7.9

Sub-replacement players take up a lot of playing time and can give away a lot of value while they do it. The players these numbers represent tend to the shuttle-riders who go from AAA to MLB and back a few times per year, and the "warm bodies" that teams call in when they have a rash of injuries to deal with. Exactly how much value they give away depends on which WAR index you look at, but taking the Fangraphs numbers in the middle, we see that it's a little more than five wins.

Suppose for a moment that a team could somehow find call-ups and waiver players who could hit as well as the last player on the bench on most teams and pitch as well as the last pitcher in the bullpen. They would recover those five wins of value. As some point of reference, a player who is five wins above replacement is usually an All-Star. It's not likely that teams could reclaim all of that territory, but if they could manage even some of it, the effect could be like signing a two-win player, whom you know as that solid, average everyday player that your team has.

The value comes from having fill-in players who aren't *quite* as awful as everyone else's. It's not glamorous, but it can make a big difference. Here is where another of our not-so-hidden-forces is lurking. *Smart teams think about the end of the bench.* They think even beyond the end of the bench into who their "depth signings" are. They focus on player development, not just for the prospects who make it onto the "Top 100" prospects list, but for the pitcher whom they'll need to handle a spot start in one end of a double-header in June or the bench bat who fills in for a game or two in center field when someone needs a day off.

In the off-season, it's the free agents who sign nine-figure contracts that get the attention of the baseball press. That's great if you cheer for a team that can afford one of those deals, but winning the battle of the bullpen, bench, and beyond gang isn't about money. Most of these players are either minor leaguers poised to make their debut or veterans who sign minor league deals hoping for another shot at the majors and the minimum salary. The teams that win this race are the ones who do their homework and can identify those tiny little flecks of gold.

WHAT IF WAR isn't the answer to every question in baseball? WAR is remarkably powerful in its ability to pull all the pieces of the game into one framework and to put everyone on the same scale. It takes into account context that "traditional" stats don't. It has the ability to incorporate new data and new ideas as they come along. That's what makes it the best single-number measure of a player's value. It will also never be perfect. When you try to mathematically model something as complex as baseball, you're never going to get it completely right.

I like to think of it as the beauty yet unseen in baseball. Art, in its many forms, is a way to express things that ultimately defy full expression. If someone creates a piece of visual art or writes a song about love or bravery or that contented feeling you get when your favorite pair of socks is in the drawer, it reveals some piece of the unexplainable. Sometimes, it brings an idea into being. As an "analytics guy," I think about data in a similar way. If I research some piece of the game of baseball and I discover some morsel of truth about it, then I've created something. It might not be profound, but I've brought an idea into being. It's just that instead of the paintbrush or interpretive dance, my medium is a spreadsheet. Some people like to write songs about baseball. I like to run regressions about it. The neat thing about WAR is that when we discover those pieces, we can update the formula to include them. We may never be able to fully understand everything going on in baseball, but we can draw closer to it.

There's a perfectly boring reason that measures like WAR exist. We want to model value in baseball as accurately as we can. Baseball is a game of limited resources and teams want to spend their resources in the ways that will best help them win. WAR is very good at picking out what's valuable and which players are good at those things. WAR is quite functional. It's also a bit of a group art project. If all you ever do is focus on getting to the right answer or worse, just assume that WAR has it all figured out, you miss out on the very necessary creative piece of the process. Every once in a while, you have to slow down your breathing and think about not just what you have, but the places where there is still beauty that we haven't yet found. In baseball analytics, it means appreciating the ways that the game is changing and the ways that our numbers, even the ones we're most proud of, might not be ready to deal with that change. It's okay. José Canseco and Abe Lincoln and the dinosaur will be there to give you some advice.

Chapter 11

Actively Stupid

I was up earlier than normal that day because I needed to be in my seat before the bell rang. I was 23 years old and this wasn't one of those anxiety dreams where you're suddenly back in grade school and not prepared for anything. This was real life and I was on a mission. I did my graduate studies at DePaul University in Chicago, and, as part of my training, I had been assigned to observe a boy who was receiving mental health services from our university's training clinic. His therapist wanted to know how things were going for him at school, and so for the first time in years, I was squeezing into a little desk.

The school served children who lived in one of Chicago's public housing communities, and while I knew that Chicago didn't invest a lot of money in either the school buildings or the students of this neighborhood, there was a surprise waiting for me when I got to the classroom. I identified the young boy I was supposed to observe and began making notes on the form that I was supposed to fill out. I wasn't really focused on the teacher, who began a lesson after the bell. In fact, it was two lessons. Midway through the hour, he asked the students to exchange books. I had been so busy with my task that I hadn't noticed that he was alternating between discussing prepositional phrases and solving for X. The reason he asked them to trade books was that there were only half as many math and grammar books as students, and so they had to take turns using them. To this day, that moment haunts me.

Solving the problems of inequality in education is well beyond the scope of this book, but it doesn't take a Ph.D. to figure this one out. How were the students supposed to learn the skills they'd need later in life when they literally didn't have enough books? The families these kids came from were mostly low-income and the kids had multiple stressors in their lives. If anyone should have gotten *more* resources devoted to them, it should have been them.

When people think about "stress" in life, they normally think about very impactful, *single* negative events, like the death of a loved one. There's another kind of stress that people experience, some more than others. Chronic stress is the constant, wearing stress of everyday life. If you live in a neighborhood where a lot of crime happens, you always have to be a little bit more vigilant to what's going on around you. If your family doesn't always have enough food, you always have to be thinking about whether or not you'll need to find something to eat. Even if nothing especially bad happens, it's the constant worry that gets you, and it gets you even if you don't fully realize in the moment that it's happening.

Researchers have shown that over time, it's those chronic stressors that cause the most problems. For the kids in the public housing community I worked with, it was an onslaught of them. Sadly, there was a lot of community violence. The buildings they lived in were crowded and poorly kept. There was a lot of noise. Sometimes the kids went to school hungry. The fact that no one bothered with making sure they had the proper resources in their schools was just another thing that they had to deal with. If for some reason you wanted to design an environment that would ensure failure, it would have been this.

FAST-FORWARD NINE YEARS. I was 32 and on an airplane bound for Orlando. I wasn't going to see an anthropomorphic mouse and his goofy friends; I was going to a conference where I would hang out with other people who shared my third fact of being mental health researchers. I appreciate a good airplane ride because it's one of the only times I have a few hours to myself to indulge in a good book. For that trip, I had packed *The Bullpen Gospels* by former major (and minor) league pitcher Dirk Hayhurst. Hayhurst's book didn't contain a lot of actual baseball. He was more interested in telling the story of what happened outside the white lines, and in that book, he focused on his time in the minor leagues.

There was a passage in the book that surprised me. For those who exclusively follow the majors and know the minor leagues only as the mysterious place where future major leaguers hone their skills, you might assume that minor leaguers are well-cared for. After all, they are professional athletes and MLB organizations have a vested interest in them becoming productive players. Hayhurst told a different story.

Minor leaguers make surprisingly low salaries—there have been lawsuits on the topic alleging that MLB is in violation of federal minimum wage labor laws—and until recently, teams paid little attention to the food their players were eating. Most players had to scrimp. Hayhurst painted an oddly bleak picture of players subsisting on a diet of plain pasta and peanut butter and hoping it lasted through the week—and that's when they could get to a grocery store. When on the road, they often ate the fast food being sold at whatever rest stop the team bus pulled into, because it was cheap, calorically dense, and available. For people whose entire livelihood revolves around keeping their bodies in top shape, this made no sense.

As I read more on the topic, I learned that minor leaguers often lived six players to a two-bedroom apartment. Low wages meant that they couldn't afford much. They did what they could and pooled their resources, but there are only so many property managers that will rent to you if they know you'll only be in town for six months and you have a job where you can be transferred to another city at any time. Players were sleeping on air mattresses or inflatable pool floaties. Sometimes, they skipped meals.

After reading Hayhurst's book, my head snapped back to that morning in Chicago. The minor leagues are a training ground where young players learn the skills that they will need to become big leaguers. Why were teams not giving them every resource that they could? Why were they playing hunger games with minor leaguers?

IN CHAPTER 8, I asked the question of whether analytics had ruined baseball and suggested that the real culprit wasn't that teams were trying to find ways to win, but that everything had become an exercise in efficiency. From an asset valuation point of view, minor leaguers are an expense. You hope that some of them turn into productive major leaguers, but history tells us that the majority of them will never wear a big-league uniform. Most of them are there to provide live batting practice to the prospects who actually do have a chance.

Since the days of *Moneyball*, it's been taken as an article of faith that the best way to run a major league team is to look for "market inefficiencies." It isn't that the asset management model is wrong, but there is a side effect of it that doesn't get talked about. MLB front offices are now overrun with people who are used to thinking about things in terms of "business cases." When I've spoken to "friends" who work in MLB front offices, they talk a good game. They want to help minor league players along their way. Those are the assets. You want them to appreciate. They get that if paying players more or improving conditions for them would eventually produce better major leaguers and the cost-benefit ratio works out, it's worth looking into. But for the longest time, very little was done, and minor leaguers were still scrounging for housing and food. There were eventually some teams who were quietly doing more, but it took until the 2022 season for MLB teams to agree to provide guaranteed housing to their minor leaguers. It made me wonder whether anyone on duty had any idea about how human development works.

I don't mean that as (too big of) a dig. When you've studied business and finance, it's not that you don't understand that the effects of stress are "a thing." It's that you probably understand it *vaguely*. I've sometimes wondered what would happen if teams hired a director of health and well-being, someone in charge of ensuring that the players in an MLB organization, majors *and* minors, were eating and sleeping as well as possible. The potential benefits are obvious, but the more important word in that title is "director." It's one thing in a front office to have someone in the corner saying, "Hey, six players in a two-bedroom apartment sleeping on air mattresses is a bad idea." It's another to elevate that to the level of "something we need a director for." Directors have a budget. Directors have staff. Directors get invited to meetings.

There's a concept in public health called "Health in All Policies," which is exactly what it sounds like. When a government or organization makes decisions about anything—even things that aren't directly health-related—it should consider the policy's impact on the health of the community. Zoning codes that promote "active living" in a neighborhood mean people spend more time walking and less time in cars. It doesn't seem at first glance that zoning laws would have an impact on health. They do, but you have to connect the dots to get there.

The baseball version of Health in All Policies could be similarly powerful. If a team wanted to switch bus charter companies for their AA affiliate, there could be a voice in the room who says, "Hey, that company uses the really small buses. The players will be cramped up while trying to catch some sleep, and sleep is important. I realize that this new company is cheaper, but it's worth the money to spring for the extra space so they can get some shut-eye." That's the sort of thing you don't immediately think about if you're just trying to get a contract done on the cheap. If you center wellness and health in your decisions, you end up with healthier, happier, and hopefully better players. To get there, you need someone in the room who can pick out the places where a seemingly innocuous decision might have an impact far beyond what teams might have considered and that might be worth the extra money. That person has to be at the table, figuratively and literally.

You also want someone who can do more than just react to circumstances. A director isn't a worker bee. They should have a few ideas of their own to proactively promote health within the organization and should be able to monitor and make adjustments to what's going on. They'll probably also have to show the business case for their proposals. MLB teams aren't charities. The problem with health promotion is that it doesn't always get results right away. The bet you make is that over time, investing money in food and housing gradually makes things better for players and that it eventually shows in their results on the field. That might take three to five years—an eternity in a front office. The person in that director's chair would have to know how to show measurable progress along the way.

The asset-value model is one of the very much not-at-all-hidden forces that shapes baseball and whether we like it or not, it is the dominant model in how MLB teams are run. *To get something done in MLB, you must speak the language of investment.* In good news, we can make the business case that improving conditions for minor leaguers is likely to have a positive return.

FIRST, WE NEED to talk about why poor working conditions for minor leaguers are a *problem* and not just a fact of life. Players from the United States and Canada are usually drafted either out of high school (at 18 years old) or their junior or senior year of college (at 21 or 22 years old). Players from outside the United States and Canada are commonly (ahem) officially signed at the age of 16. The median age for an MLB debut hovers around 24 years old. There's a lot to learn in that intermezzo. Players are growing physically, but there's also a lot of mental work to do in becoming a major league player. There's a reason that they call it player *development*.

There's a name for the condition that minor leaguers find themselves in when they are worried about where their next meal is coming from. Food insecurity is not the same thing as hunger, though they are obviously related. The problem isn't necessarily deprivation. There might be food to place into your mouth and chew, but it might all be junk food. There might be a $10 bill in your wallet today to go to Chipotle and buy a burrito, but tomorrow is another day. If you buy that burrito today, can you make it to the end of the week? It's not the lack of food that's the problem. It's the worry.

This is a well-known problem in the world beyond baseball, and one that has drawn a lot of attention from researchers and public health professionals. Food insecurity has been linked to both physical and mental health problems. On the physical side, it's associated with obesity. When they have to eat what's available and don't know what tomorrow will bring, people often load up on empty calories because those tend to be plentiful and cheap. That changes the body's metabolic processes as it attempts to cope with an unhealthy diet.

Food insecurity also increases the risk of depression, anxiety, substance use disorders, and suicidal ideation. There's evidence that it leads to higher levels of risk-taking behaviors, the kind that can put you in the hospital. That last part is particularly important. Risk-taking behaviors are controlled by a part of the brain known as the prefrontal cortex. It's the part of the brain that sizes up the risks and benefits in a situation and tells you that your harebrained idea might not be the best course of action. It's also the part of the brain involved in things like pattern recognition and learning. If food insecurity is messing with the prefrontal cortex, then that's a major issue for people who are trying to learn to be big leaguers.

Studies of college students—now we're getting into the same age bracket as many of our minor leaguers—show that food insecurity is related to lower academic performance (i.e., GPA), even if you statistically control for their high school grades. While our players aren't majoring in chemistry or philosophy, the minors are for learning new skills. If food insecurity affects someone's ability to learn in community college, it's probably doing the same at curveball college. This is not just "roughing it" for fun, so that when you get to the majors, you can laugh about how much you had to overcome. This is four or five years of actively doing harm to the most important part of the talent pool in an organization.

The housing question is another one where the science is pretty clear. Crowded housing conditions means close quarters, and some people really need their personal space. It also means that you have four or five roommates, some of whom are also in precarious financial positions, but on whom you are counting to make the rent. If one of them slips up, that's a problem, and you have to worry about it all month. Research tells us that people who live in crowded conditions often end up sleeping less. It can be noisy and if someone else is a night owl, it can be hard to find that dark, quiet place that a lot of people need to fall asleep. If you don't have enough money for a bed or a mattress, it can be hard to get comfortable.

As the father of five kids (fact four), I can personally vouch for the effects of having a few sleepless nights, but people don't often realize the impact that even a moderate reduction in sleep can have. Most adults need seven or eight hours per night. What happens if you get six? It feels mostly like a full night of sleep, but eventually your body knows the difference. In fact, after about two weeks of this sort of sleep pattern, some of the effects are the same as if the person had stayed up all night. Concentration becomes much harder. People miss things and are slower to react. For someone who's trying to learn some very high-level skills and react to 98 mph projectiles, that's not a great combination. That's to say nothing about the fact that these are people who make their living through great physical exertion. The body needs time to rest, heal, and lay down new neural pathways in the brain to code for all the skills that it learned that day. Sleep is the most important workout that an athlete does. It's an interesting decision to place players in a situation where sleep is hard to come by.

For some players, there's also the stress of living in a new country and acclimating to a new culture. The majority of players in affiliated baseball born outside the United States come from countries where the primary language is Spanish. It's hard enough to learn to be an adult. Now try doing it in a place where you don't speak the dominant language, at 19, and in a league where your team might not have a Spanish-speaking coach on staff. What if the reason that some players don't come back next year is that while they could hack it, only about a quarter of their teammates (and none of their coaches) even spoke their language? You might be in a city where there isn't a big concentration of Spanish-speaking residents. What if the realities of being that far from home caught up with you? What if you might have had a chance at MLB if you stuck with it, but when you thought about spending a few more years chasing that dream, it just wasn't what you wanted out of life? We can see that very thing happening in the data.

Figure 35. Percentage of players born outside the United States/Canada, by level, 2005–2019

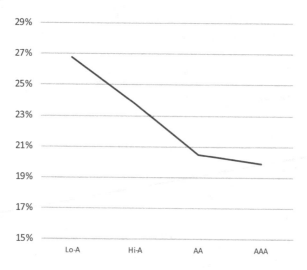

The percentage of players born outside the United States and Canada goes down by a couple of points at each level along the minor league journey. There's no reason to believe that players from outside the United States are more or less talented overall than their American-born teammates, but they are more likely to "wash out" at the end of every year. We can even do a more sophisticated analysis and control for things like how good a season the player had, and the effect is still there. In fact, for players born inside the United States, age and performance are the best predictors of whether a player will wash out. That makes sense. If you're not good or if you're getting "too old" to be considered a prospect, you won't be asked to come back. That link isn't as strong for players born outside the United States. More of them leave, especially early in their minor league careers, and even a few whose performance would usually get an invitation back for another year. Clearly, something is going on. If teams want a market inefficiency, providing good support for player acculturation might be a good start.

WHEN THE HUMAN body is under stress, it produces more of the chemical cortisol. Cortisol can be useful in the body. One of its jobs is to stimulate the production of adrenalin during dangerous situations. This is the well-known "fight or flight" response, and it's a great system if a large predator is headed your way. The problem is that when you're constantly under low-level stress, your body is constantly producing low levels of cortisol. The fight or flight system was never meant to do that.

Cortisol is pretty easy to study. You can measure it with a simple cotton swab to the inside of someone's cheek. You can inject it into someone to artificially change their levels of cortisol short-term and see how they react. We know a lot about it and how it impacts human behavior. The results aren't good. Memory and learning of all kinds seem to be negatively affected, not to the point where a person loses the ability to learn, but to the point where they can't learn *quite* as much as someone whose body isn't hopped up on cortisol. It's like trying to have an important conversation in a noisy room. You might be able to get through the conversation, but it's harder than it has to be and there will be times when you miss something. Over one day, the thing that you miss might not make a difference, but over five years in the minors, it becomes a slow bleed of what could have been, but never was. If you prevent the stress, you reduce the cortisol levels and reduce the noise in the room.

It's odd. Minor leaguers are literally the future of the organization. I had always assumed that making sure they had every advantage in developing their baseball skills would be a given. There are mistakes where it's clear that someone was close, but not exactly right. Then there's using a sledgehammer instead of a screwdriver. This is the latter. Major league teams have been using an actively stupid way to structure their developmental programs. Why would anyone build a classroom next to an anxiety factory?

I STILL NEED to make a business case and show the proof. Fortunately, baseball gives us a way to test out the theory. For players who enter MLB through the Amateur Draft, they are given a signing bonus, and the sizes of those bonuses are widely reported. First round picks are usually handed seven-figure checks. By the 10th round, you might get a thousand dollars and a free hat. The players who get the multi-million dollar bonuses have a reservoir of funds from which to draw during their minor league adventure. If they take care of their money, they don't need to worry too much about where their next burrito is coming from.

Let's stop for a moment, because there's an obvious elephant in the room. The size of a player's signing bonus isn't random. It's most correct to say that it's a reflection of *perceptions* of the player's potential on draft day, but if we believe that MLB teams have some idea what they're doing, then we have to accept that if players with bigger bonuses are more likely to make the majors, then maybe teams knew that talent was there all along. Or do we?

Minor league stats aren't always great indicators. Sometimes teams will ask their players to work on specific skills in games, rather than just play to the best of their abilities. A power hitter might be asked to work on contact skills and not hit the 35 HR that they're capable of, because the team knows the power is already there. We will have to live with this limitation. I started with draft bonus data from 2000 to 2015 and minor league data through 2019. The lack of a minor league season in 2020 due to the COVID-19 pandemic made it difficult to research things further.

The first thing I looked at was whether draft bonuses told us anything about players when they started their journeys. For batters, I used OPS (which is on-base percentage plus slugging, an easily calculatable measure that's a pretty good proxy for hitting talent) at Low-A. I normalized it by dividing it by the league's overall OPS, which produces a statistic known as OPS+. Some minor leagues have a large number of hitters' parks, and this is a way to make sure that we're crediting the hitter, and not the park. Draft bonus was significantly associated with OPS+, but not strongly. Bigger bonuses likely meant a bigger bat, but there's a lot of "yeah, but not always" in there as well.

Next, I looked at whether signing bonus predicted whether a player would "pop" once promoted. We expect that a batter who hits "about average" at Double-A will probably reach "about average" at Triple-A after a little bit of adjustment, but sometimes, players move up and break out well beyond what we once thought that they were. When we talk about statistics, we often look at "on average" and "across the league" but human development doesn't always follow gently sloping lines. Sometimes, you finally pick up some little trick and it changes everything. When those breakouts happen, they are immensely valuable to an MLB organization. Think of the light-hitting infielder who suddenly goes from hitting .240 to .290 and no one saw it coming.

I took all cases in which a player was promoted a level from one year to the next. I limited the sample to those cases where players had an OPS+ of at least 95 in year one. The reason for that limitation is that a player who goes from a 62 OPS+ to a 74 is still a well-below average hitter in the minors. Clearly, they made some strides, but they're still not likely to be a useful MLB player in the future. The math here starts to get a little gory, but I looked to see whether signing bonus predicted the chances that a player would break out. (For the initiated, a logistic regression was involved.) The answer was yes (but barely) for promotions from Low-A to High-A, but not for High-A to Double-A and not for Double-A to Triple-A.

Signing bonuses aren't great predictors of where players will start at Low-A and they aren't great predictors of breakouts. They also aren't great predictors of whether someone will eventually make the majors and do anything useful once there. Signing bonuses aren't completely devoid of information, but they aren't the clear signals that we might hope for. The careful reader will note that I've been looking only at batters so far. I re-ran that entire suite of analyses for pitchers and I could rewrite the last few hundred words and barely change anything other than the word "batters" to "pitchers" and "OPS" to "ERA."

I want to stop here and suggest that the data are pointing us toward something: humility. People like to think that they can predict the future, but it isn't that easy. Not all minor leaguers are going to become major league quality players, but the data suggest that even MLB organizations aren't always sure who's who. It makes sense to set up an environment where as many of them as possible will have a chance to succeed.

November 2, 2013—AFL East at AFL West (All-Star Game)

AFL East	AB	R	H	RBI	AFL West	AB	R	H	RBI
Ramsey, lf	2	0	1	0	DeShields Jr., lf	2	0	0	0
Williams, cf	2	0	2	1	Romero, lf	2	2	2	3
Goodwin, cf-lf	5	0	1	0	Naquin, dh	4	1	1	0
Bryant, 3b	4	1	1	0	Buxton, cf	4	1	1	1
Cron, 1b	4	0	1	0	Moran, 3b	2	0	2	0
Lindsey, 2b	1	0	0	0	Cecchini, 3b	2	1	1	1
Travis, ph–2b	2	0	1	0	Bonafácio, rf	2	0	1	0
Piscotty, dh	2	0	1	0	Rodríguez, rf	2	0	0	0
Parker, ph-dh	2	0	0	0	Seager, ss	3	0	0	1
Soler, rf	1	0	1	0	Semien, ss	2	0	0	0
Almora Jr., rf	2	0	0	0	Hedges, c	3	0	0	0
O'Brien, c	2	0	0	0	Alfaro, c	1	0	0	0
Nieto, c	1	1	0	0	Nicholas, 1b	4	2	3	2
Russell, ss	2	0	0	0	Betts, 2b	1	1	0	0
Hanson, ss	2	0	0	0	Rosario, 2b	2	1	1	0

AFL East — 000 000 110   2 9 2
AFL West — 002 202 12x   9 12 0

2B—Williams (1); 3B—Piscotty (1), Naquin (1); HR—Nicholas 2 (2; 4th inning, off Bedrosian, 1 on; 7th inning, off Familia, 0 on), Romero 2 (2; 6th inning off Montgomery, 1 on; 8th inning off Knebel, 0 on), Cecchini (1, 8th inning, off Barrett, 0 on); HBP—Nieto (1, by Bassitt); SH—DeShields Jr. (1); SB—Buxton (1), Betts (1); CS—Goodwin (1), Ramsey (1); DP—East 1 (Hanson-Travis-Cron), West 1 (Hedges-Seager); E- Bryant 2 (2); WP— Bedrosian (1); LOB—East 9, West 9; T—2:47; A—6,529

AFL East	IP	H	R	ER	BB	SO
Sanchez	2	2	0	0	1	1
Crick, L (0–1)	1	2	2	1	1	0
Bedrosian	1	1	2	2	1	1
Stroman	1	1	0	0	1	2
Montgomery	1	3	2	2	1	1
Familia	1	1	1	1	0	0
Knebel	0.2	1	1	1	0	1
Barrett	0.1	1	1	1	0	1

AFL West	IP	H	R	ER	BB	SO
Meyer, W (1–0)	3	3	0	0	1	3
Rodriguez, H (1)	1	0	0	0	1	0
Giles	1	1	0	0	1	0
Sampson	1	1	0	0	0	1
Bassitt	1	1	1	1	0	0
Garcia	1	2	1	1	0	0
Goforth	0.2	0	0	0	0	0
Dufek	0.1	1	0	0	0	0

THIS IS THE box score from the 2013 Arizona Fall League "Fall Stars" Game. The AFL is a cooperative developmental league that MLB holds at Spring Training sites in Arizona each autumn after the regular minor league seasons are over. Each team sends a few players from their farm system, often their top prospects, who then form combined teams for a little after-school competition. This Fall Stars game, like most All-Star games, was more about the exhibition (and marketability) of having all the "good" players on the field at once, and less about the game it produced (a 9–2 snoozer).

Looking through this box score, we can see a flashpoint in time. We see players who a decade later became stars and starters, some who became role players, and some who never put on a major league uniform. Even the ones who make it to this level sometimes trip and fall before they have a chance to make their mark. We know what happened to Mookie Betts and Kris Bryant, but what about the names in this box score that you don't recognize?

There are going to be players who overcame the obstacles and made the majors despite being 10th round picks. The problem is that we never interview the ones who *didn't* make it. If all you ever study are the players who do make it, then success sounds easy. Let's find the ones who didn't and ask *why not?* If minor league life really is filled with obstacles to success, maybe we could go knock a few of them over?

Returning to our minor league data set, I found hitters who had 250 PA at one level, and then in the next year were promoted upward, where they again logged at least 250 PA. I controlled for OPS+ in year one and looked to see whether draft bonus size was associated with how the player did the next year. I looked at all rungs on the minor league ladder (promotion from Low-A to High-A, High-A to Double-A, and Double-A to Triple-A). At each step, players with an extra zero in their signing bonuses (for example, moving from $10,000 to $100,000) had a one to two point advantage in how their OPS+ moved (i.e., 99 to 100 OPS+) after the transition. Those with a bigger bonus kept a little bit more of their performance from the year before.

There are two possible explanations for this, and both might be a little true. One is that a big signing bonus is a signal that the team always knew that the player was "built" for moving up the ranks, while others would flounder. Given what we saw about how signing bonuses don't seem to relate that well to other measures of talent or developmental potential, it would be a little surprising if signing bonus was suddenly doing its job as a signifier. The other possibility is that this is the skill bleed that we know happens in other areas of life to people who have to spend a lot of time worrying.

For pitchers, this skill bleed effect doesn't show up as clearly, but something more insidious does. We can look at the rates at which players "wash out" of affiliated baseball. In theory, the only factors that should play into the decision for a player not to be asked back should be performance, or perhaps a player getting a little old (and by "old," I mean the geriatric age of 27) to be considered a candidate for further improvement. We can control for both of those, but signing bonus is still a predictor. There might be some players who are leaving before their performance says that they should. Maybe someone washed out before they could break out because they ran out of money.

Even if chronic anxiety and financial stress isn't the entire story, there's a pretty good case that it's mixed in there somewhere, and given what we've seen, it's probably a bigger part of the story than we'd like to admit. The idea that deprivation builds "character" is mostly survivorship bias mixed with some toxic cultural messages. Congratulations on "making it." What if 10 others could have made it if we hadn't made their lives so hard?

The point of spending money on minor leaguers isn't what it buys. Minor leaguers don't have to be millionaires, but there's a threshold below which people have to worry about basic needs. If you listen to minor leaguers tell their stories through the media (mostly anonymously), you'll find that they worry about eating, they worry about having a literal place to sleep, they worry about making ends meet in the off-season. And they worry about the future. If there's a business case for spending money to improve minor league working conditions, the point of the money is the worry that it can get rid of.

IN THE LAST chapter, we saw that MLB teams end up employing a lot of players (an average of 28 batters and 29 pitchers per team in 2022). Some of the extras were plucked from the waiver wire, and some were veteran "depth signings" who were willing to hang out at Triple-A in the hopes of that one last shot in MLB, but a lot of them were players who had been drafted by the organization and were being called on to fill a role.

Between 2018 and 2022, a total of 1,288 players made their MLB debut, and 73 percent of them came through the Rule 4 Draft system, which governs the players from the United States and Canada. Of those draftees, about one third of them were drafted after the 10th round and likely got a bonus that had four digits in it. In those same years, 5 percent of plate appearances were taken by batters who had received a signing bonus of less than $10,000 and who were in the first 250 PA of their career. For pitchers, the number was 7 percent.

A small, but important amount of playing time is being handled by players who had very little financial cushion to work with as they worked their way up through the minors and are just emerging from the minor league meatgrinder. They haven't yet really had a chance for that major league minimum salary to kick in (as if someone could quickly undo five years of living hand-to-mouth). How well those players have developed is going to have a direct impact on a team's fortunes.

We saw a moment ago that the skill bleed associated with a smaller bonus was about one point of OPS+ over the course of a year, and about five points over the course of a player's journey from low-A to MLB. It's the difference between being a league-average hitter (100 OPS+) and 95 percent of a league-average hitter (95 OPS+). Both of those players will probably stick at the major league level, but one could have been more, and the driving force behind that gap seems to be the size of the signing bonus, and more accurately, the financial cushion it would have provided. Again, the math here gets a little gory, but given how many plate appearances these low-bonus/early-career players are responsible for, that might be a few extra hits over the course of a year that a team loses, enough to push a game one way or the other. That's just assuming that whatever damage was done by the minor league lifestyle simply disappears when the player steps to bat for the 251st time.

When I looked a little deeper, I didn't find evidence that if low-bonus players did stick in the majors, there was any sort of "catch-up" effect once they got to MLB. Maybe the low-bonus players that make it to MLB are contributing, but you can't undo what's come before. The effects of minor league deprivation could last for years. So could the benefits of fixing it.

ALLOW ME TO introduce Matthew. The Matthew Effect is named after a passage in the Christian Gospels, which says, "For whoever has will be given more, and they will have an abundance. Whoever does not have, even what they have will be taken from them." (Matthew 25:29, NIV). It's often shortened to "The rich get richer and the poor get poorer." The term "Matthew Effect" was coined in 1968 by researcher Robert Merton, and the effect pops up in a number of interesting places.

The most famous example applied to sport is the study of ice hockey. Canadian psychologist Roger Barnsley noted that players in the NHL (and other professional hockey leagues) were much more likely to have birthdays in the early months of the calendar year. Canadian youth hockey programs commonly had a cut-off date of January 1 for deciding what age group a young person was in. For example, someone who turned 9 on January 2 would have to wait 364 days to qualify for the nine-year-old division, but once there, would be nearly 10 years old. A young person born on December 31st would enter that same league having just turned nine. The older child would have almost a year's advantage in physical and cognitive development and would probably be seen as a "better" player and would be given more opportunities for skill development. Over several years, because of these extra opportunities, conferred by nothing more than their birthday and an arbitrary cut-point, they'd be more likely to end up as the better trained hockey players. What begins as a small and random advantage can compound on itself. That's the Matthew Effect.

We see something like this happen in minor league baseball. Some players are given large signing bonuses and are able to blunt the effects of the poor conditions of minor league life. Signing bonuses don't do a great job predicting initial performance, nor do they do a good job predicting which players will have a big breakout, and they only do a mediocre job of predicting who will eventually make it to MLB. They do a good job predicting two things. One is how much skill a player will bleed away on their way through the minors. The other is that even controlling for performance, a player with a bigger signing bonus is more likely to be promoted and get an opportunity at the next level.

MLB teams have set up the minor leagues to be a toxic sludge of chronic stress that players must wade through. A few of them have a way out of the sludge. Should we be surprised when the big signing bonus guys end up in the majors? Maybe the talent was there all along, but what if the ghost in the machine is baseball's version of the Matthew Effect? If you invest more resources and give more opportunities to one player, but not another, those resources themselves are eventually going to make a difference. Not everyone is going to make the majors and some players will beat the long odds no matter what, but everyone drafted is a gifted athlete, and sometimes people will surprise you if you give them the chance.

SUPPOSE THAT A pitcher on the double-A team is messing around with some slider grips and wants to try something in a side session. The obvious next step is to bring over the pitching coach and ask, "Hey, can you watch this and see what you think?" What if your team didn't have a pitching coach? That sounds like a mistake to even ask the question. What kind of baseball team wouldn't have a pitching coach, and at that, a very carefully selected one? Pitching is serious business, literally. You want players to have access to all the resources that they need to hone their pitching skills, including mentorship from a good teacher of the craft.

If someone came to the front office and said, "Hey, we somehow forgot to hire some pitching coaches for the minor league teams, can we get a budget allocation to do that?" it would get approved in about five minutes, and four of those would be because someone was in the bathroom. No one would ever think of saying, "Do we really need them? I mean, our tinkering pitcher might just throw a side session and see how it feels and maybe discover something nice without anyone's help."

As someone who's both a researcher of children's development (fact three) and a dad (fact four), that's what all of this sounds like to me. Humans learn when they are put into an environment where they can focus on learning. When you build a structure that makes them worry about everything else, the brain has to devote resources to thinking about survival.

Finding good players who are "cost-controlled" is an obsession in front offices, and from an asset management perspective, it makes sense. When you draft and develop minor leaguers, you get to pay them less than the prevailing open-market price for talent. It's generally accepted that teams will pay between $8 and $10 million on the free agent market for a "win" of value. In the language of WAR, that means a player who is projected to be better in ways that will raise the team's expectations by one win. Eventually, if you get (or prevent) a few extra hits that someone else wouldn't have gotten, one of them will push across the run that wins you a game. Teams don't get to "cost-controlled" without some investment. You need to scout those players, pay signing bonuses, and then operate a minor league system. Even accounting for all of that, the overall cost per win of a cost-controlled player was about half that of a free agent player.

In Chapter 10, we saw that teams employ a lot of players who are below "replacement level." Many of them are these same minor leaguers who are called up to "do a job." They might be small assignments, but there are a lot of them. It's a good idea to have a pool of players who can handle those jobs and can be slightly less awful than everyone else's pool. That could provide a very large boost to a team.

This is where we get down to raw numbers. Minor leaguers make between $10,000 and $15,000 per year. If teams were to simply raise each player's wages to $50,000—enough that they would not need to worry about things like food and wouldn't have to split their time in the off-season working at Target, rather than working on getting to Target Field—it would cost the team somewhere around $4 million in new spending. Teams could also opt to provide direct support around things like meals and off-season training. Players wouldn't have to worry as much. If that turned back the skill bleed and made those low-bonus players a little bit better, then a team could easily clear enough value to justify the cost. The next decade will belong to the teams that embrace a not-so-hidden force in the game: *Understanding how human growth and development works is a strategic advantage.*

THE FIRST QUESTION out of anyone's mouth when any big change is proposed—and we're talking about big changes in how MLB teams approach player development and, more importantly, a lot of money—is, "Are you sure?" Humans want certainty before they change anything. The honest answer is "Pretty sure." It's the honest answer to just about anything. I suppose if the price for something is a few million dollars, "Are you sure?" is a reasonable question. That money is going to come from the payroll budget. There's no other area from which a team could reasonably re-direct that much money. There's a pretty good case to be made that money invested in minor league living conditions goes further than in free agency, and it's not like free agency is without its risk. There, you're dealing with players who are older, often on "the wrong side of 30," and all your risk is tied up in a couple of individuals.

Spending that money on minor leaguers works differently. For one, the money gets spread out over a hundred or so players. Some will see a great deal of benefit. For some, this won't move the needle. From a major league roster construction point of view, a team doesn't need *everyone* to benefit. There are only so many spots on an MLB roster, and teams can simply select from the ones who did get a boost. It's a way to diversify risk, while skimming only the upside.

Then there's the objection that's going to be hardest to argue against, because it's not based in reality. It's the idea that improving conditions for minor leaguers will somehow deprive them of some key formative experience. Minor Leaguers need to be "hungry for it" (literally?) They shouldn't be "coddled." Then, there's the ever-popular, "If I had to go through it, so should they."

Deprivation isn't a virtue and suffering doesn't produce character. It produces cortisol. There's a difference between surviving deprivation and overcoming *adversity*. In Chapter 7, we briefly talked about the concept of "scaffolding," borrowed from the fields of child development and education. You provide an environment in which the child can approach a problem. You begin by teaching the basic principles, and then as the student masters those, build the "scaffold" higher from the base you've created to teach more advanced skills. It's a measured process. You most certainly don't just say, "Here, figure it out." You support the student as you walk along together.

Learning to become a major league player is like that. It's a gradual, multi-step process that's hard to accomplish, and there will be plenty of adversity along the way. It takes showing up every day ready to learn and pushing yourself even on the bad days. Or bad weeks. It means working on your weaknesses. It means being willing to listen. It means taking extra grounders. You'll get plenty of chances to see how players handle adversity. At the same time, you make a pact with the players. If you're willing to go all-in on building yourself into the best player possible, we are going to create an environment where you can build that scaffold.

The payoff might not be as flashy as a free agent signing. It's a thousand tiny daily victories that add up a little bit at a time. It might take the form of a spot starter who gets called up to start the second game of a double-header, manages to get through five decent innings, and is barely seen again. That's still valuable, and you can only get to that value if you understand the human side of the game at a deep level. At the very least, it means not being actively stupid about development.

Chapter 12

Five More Facts

The hardest thing to do in life is to write your own five facts speech. The words eventually write themselves, but you have to build the five facts that go in each of the spots. We spend a lot of time as a culture telling young people, "You can be anything you want." Sometimes that's true, but we never tell them the other part. At some point, you have to pick something and there's no going back in time to see what would have happened if things had been a little different. The hard part is the day that you wake up and realize you *are* a mental health researcher from Atlanta with five kids. Whether you chose that identity purposefully or accidentally, you have to hope that when you get to the other side, you like all five of your facts. I grew up in Cleveland. I'm from Atlanta. I'm a researcher in children's mental health. I'm married with five amazing kids. I love baseball. What do you really know of me from those five facts?

Over time, everyone's five facts change bit by bit, even the ones that don't seem like they'd be up for negotiation. I used to introduce myself as someone who was *from* Cleveland and lived in Atlanta. One day, I heard myself saying that I grew up in Cleveland and am *from* Atlanta. At some point, you realize that who you are has changed even if you can't pinpoint the moment when.

November 2, 2021—Atlanta at Houston (World Series, Game 6)

Atlanta	AB	R	H	RBI	Houston	AB	R	H	RBI
Rosario, lf	4	1	0	0	Altuve, 2b	4	0	1	0
Soler, dh	3	2	1	3	Brantley, lf-rf	4	0	2	0
Freeman, 1b	4	1	2	2	Correa, ss	4	0	1	0
Riley, 3b	4	0	0	0	Álvarez, dh	4	0	1	0
Duvall, cf-rf	4	0	1	0	Gurriel, 1b	4	0	0	0
Pederson, rf	0	0	0	0	Tucker, rf-cf	3	0	0	0
Heredia, cf	0	0	0	0	Bregman, 3b	3	0	0	0
Albies, 2b	3	2	2	0	Siri, cf	2	0	0	0
d'Arnaud, c	4	0	0	0	Díaz, ph-lf	1	0	0	0
Swanson, ss	4	1	1	2	Maldonado, c	2	0	1	0
					Gonzalez, ph	1	0	0	0
					Stubbs, c	0	0	0	0

Atlanta — 003 030 100   7 7 1
Houston — 000 000 000   0 6 0

2B—Freeman (3); HR—Soler (3, off L. Garcia, 3rd inning, 2 on), Swanson (2, off Javier, 5th inning, 1 on), Freeman (5, off Stanek, 7th inning, 0 on); DP—Atlanta 2 (Fried-Swanson-Freeman; Albies-Swanson-Freeman); E—Fried (1); LOB—Atlanta 3, Houston 5; WP—Javier (1); T—3:22; A—42,868

Atlanta	IP	H	R	ER	BB	SO
Fried, W (2–2)	6	4	0	0	0	6
Matzek	2	1	0	0	0	4
Smith	1	1	0	0	0	0

Houston	IP	H	R	ER	BB	SO
L. Garcia, L (1–3)	2.2	2	3	3	1	3
Raley	0.1	0	0	0	0	0
Javier	1.1	1	2	2	1	3
Taylor	0.1	1	1	1	1	0
Maton	1.1	2	0	0	0	1
Stanek	1	1	1	1	0	2
Pressly	1	0	0	0	0	0
Y. Garcia	1	0	0	0	0	0

UNTIL THIS NOVEMBER night, I had never lived in a city that was celebrating a major sports championship. This technically isn't true. I lived in Chicago in 2005 when the White Sox won the World Series, but I lived on the North Side. The next day, I might as well have told everyone that the Texas Rangers had won. It would have gotten the same response. That night, as Yuli Gurriel's ninth inning ground ball was picked by Dansby Swanson and then thrown across the diamond into the outstretched glove of Freddie Freeman, Atlanta won the 2021 World Series, and its first championship since 1995. I was happy. It surprised me how happy I was. This was, after all, the team that had broken my heart when David Justice hit *that* home run off Jim Poole, but it was the moment I realized I was from Atlanta.

A lot had happened since 1995. I turned 20, then 30, then 40. I moved from Cleveland to Chicago, then back to Cleveland, and then Atlanta. I found a career and then realized I needed a different one. I became a husband and then a father to one, then two, then three, then five kids. The one constant was my love of baseball. When the changes came, baseball was a friend that marked the good ones and consoled me during the tough ones. Now my friend is trying to write its own five facts. It's a new ballgame. I suppose after a century and a half, you have to decide what you want to be when you grow up.

After the 2021 season, franchise owners locked players out after the collective bargaining agreement between the two had expired. The labor negotiations that followed centered around who would get what portion of the large pile of money that comes into the bank accounts of MLB and its 30 teams. There was a side plot though. They were also talking about what *the* game of baseball would look like afterward. Coming into the 2022 season, MLB implemented the universal designated hitter, ending the run of pitchers batting in the National League that had begun in 1876. A year later, MLB implemented a pitch clock and a ban on infield shifting. Baseball is an evolving game, and MLB has not been shy about its willingness to overturn a few traditions. The adjective that you choose to describe that evolution is a bit of a baseball Rorschach test. Ed from Lakewood is probably out there right now complaining about all of it.

Being on the "wrong side" of 40 now, I have a little more sympathy than I used to for the people who don't want MLB to mess with *the* game of baseball. I think that the moment you stop wanting baseball to change is the day that the last player who is older than you are retires, and it usually happens around 40. For me, that moment wasn't exactly glorious. In Game 4 of the 2019 World Series, Washington Nationals reliever Fernando Rodney had a disastrous seventh inning. After Tanner Rainey had walked two Astros, Rodney relieved him and gave up a single to Michael Brantley and a grand slam to Alex Bregman. After walking the bases back to loaded, Rodney departed the game. I didn't realize Rodney was the last man standing when it was happening, but when I looked it up later, I needed a moment to compose myself. If there's a bit of sad wisdom that comes with age, it's understanding that sooner or later, the world you once knew fades away. If there's something that I hope people have realized through this book, it's that, like it or not, baseball is a changing game. Change is inevitable.

HOW DID WE get here? Through this book, I've tried to highlight some of the forces that have molded the game into its modern form. Some of them will continue to slowly shape the game. Over time, players have gotten bigger and stronger. They throw faster and they hit the ball harder. What was once a game of the legs has become a game of the arms. Some of those changes were choices. MLB, for entirely obvious reasons, has grown its brand internationally. That's brought in more fans and more dollars but also more talent. The result for MLB as a business has been excellent, but it's had an impact on the field too. The most important ratio in the game is the amount of talent currently playing baseball compared to the number of roster spots available, and right now, there's a lot of talent fighting for a stagnant number of roster spots. One of the major questions that MLB will have to answer in the next decade is the matter of expansion. As the talent pool continues to grow, there are only two ways to create more roster spots. MLB already added a 26th space on the active roster.

Expansion might happen, and it might provide 52 new jobs for 52 players who would otherwise be on the edges of the game, but eventually the talent pool will overtake even that. As bigger, stronger players continue to cram their talents into a strip of dirt that is 60 feet, six inches long and a box that is 90-foot square inside a park that has fences a mere 320 feet away, the game will continue to struggle to fit those players inside those suddenly not-so-friendly confines. MLB will face a choice about living with that struggle or changing the physical structure of the game. There are only so many cities that you can expand to.

The evolution that has changed baseball the most has been the short-burst reliever, and MLB still hasn't quite figured out what to do about that. Baseball has always been a game best understood from the pitcher's mound and there have always been substitute pitchers, but the idea that a pitcher would enter the game to *perform a task* has altered the game on a fundamental level. Before the emergence of the short-burst reliever, a pitcher was prized for the length of time he could stay on the mound and remain effective. But now there's a new way to be a good pitcher, and there are a lot of pitchers who can fill that role. Teams have traded length for maximum effort and made up the difference in volume. It's why it seems like every game involves five or six pitchers per team. When everyone can throw at maximum effort, the strikeouts will start to flow.

In the batter's box, the strikeout problem, which is effectively the same thing as the length-of-game and lack-of-action problems, has become impossible to ignore. Some of that surge is an improvement in the quality of pitching, but some of it is a response to the environment that batters find themselves in. The (ahem) "differently behaving" ball of the late 2010s incentivized players to swing real hard in case they hit it, and somewhere along the line, swinging and missing became seen as an unfortunate side effect, rather than a moral failing.

If there is a thread that runs through all of this, it's the tension that has grown between efficiency and entertainment in the game. Whether you choose to call them problems or innovations, the strikeouts and the death of the bunt and the "power game" and the starters who only throw five innings all have perfectly reasonable explanations behind them. Everyone is behaving rationally, and yes, that's the result of analytically-driven thinking. If you put 30 teams into a competition with the mission to out-play each other, when they discover something that will make that easier, you can't expect them to simply forego that knowledge. Or can you?

MLB has begun to strike back. They will never be able to outlaw teams and players trying to figure out ways to get the most they can within the rules, but MLB has the power to change those rules. While the 2–2 symmetrical infield and the three-member outfield feels balanced, the best defense a team can play is sometimes the shifted infield or the four-member outfield. When I say "sometimes," I don't mean a dozen times through the year. It's possible that, left unchecked, the "standard" formation would have become the strange exception. The problem that MLB faces is that the standard formation is so deeply ingrained into the minds of fans that it feels like part of the game itself, and MLB has chosen that feeling of comfort over innovation. Efficiency for its own sake is no longer the way of MLB. Baseball is a game, but MLB is an entertainment company.

MLB has still has more decisions to make about what it wants *the* game of baseball to look like. It's a tough situation to be in. Not only does MLB have to deal with the fall-out of deciding something, but they run the risk of making a decision and having it not work to deliver the result that they were hoping for. Eventually, MLB will choose their own adventure, but that tension between efficiency and entertainment will define the next couple of decades in baseball history.

As the game changes, it will mean that the numbers we use to describe the game will change. In the "dead ball" era, as late as 1918, a single-digit home run total (Gavvy Cravath's eight) was enough to lead a league. We recognize that the game was different back then and we should adjust our eyes accordingly. Maybe it doesn't feel as emotionally salient to talk about 1918, because there aren't many current baseball fans who were even alive then. When we're talking about how the game has changed since the 1970s or '80s, it suddenly becomes a different story. The new ballgame is different than the baseball than a lot of fans grew up with. Pitching was the obvious first casualty. The idea of a pitcher throwing even 200 innings in a season has quickly disappeared. In 2022, a *total* of eight pitchers made that mark. It's hard because, even for those who aren't into the numbers, the numerical vocabulary of .300 hitters and 20-game winners that baseball has developed over the years has some new words in it and some of the old ones aren't used that much any more.

If there's a bright side to the new ballgame, it's that we're beginning to understand things that we previously had very little ability to appreciate. The catcher is so much more important than anyone had ever recognized. Understanding the human element of the game—not magical thinking about players, but a real scientific understanding of how humans grow and develop—has become tremendously valuable. We've realized that there's more to the game than just athletic ability. You have to pay attention to all of it if you want to survive.

We're also starting to see that there was a little bit of wisdom that we learned in Little League. Figure 36 shows the average number of players from each team that ended up with their own line in the box score through the years.

Figure 36. Average number of players used, per team per game, 1950–2022

Over time, the number has gone up. It's not quite "everyone plays," but more than ever, baseball is a team game, won or lost by the entire roster. Baseball has long been a game, much like the United States culture that it came from, that has valued its individual players. There are baseball cards and

Hall of Fame plaques with one name each on them. In the new ballgame, when you root, root, root for the home team, you'll probably get a chance to root for most everyone on it at some point.

THE DANGER OF writing a book like this is that by the time someone is reading it, the trends I've identified might be old news and the questions I've asked may have already been answered. They may have even been answered years ago. There may be new questions that I didn't even know to ask. Books represent a picture of a moment in history, but they stick around for years afterward. I can only hope that those years have been kind. MLB has its own five questions to answer. If there's one small saving grace for me, it's that not only does MLB have to answer them now, but that they've been answering these same questions for years, and will probably have to answer them years from now. The details will change, but the questions themselves won't. MLB continually has to write its own five facts speech. We all do.

1. What is the role of technology in the game?

When I was a kid, there was a video game called *Base Wars* that imagined futuristic baseball as played by robots with guns. On a tag play, the question of safe or out was settled by a battle between the runner and the fielder. Every once in a while, one of the players exploded. We'll hopefully never get *there* but now we have the question of whether a robot should call balls and strikes. The arguments on either side are well-worn. The strike zone called by humans is not uniform and it's not even the rectangle that the rulebook calls for, but the mistakes and inconsistencies have become part of the game. The hidden detail that never gets mentioned is that there would still be an umpire behind home plate, mostly to relay the calls that the computer system made, but there would still need to be rulings on check swings and foul balls and safe-out plays at home. Otherwise, the runner and catcher would have to fight it out.

The home plate umpire would be there for another very specific reason. Sometimes the machine blinks. The technology that would be used would be a couple of sensors and a computer, and a sensor can get misaligned because someone bumped it. If the system shuts down, it would fall to the home plate umpire to reclaim the job of judging pitches. What happens though if the sensors are still feeding information into the system, but something is a little out of place? What happens when Ed from Lakewood finds out that the called strike that looked a little off to everyone in the stadium was the result of a mechanical error?

Technology can improve many things in life. It might even be an improvement in calling balls and strikes, but it's only as good as the humans who design it and operate it. Robot umpires have been sold as a way to get rid of the mistakes. With human umpires, we recognize that there will be a few wrong calls because all humans make mistakes. We expect perfection from technology. MLB might want to have a plan ready in case perfection doesn't actually happen.

Robot umpires also aren't the technology that fans should worry about. In 2021, MLB introduced its new FieldVision system. The system tracks not only the motion of the ball in flight, but everyone on the field as well. That of course includes the batter and pitcher, but also the fielders, runners, umpires, and even the base coaches. It renders all of them in stick-figure forms, with the ability to tell not only where each player went on the field, but fine-grained details about where each limb and joint went. You can see the extension of the arm or the bending of the knee. In theory, it will allow for teams to look at things like in-game pitching and hitting mechanics. I'm sure they'll come up with all sorts of fun ways to uncover players who have hidden talents that no one else recognized.

You can also see where the third-base coach touched his hat and his belt to give the bunt sign. You can see the little tell that the pitcher does before throwing a curveball. Watching players' behavior to look for clues on what they're going to do next is part of the game. If a pitcher is tipping pitches, that will be quickly shared on the opposing team's bench. Now imagine being able to figure that out with the speed and capacity of a computer. What happens when the job of reading the other team's body language can be done more efficiently?

2. (How) should MLB regulate innovation?

This one goes beyond the infield shift, though the infield shift was the most obviously visible innovation in baseball. It was the result of people being willing to think differently about the game and to try out new ideas that ended up working. If there's one thing that's for certain, MLB teams aren't going to stop looking for the next edge. They have been ever since William A. "Candy" Cummings threw the first curveball in 1867.

Most people think of a baseball team as the 26 players in uniform, and maybe their manager and coaches. The sheer number of people it takes to run an MLB team, even before you get to the accountants and janitors, is something that doesn't get talked about. If there's an advantage to be had (or copied) in MLB, there are plenty of eyes out looking for it. Every MLB team is fully invested in data modeling, and as the available data sources get more detailed, there will be more ways to find a small edge, even if it means a big change to the game. The next infield shift is out there waiting to be found.

In Chapter 9, we talked about the tension between a desire to change the rules to alter the flow of the game and the tradition that players should simply figure out their own counter-measure. Figuring out a response might take a while and sometimes the game can get stuck. But when something comes along to make the game "more boring" and the players can't figure out a counter-move, perhaps MLB should simply strike those innovations down?

It's not always that easy. While the process of finding inefficiencies in the game has been sped up by the availability of big data sets, *implementing* those innovations is a different story. Data sets behave in very predictable ways. Humans are much more temperamental. There's always friction. The infield shift didn't just appear from nowhere. In 2010, there were a total of 2,463 balls hit into play against the shift. By 2022, there were 66,942. During that time, there was a growing awareness of the effects—good and bad—of the shift, but it took a decade or so for the full growth of the strategy to take place.

That 10-or-so-year lag seems to hold pretty steady in baseball. In Figure 37, we can see the percentage of all saves in MLB games that lasted exactly three outs.

Figure 37. Percentage of saves awarded lasting three outs, 1950–2022

The first step toward the short-burst reliever model was the use of one-inning closers, beginning in the late 1980s. Before then, about 20 percent of saves lasted one inning, but the period of rapid growth is obvious on the graph. Depending where you count from, it took 10 to 15 years for the one-inning closer model to fully blossom. As it did, teams started using the one-inning model with other relievers. We've seen how the game has evolved as a result.

This is a problem for MLB because if it wants to clamp down on innovations in the name of interesting gameplay, it can take a decade between the introduction of the idea and its use spreading widely enough to where it's a "problem." Past that, it's going to take a few more years until the nature of that problem is understood, and all the while, the strategy is becoming more ingrained into the cultural fabric of the game. MLB not only has to figure out what banning certain strategies might do, but how to convince the public that they aren't banning a time-honored tradition when they do it.

3. What responsibility does MLB have to its past?

Baseball is a game that prides itself on continuity, and for a lot of people whose fifth fact is that they love baseball, it's been a through line in their lives. A 2017 study found that the average age of a fan of MLB was 57 years old, giving it one of the oldest fanbases among the major sports. Baseball is a storyteller's game and for many people, there is a lot of their story wrapped up in it. As a psychologist, I know that you have to respect someone's story. It also means that there are a lot of—what's the polite term?—grumpy old people watching the game. Maybe some of them are even reading this book.

Baseball has never stood still. One of the beauties of the game is being able to watch how it has grown and changed and even how it even mirrored changes in the world around it. The thing is that most of those changes have been gradual. Despite what I just wrote about innovations taking 10–15 years to fully develop, there is concern that the availability of data and the ability to process those data quickly and perhaps most importantly, the near-dominance of "efficiency" as the standard by which all things are judged in baseball, will shorten the time between those changes.

Figure 38. Average number of outs recorded by starting pitchers, 1950–2022

We can see the average number of outs that starting pitchers recorded through the years. There's been a slight downward trend for a long time, but the end of that graph ends with a *thwump*. If you go back through this book and look at some of the graphs, you'll see a few of those very sudden, very sharp, and very recent *thwumps*. People can generally handle change in life. We've all seen our own five facts change over time, and if you talk to fans long enough, they'll tell you that they understand that nothing really ever stands still. Even baseball. As a psychologist, I know that big, sudden changes are different, especially for people who have held onto baseball as that fixed point in the storm of life. The game will move in its own way and I can make graphs about how it has moved, but sometimes it's a good idea to appreciate what a graph might feel like to someone else.

4. What is the role of fun in the game?

It's supposed to be fun. It's supposed to be emotional. It's supposed to make you stand up and cheer or sometimes cry over the home run that made someone else cheer. A game of baseball is a nine-act work of art and the purpose of art is to make you feel something. Those are real people on the field. They experience joy and frustration and boredom out there too.

So much of the new ballgame is wrapped up in the search for "efficient" baseball. But baseball is at its most fun during those moments of uncertainty, and efficiency is not a friend of the uncertain. There's beauty in being efficient too. It involves diving in and having a deep understanding of the game and how all the gears work. It's the sort of thing that tickles my toes, but it's not for everyone. MLB is going to have a hard time putting that genie back in the bottle, even if they do change the rules. Even then, teams will start researching the new ones. It's not like MLB can ban math.

The other place where baseball will have to answer the "question of fun" is not only on the field, but also in the stands. If you want to understand this one, ask yourself the question, "Why do people flip out about bat flips?" We like it when players show emotion on the field. After an RBI double in a key situation, it's common for the camera to catch the batter at second base celebrating and shouting back to his teammates in the dugout. It was a tense moment and the batter won the confrontation and pushed his team closer to winning. There's a lot to celebrate. We would understand if the pitcher did the same had the plate appearance turned into a strikeout. It's an oddity though that when a player hits a home run, it's suddenly rude if you do anything other than run around the bases efficiently. If you admire the ball after you hit it or if you casually dispense of that burdensome toothpick you are holding or do anything other than pretend that you are jogging out to get a can of beans from the store, that's not okay.

In the stands, there are approved times to cheer as well. If a game event happens, cheering is fine and if the scoreboard has one of those animations saying, "Make Some Noise!" then that's fine too. In between though, you can hear the conversations going on around you because it would be weird to be "too loud" then. Baseball is a game filled with contradictions and unwritten rules about who is allowed to have fun when. Baseball fans who go to other countries to watch a game are often surprised by what they find there. The game on the field is more or less the same, but the cheering is more constant. There are sometimes drums and songs. It's a different experience.

The expression of emotion is governed by the culture that a person is part of. Culture refers to a lot more than what country a person comes from. It might also refer to how old someone is or what social class they come from, and in a game where the fans are, on average, 57 years old and able to lay out the money for tickets and parking and "nachos," the culture of older, wealthier people in the United States (and Toronto) will make up most of the crowd. It gets interesting when people who are much younger than 57 and who were raised in places other than those which are politely called "upper middle class" in the United States end up on the field or in the stands.

If MLB is planning to base its decisions on what the game will look like to shape the game toward a "fun" experience, it may want to think very carefully about how fun is being defined and, more importantly, who is defining it.

5. When does it become mutant baseball?

There's a certain luxury that I have as an "analytics guy." I get to be linear. I specialize in questions that have *an* answer. They might not be interesting or useful answers, but eventually, I can say that *the* answer is 12 or 47 or 107.9 and that's the end of it. MLB doesn't have such an easy task. There aren't correct answers to any of this. In theory, baseball could have its batters run to the left or have 10 fielders or play seven inning games, but would that still be baseball? Some of those questions even sound heretical to ask.

Take the issue of tied games. One way for MLB to cut down on the number of games that go into their fourth and fifth hour is to declare that after 12 innings, a tied game will simply remain that way forever in the record books. As the "analytics guy," I can tell you that from 1993–2019, that would have affected 1.4 percent of all games. From 2020–2022, the era of the "ghost runner" rule, the percentage dropped to 0.2 percent. Ties are already technically possible in an MLB game, though only in very special circumstances. You first need a game that is past the point of being "official" and has a tied score, but then is delayed by rain and is unable to be continued. At that point, MLB considers the game suspended and it's supposed to be continued from that stopping point at a later date. If the suspended game is between two teams who will not meet again during the regular season and if the game ends up having no bearing on the playoffs, then it is considered a tied game. That doesn't happen often and means that ties are only allowed to happen if no one would notice.

Allowing ties would solve the problem of long games, but at what cost? The poetic lore that surrounds baseball is that it's a game that could, in theory, continue forever. While that would be interesting, everyone would eventually go home around the 21st inning. It's not that the game would stop running if ties were allowed, but it might not feel like baseball anymore.

What if things had been a little different? Using data from 1901–2022, I retroactively turned all games that were still knotted up after 12 innings to ties and gave each team a half-win as a result. It's impossible to know if players or managers would have behaved differently if the tie rule had been in effect, but ignoring that, we see some interesting results. In 1915, 1948, and 1964, the Red Sox, Cleveland, and the Cardinals (respectively) would have missed the World Series that they eventually won. In 1993, the National League West race that saw Atlanta win 104 real games to San Francisco's 103 would have swung to the Giants by half a game. In 2003, the NL Central Division would have been won by the Houston Astros, rather than the Chicago Cubs, and the Cubs would have missed the playoffs. Perhaps some other overzealous fan would have interfered with Astros left fielder Lance Berkman during the NLCS. As someone who grew up in Cleveland hearing about the heroes of 1948 and then lived two miles from Wrigley Field in 2003, it would have changed part of my own story.

Of course, things *didn't* happen that way. Ties aren't part of baseball and they probably won't be. The mutant baseball line is a tough one to walk, and there are some things about *the* game of baseball that simply aren't open for negotiation. It will still be one, two, three strikes you're out, even in the new ballgame.

IN THE WINTER of 2021–22, I found myself in a strange position. During the negotiations over a new collective bargaining agreement, there was a sticking point around how MLB might reform its arbitration process. The process is often contentious, especially during the hearing when the team has to say that the player isn't actually *that* good and the player says that the team is being cheap. And at the same time, both parties know they'll be reunited in a few weeks at the start of Spring Training.

Before they submit their numbers, there's a calculation. When both sides get into the room, they know they have to pick a number they can defend, and arbitration is a process that heavily relies on precedent. A couple of similar players who were at the same career point and had similar numbers may have received salaries of around $3 million over the past few years. As the player's agent, you may ask for $3.2 million and leave out the worst of those comparison players when you make your case. Maybe the team offers $2.8 million and does the opposite. Neither side can go too far afield from $3 million, but they will shade their arguments (and their offers) accordingly. If the player's agent offered a salary of $10 million for that player, it would be laughed out of the hearing room.

What if we could do away with the hearing? What if everyone could agree on a scale that told us how much the player was worth and then that became his salary? That's when they started talking about WAR. I am proud to be an "analytics guy." I have worked at *Baseball Prospectus*, one of the places where the hammers of WAR were forged, for more than a decade, and I've written extensively about WAR and my own concerns about places where it needs fixing. (Chapter 10 of this book is based on some of those writings.)

Basing the arbitration system on WAR allows for a simple mathematical assignment of salaries for arbitration eligible players. No more messy hearings. In theory, the algorithm could be based on any stat at all (how many hits did the player get on Tuesdays!) They could have created something based on batting average or ERA, but there's a recognition within the game, even if not within its fanbase, that WAR is the best measure of value available for MLB players.

I think most people stopped processing the story at that point. This was another victory for WAR, and as someone who's been knee deep in those waters for a long time, I suppose I should have felt honored. It was a tribute to how far the analytics movement in baseball had come, but WAR wasn't the point. Getting rid of the hearings was. There's a devil waiting in that snare. The initial proposal was that there would be a pile of money—it was never really disclosed how much or where it would come from—that would be designated as the "arbitration pool." WAR was to be the pizza cutter that divided that pie among the eligible players. It seemed like the perfectly unbiased solution.

It's a terrible idea. For a long time, the analytical movement struggled to find its voice within the game. We were a collection of outsiders who were told that our opinions didn't matter because we had never played. The problem was that we had hard data to back up our opinions and eventually the data won out. Because we were shut out for so long, Sabermetricians took to operating independently. If they didn't want us, then we certainly didn't need them. WAR grew up in that environment of independence.

Over time, the formula for WAR has changed as new information has come available. If there's something to be said for batting average, it's not a great statistic, but at least everyone knows how to calculate it and the formula has been the same since 1888. With WAR it's not that easy. For example, how do we include the role of luck? When we study pitching, we know that there are certain things about individual pitchers that are relatively stable across time. High strikeout pitchers in one year are likely to be high strikeout pitchers in the next year. We can reasonably assume that striking batters out is a talent that some pitchers have more of and others have less. There are other places where pitchers do not get consistent results from year-to-year, and seem to be random. Should we credit (or debit) a pitcher for something that is a matter of chance? Should we try to split the difference and figure out how much we should credit to skill? Those aren't questions with easy answers, but eventually you have to pick an answer and mathematically model things accordingly.

Now imagine that one day, the people who hold the sacred spreadsheet say, "We're switching." Maybe some mental health researcher in Atlanta found something new that changed the way people thought about the problem. Would they have the power to do that? Would it have to be approved by someone? One of the glories of WAR is that it's not a static process. WAR is supposed to change. It's a live thing that represents the best knowledge that we have about how value is created in baseball. There are assumptions that people honestly disagree about, but sometimes as more data emerge, people change their view. That could lead to millions of dollars changing hands. With real money in play, the independence that birthed WAR was suddenly threatened. MLB eventually sidestepped the immediate problem by creating its own internal version of WAR to use for distributing pre-arbitration bonuses to certain players, rather than replacing the arbitration system fully. It's still not entirely clear what happens when a measure that's supposed to change as researchers learn more collides with people who have several million reasons to be very interested in those changes.

In the new ballgame, the Sabermetric movement will have its own challenge. What happens when a group of researchers goes from an independent voice crying in the wilderness to having the ability to move mountains of cash? Baseball researchers, myself included, have spent a long time working for this sort of recognition and respect and even power. Well, now we have it and we have to figure out how to wield that power responsibly.

THERE'S ONE MORE not-so-hidden force in the game of baseball. It's the most terrible of all of them because it eventually ruins everything: dumb luck. As a culture, we use the word "luck" in a very different way than a mathematician does. Luck is, by definition, random and unpredictable. There is some of that type of luck in baseball, but we tend to use the word for the things that we *didn't* predict.

At the beginning of every year, people who write about baseball are often asked to predict what will happen in the upcoming season. Who will win each division? Who will win the World Series? Who will win the Cy Young Award? I desperately try to avoid those. Fortunately for me, the internet seems to have lost my prediction from March 2015 that the Oakland A's would win the World Series. They went 68–94 that year. I guess they just had bad luck. It certainly had nothing to do with me completely misreading their situation. When we say that a team or a player caught a lucky break, most of time we really mean we didn't see *that* coming, and perhaps we should have. Maybe we're just not comfortable with the truth that baseball changes faster than even its most ardent fans and the so-called experts realize. If the game hasn't humbled you yet, it's because you haven't been around very long.

I used to apply for baseball jobs. I used to think that I wanted to make a full-time career for myself inside the game. I've interviewed a few times here and there and done some work on the side for some teams, but I never landed *that* job in the front office. There's a really simple reason why. I don't have the skills that I would need on "the inside" and at this point I've spent a lot of time developing my other talents. Maybe it's all for the best. I may love baseball, but I've found a home that I don't want to leave, a career that pays the bills and provides fulfillment, and a wife and five kids whom I don't want to uproot every few years. Some of your five facts end up being more important than the others. I love baseball, but one day, I realized that the dream was over. The therapist in me knows that people cope with those sorts of realizations in different ways. I decided to write a book.

Years from now, someone else will write another book about how it's a new ballgame and they'll have a good laugh about how inefficient they all were in the old days. Ed from Lakewood will still be complaining about how the game was so much better back then. The "back then" they'll all be talking about is right now. The game will have changed again, and so will I. I look forward to reading that book and seeing what *the* game of baseball has come up with. By then, my five facts speech will have changed too. I was born in Cleveland. I am from Atlanta. I'm a retired mental health researcher. I'm married with five grown kids and perhaps a few grandkids. And I love baseball.